KU-052-337

Whole School Approaches to Special Needs

A Practical Guide for Secondary School Teachers

Edited by
Arlene Ramasut

 The Falmer Press

(A Member of the Taylor & Francis Group)
London • New York • Philadelphia

UK The Falmer Press, Falmer House, Barcombe, Lewes,
East Sussex. BN8 5DL

USA The Falmer Press, Taylor & Francis Inc., 242 Cherry Street,
Philadelphia, PA 19106–1906

132816

Selection and editorial material
© copyright A. Ramasut 1989

*All rights reserved. No part of this publication may be reproduced,
stored in a retrieval system, or transmitted in any form or by any
means, electronic, mechanical, photocopying, recording or otherwise,
without the prior permission in writing from the Publisher.*

First published 1989

British Library Cataloguing in Publication Data

Whole-school approaches to special needs: a practical guide for
secondary school teachers.
  1. Great Britain. Schools. Students with special educational
  needs. Education
  I. Ramasut, Arlene
  371.9′0941

  ISBN 1-85000-569-9
  ISBN 1-85000-570-2 Pbk

**Library of Congress Cataloging-in-Publication Data
available on request.**

*Typeset in 10/13 Bembo by
David John Services Limited, Slough, Berks.
Printed in Great Britain by
Redwood Burn Limited, Trowbridge, Wiltshire*

For George Morgan

(1895–1988)

who stood against inequality

Contents

Contents

Section III : Cross-curricular Issues

Foreword

The great concern for meeting special educational needs of children has generated a considerable volume of literature in the last few years. However, most of the existing books on the subject are academic and theoretical accounts of how schools should meet special needs, and are often also fragmented accounts that look at special needs provision isolated from the remainder of the school population.

This book is different in many ways. It is above all a *practical* guide for teachers and headteachers, with many of its chapters written by serving teachers or by those who train teachers and directly supervise their classroom practice. The second section of the book, for example, contains the most detailed advice yet to teachers on how to implement whole-school strategies aimed at low achievers in the curriculum areas of Science, Mathematics, English, Modern Languages, Music and Physical Education. These chapters also contain lists of resources for teachers that will be an invaluable guide for anyone wanting to turn the theory of integration into living practice in their schools.

The book is different from those already published in other ways too. The chapters written by academics and non-classroom-teachers are practically orientated and concentrate on outlining how schools can actually organize themselves to meet the special needs of all pupils, from the most to the least able. Chapters on this theme cover teachers' attitudes to children, pastoral care, promoting children's self-esteem, generating some degree of academic success for all pupils, successful classroom management, improving language communication and the important area of gender differentiation within special needs provision, since there is evidence that sex differentiation is much greater for lower ability pupils than it is for those of higher ability.

It is clear, then, that this book is not just 'another special needs education book'. Its practicality, the range of its themes and the links it makes between the academic research literature and the day-to-day life of schools make it a unique contribution to its field.

David Reynolds
University College, Cardiff, Wales

Acknowledgements

The idea for the volume grew out of my work, over many years, with children and young people in ordinary schools who were deemed by the system to be failures but who invariably responded to encouragement and good teaching with willingness, humour and style.

My thanks are therefore due to all my ex-pupils who taught me so much about teaching and particularly to Anthony Abdulrub who often reminded me how much I was learning from his school experiences!

To the contributors of this book, I am indebted for the wide-ranging thought-provoking yet pertinent issues which have been raised and for the many and varied suggestions and techniques put forward to relieve a frequently beleaguered situation.

Finally, special thanks must go to Miss Nicola Perry and Mrs Diana Taylor for their staunch and efficient secretarial support at all times and to my husband and children for their constant encouragement.

List of Abbreviations

APU   Assessment of Performance Unit
BTEC   Business and Technical Educational Council
CDT   Craft, Design and Technology
CGLI   City and Guilds of London Institute
CPVE   Certificate of Pre-Vocational Education
CSE   Certificate of Secondary Education
DES   Department of Education and Science
ESN(M)   Educationally Sub-Normal (Moderate)
GCSE   General Certificate of Secondary Education
GOML   Graded Objectives in Modern Languages
HMI   Her Majesty's Inspectorate
ILEA   Inner London Education Authority
INSET   In-Service Training
LEA   Local Education Authority
MSC   Manpower Services Commission
NCDS   National Child Development Study
NFER   National Foundation for Educational Research
RSA   Royal Society of Arts
SEN   Special Educational Needs
SNAP   Special Needs Advisory Project
TGAT   Task Group on Assessment and Testing
TVE   Technical and Vocational Education
TVEI   Technical and Vocational Education Initiative
WJEC   Welsh Joint Education Committee
YTS   Youth Training Scheme

Introduction

The Warnock Report of 1978 succeeded in focusing attention on the needs of a large minority of our school population. It reminded administrators and planners that many children in need of special help were already in the ordinary schools, often struggling to swim with the tide. Those children who were thrown a life-buoy in the form of remedial help or good pastoral care, often managed to reach the shore at 16, somewhat bedraggled by the experience but otherwise unharmed. Some, however, for whom the life-buoy was inadequate, or who never managed to grab hold of it, were either drowned by the school experience or emerged fiercely aggressive towards the system which had tried to put them under. A few, the few who were given carefully planned help with just the right amount of support, did learn to 'swim'. This last group, however, represented only a small proportion of the pupils in secondary schools for whom success was always elusive.

Is the situation any different today? The Warnock Report and the 1981 Act make it clear that children with special educational needs should be educated in ordinary schools wherever possible. The Report recommended that schools should plan teaching and allocation of resources in the knowledge that approximately 20 per cent of the population will need some form of extra help and support. Yet, why is it that we hear, so often, that the 'remedial' teachers are the first to go in a time of cutbacks? Is this an indication that schools do not value the worth of children who need extra help, or does it indicate that, in fact, schools are in the process of reorganizing their resources in an effort to meet special needs more effectively? Probably both suggestions are true. Some headteachers make it obvious through their structuring of the curriculum that the low achievers will always remain a very low priority. For teachers who are committed to equality of opportunity for all pupils, this makes working in such an environment stressful and difficult. It is hoped that those who find themselves in such a position may take heart from the collection of ideas presented in this book and find them of use in improving their own conditions and those of their pupils. Some headteachers, however, are committed to change, and their problem may well lie in persuading staff that it is part of their responsibility to teach *all* pupils effectively and well. For those who find themselves in the second position, this book will surely act as a resource in itself. A whole-school approach necessitates all staff accepting this responsibility.

The 1981 Education Act amended the law in relation to special education, introducing the more dynamic concept of 'special educational needs'. This new concept has implications for all schools, primary and secondary alike, in that it encompasses a much larger number of children than those previously considered to be 'handicapped' in the traditional sense. Since the implementation of the 1981 Act in 1983, LEAs have been required to identify all children with special needs. Furthermore, governing bodies have been empowered to ensure that schools both make known to all teachers the names of children experiencing learning difficulties and plan to meet their special needs. A learning difficulty has been defined as 'a learning situation which is presenting the child with more difficulties than experienced by the majority of other children of the same age' and may be mild, moderate or severe in nature. This book is concerned with the teaching and learning problems of those pupils who experience mild to moderate learning difficulties in the ordinary school. They may be found in special classes, in remedial departments, or in the bottom band of the mainstream. Wherever they are, they share the same characteristic: they are perceived to be the low achievers. This, in fact, is not always the case. Some are achieving well in relation to their ability and frequently this will be the result of good teaching in special classes. However, a much greater number *will* be performing below their actual potential for a number of reasons. In the past, it has been common practice to account for poor performance in two ways: either by attributing the pupil's low standards of achievement to home factors or to some fault located within the child, inherited or acquired. This book aims to refocus the view of failure and look at the problem in relation to the school. It is not, however, productive to apportion blame without at the same time suggesting ways and means of overcoming the problem.

The first section examines the ways in which the school as an institution may be responsible for creating or exacerbating problems of learning for some pupils. By highlighting certain causal factors and by showing how some schools are working towards eliminating these factors, it is hoped to make educators more aware of the range of advantages of developing a whole-school approach to meeting special educational needs.

The second section contains chapters on the curriculum. It aims to show how the teaching of low achievers can be effective in improving academic standards, be made enjoyable for the pupil and result in increased self-esteem. Each chapter contains a list of resources and materials available, as well as suggestions for further reading, and should prove to be an invaluable aid to those teachers who really want to facilitate improvement.

The final section addresses a number of issues which may be regarded as cross-curricular in that they affect teaching and learning in all subjects and at all levels. Again, it is hoped that these chapters will call attention to the possible school-based causes of low achievement and enable teachers to make changes.

For all serving teachers and teachers in training who are convinced of the need to improve the lot of pupils with learning difficulties, this book is intended as encouragement. Progress may be slow and the path strewn with obstacles but if the number of INSET courses being devoted to special educational needs up and down the country is any indication, many schools are working towards whole-school approaches which ensure that all pupils develop to their full potential.

Arlene Ramasut
UCC 1988

SECTION I:
IMPLICATIONS FOR THE SCHOOL AS AN INSTITUTION

Introduction

Meeting special educational needs in the secondary school is an area of concern for many, not least those responsible for making decisions at an institutional level. The current political and economic climate has exacerbated an already difficult situation. Centralist tendencies in terms of control of education are, as yet, uncharted waters. Teachers are working against a backdrop of deteriorating school buildings and diminishing resources, of falling rolls and redeployment, of imposed conditions of service and low perceived social status. Those who cope with the stress imposed by the situation and still care about the future of the often large minority of pupils in schools who are experiencing learning difficulties are to be acknowledged for what they are, true professionals.

Working with such teachers on in-service training courses has highlighted for me their main concerns in ensuring a better deal for up to 40 per cent of their school populations. The Warnock Report and the subsequent enactment of the 1981 Education Act has encouraged them to review their present provision for pupils with special educational needs and to question its limitations. Teachers across Britain have examined the philosophy of separate provision and rejected it as inadequate for most children in the 1980s. The question which must then be posed is, how can schools organize themselves to meet the special needs of all pupils from the most to the least able? A variety of models already exist, some more effective and fair than others, and the first chapter includes a description of these together with an examination of what is meant by the term 'integration'.

Teachers are concerned about the implications of 'integration' and particularly about attitudes towards pupils with learning difficulties both of other colleagues and of teacher trainers who cannot remain free from blame. Derek Phillips' chapter examines research on teachers' attitudes to children with learning difficulties in order to develop awareness of the effects which

such attitudes have on pupils' academic performance. By increasing awareness he hopes to encourage an appreciation of the need for change.

Teachers are also worried about a perceived lack of commitment on the
part of school managers to plan for an improved service. Here, the chapter
by David Galloway shows that a different concept of pastoral care can help
prevent problems before they occur rather than acting as an inefficient system
of crisis intervention.

Mike Farrell describes one school's efforts to move away from the
model of separate provision and to replace it with a more integrated
programme, whilst Tony Kloska sets forth the philosophical and moral
arguments for a whole-school approach. David Reynolds' contribution on
effective schools further details the characteristics which good schools display
in planning to meet the needs of all pupils. This section should, therefore,
prove useful to school administrators and policy-makers as well as to teachers
who appreciate the need for change.

Chapter 1

Paving the Way for Change — Warnock and the 1981 Act

Arlene Ramasut

Background

The 1981 Education Act represents the Government's response to the findings and recommendations of the Warnock Committee Report (1978). It is the Act which has been responsible for a view of special education quite different from that described in the 1944 Education Act which previously formed the legislative basis for the provision of special education.

The 1944 Act referred to children who 'suffered from a disability of mind or body' as being in need of special provision and it formalized a system of categorization, based on a medical model of handicap. This was done in order to facilitate appropriate provision. The major disadvantage of such a system was that it was a static model which located the 'fault' entirely within the child; that is to say, the ten categories of handicap such as deaf, blind, physically handicapped, were formulated on the 'disease model' of medicine. Certification of the handicap was made by medical officers and placement often recommended by them. The educational needs of children with evident disabilities was very much a secondary consideration in terms of appropriate school placement and indeed education was talked of in terms of 'treatment'. From such a basis, then, developed a separate sector of education known as 'special schooling' and it is this concept of a separate network of highly specialized institutions with trained staff which usually comes to mind when children with special needs are thought of.

Advantages of Special Schools

The existence of such a separate network has not been without its advantages. Arguably it can be said that special schools, for example for physically handicapped children or children with visual impairment, have facilitated the accumulation of resources, both in terms of staff expertise and material equipment, which would not have been possible otherwise. It can be further argued that the gathering together of children with a similar identifiable handicap has allowed for and helped in the formation of pressure groups to work on behalf of the children and to focus attention on their needs. Certainly many special schools have benefited from the concern and support shown by their local communities in terms of fund raising; would they be able to raise money in quite the same way if the children were dispersed in ordinary schools? Separate special schools also make life easier for all the agencies which are frequently part of the schools' support services. Visits from speech therapists, psychologists, medical officers and social workers are perhaps more easily accommodated in the special school regime than in the ordinary school.

In terms of the all-round education offered to children in special schools, it can again be argued that they have benefited from the way in which it is offered. Such schools are usually staffed by teachers and ancillaries who have a commitment to children with special needs and who make every effort to provide them with wide-ranging experiences of success in all aspects of life. Whether the educational diet is actually 'special' or different from that offered in the mainstream remains, however, a moot point.

The ordinary schools, too, have perceived the existence of special schools as a benefit to them in that 'difficult to teach' children have been removed from their classrooms in great numbers since the 1950s. Indeed the number of children 'diagnosed' to be ESN(M) – educationally subnormal (old terminology) – or maladjusted in England and Wales rose consistently from 1950 to 1978, according to Galloway and Goodwin (1985), with only a minimal decrease up until 1982, and that at a time of falling school rolls. It must also be noted that Galloway's figures do not include the large numbers of pupils in separate but 'non-designated' provision such as 'on-site' units, set up by the schools themselves out of existing provision, which have proliferated since the 1970s. Swann's (1985) figures show that between 1978 and 1982 the proportion of secondary-aged children with behaviour problems and learning difficulties in the old category ESN(M) and maladjusted rose by 8.5 and 10 per cent respectively, and again these figures did not include pupils labelled as disruptive or disaffected.

The 1981 Act does not then appear to have affected the removal of pupils from mainstream schooling in these two most difficult to define areas of special needs. This fact must surely give rise to debate about the criteria employed in deciding where a child should be educated and the motives of the schools in reaching such decisions.

Disadvantages of Separate Provision

What separate provision for children with special needs perhaps did not do before the Warnock Report was to examine the disadvantages of such a system for the children involved and for their families. One of the clearest findings of the three-year research project on the integration of children with special needs undertaken by Hegarty *et al.* (1981) for the NFER was that parents wanted integration for their children. The desire for 'normality' appeared to override other considerations even when the parents had nothing but praise for the special schools. Normality, whilst being difficult to define, emerged from the parents' comments as pertaining to the promotion of independence and was viewed as being an end in itself for which to strive. Special schooling, whilst offering support and help which may be difficult to reproduce in another setting, may be said to offer a 'cocooned environment' from which many children emerge at 16 unprepared for the harsh realities of adult life. Indeed, separate special schooling often means that handicapped children are socially isolated in their home environments, not knowing or having friends to play with in the evenings, weekends or holidays. Parents of handicapped children are perhaps more aware of this than anyone and the 1981 Act has provided recognition of the role of parents in education decision-making. It can be argued, however, that the very nature of the statementing procedure is so tortuous as to make true parental participation extremely difficult to achieve. Support groups such as SNAP (Special Needs Advisory Project) in Wales are being set up by voluntary workers to ensure that the voice of parents is not just heard, but listened to when educational placement is under consideration.

The Warnock Report and the 1981 Education Act

The Education Act (1981) has been greeted with a variety of responses ranging from those who see it as a 'parents' charter' to those who feel that it did not go far enough in legislating on the Warnock recommendations. The Warnock Report (1978) contained some 225 recommendations in the summary and provided the philosophy for the 1981 Act. The Act has amended the law broadly in line with the concept of 'special educational needs' as proposed by Warnock but has not gone as far as the equivalent law in the USA (Public Law 94.142) in terms of legislating for integration. It is generally regarded as being an 'enabling' act based on a consensus of what constitutes good practice but its impact on children with special needs in the ordinary schools will depend on the way in which it is interpreted by local education authorities. In fact the 1981 Act allows considerable scope in interpretation and this has been levelled as a major criticism in that LEAs which choose not to recognise the underlying message of the Act have been provided with sufficient excuse for delaying change. Whilst stipulating education in ordinary schools as the general principle, the Act states that this must be compatible with (a) the children receiving the special education they require, (b) the efficient education of other children and (c) the efficient use of resources. Thus, an LEA with substantial separate special provision may argue that efficient use of resources depends on the continued use of special schools in the traditional way, and never even begin to examine the implications of (a) or (b). A further danger inherent in the Act is that rather than delaying a commitment towards further integration, an LEA might interpret it as an opportunity to save money by running down separate provision but not making any extra financial resources available to the ordinary schools to facilitate proper integration programmes. Rather more likely than this extreme undermining of the Act is the likelihood that, in practice, some LEAs will limit their interpretation of special needs to encompass only those children who receive 'special education' at present, that is to say, the 2 per cent who were formally assessed under the old special education procedure and who are at present in special schools or special classes. It is not this group of children for whom concern has been expressed but the so-called '18 per cent', many of whom are already in ordinary schools and whose needs are not the subject of 'statements', who may be said to be neglected by the Act. It is this large group of children who may continue to be neglected by many schools unless conscious policies are formulated and implemented. In addition, LEAs who choose not to statement or whose junior school pupils with statements are not in receipt of special provision at secondary level must be called to account. While some authorities will already have moved to a whole-school approach and argue that statementing is unnecessary, others will be less clear about their position.

What are Special Educational Needs?

The Warnock Report concluded that up to one in five children are likely to have special needs at some time in their school careers and up to one in six could be expected to be having difficulties at any one time. We are, therefore, not only talking about the 2 per cent of more obviously handicapped children, when we talk about children with special needs. According to Warnock, a child has special needs if he or she has a learning difficulty which is substantially greater than his or her peers' and which calls for special educational provision to be made. On the surface, this may appear to be straightforward but closer examination shows this concept to be a relative one. It is relative to the nature and the degree of the child's problem in the environment of the school and the wider setting of home and society. Many studies (Douglas, 1964; Douglas *et al.*, 1968; Davie *et al.*, 1972; Wedge and Prosser, 1973) have shown the close relationship between academic perform-ance and social class so it will be no surprise to teachers to point out that some schools, depending on catchment area, will have a higher proportion of children with special educational needs than others. Other studies (Power *et al.*, 1967; Rutter *et al.*, 1979; Reynolds, 1982; Galloway, 1985) indicate that the power of the school in either exacerbating or alleviating problems is closely allied to the ethos of the school in terms of being a 'caring' community. Recognizing that every child in a school is an individual who has special needs at one time or another is the first step towards formalizing a workable system which will facilitate the identification of a need, the assessment of the degree and permanence of that need and the implementa-tion of a programme to meet that need. Such is the responsibility of every school envisaged by the Warnock Committee. Although the 1981 Act does not specifically legislate for such a structure within schools, the Act does anticipate changes in the system. The 1970 Education Act, which brought mentally handicapped children under the auspices of the Education rather than Health and Social Services Ministries, played much the same role in anticipating change and development in all aspects of the education of mentally handicapped children and young people. The fact that all children, whatever their degrees of mental handicap, now attend schools and are educated to the limits of their ability is surely a vindication of such legislation and demonstrates that legislation, however imprecise, can bring about changes in attitude.

What can be said then about special needs which will help us to understand the implications for the ordinary school? Firstly it can be said that children with special educational needs are no different from other children. In general, they have the same need to achieve as they pass through the educational system but, for all of them, the degree of success which they actually attain will be heavily dependent on well organized and enthusiastic teaching. Their difficulties will be more pronounced than those of their peers who may be able to succeed regardless of the teacher. Pupils with special educational needs will never do this. They make demands on a system which must be able to respond with a caring ethos and structured opportunity for success. Schools which do not respond to such demands know to their cost that low attainers and school failures frequently become the disaffected and the disruptive.

The recommendations of the Warnock Report and the subsequent enactment of the 1981 Act are beginning to have far-reaching effects in the ordinary schools although this is not always readily recognized. Where discussion about change has taken place, teachers themselves have identified problem areas (Hegarty *et al.*, 1981; Howe, 1985) which fall broadly under three headings: the meaning and reality of integration, the organization of the school and attitudes within the school. This chapter will examine what is meant by integration whilst other chapters in the section will examine trends in organization and attitudes of teachers towards children with special needs.

Integration

'Integration' as used in special education refers to the education of children with special needs in ordinary schools. It is based on the belief that all children have the right to be educated alongside their peers in a 'normal' environment. As such, the concept of integration reflects a growing world-wide awareness of the restrictions and isolation imposed by a system of separate special schooling and is associated with the movement for recognition of human rights in general and those of minority groups in particular.

The extent to which integration is a feature of a school's organizational policy will be open to discussion. It has been a focus of concern since the publication of the Warnock Report and although many teachers would seem to be in favour of integration in principle, there still exists much doubt as to the chances of its success in an educational climate of cutbacks and low teacher morale. However, research amongst student teachers carried out by this writer has shown a very positive attitude towards integration even before appropriate allocation of resources has taken place. The confusion which surrounds the issue is not helped by the fact that integration is not simply a new form of provision, but can be conceptualized as part of a continuum ranging from minimal contact between a special school and an ordinary school to the full integration of a child in an ordinary class. Furthermore there are several models of integration which exist at different levels serving to complicate the issue even more. Two of these models are described in subsequent chapters. They are clearly recognizable from the traditional remedial department which is still part of the organizational structure of many secondary schools. Being in the forefront of change, such organizational initiatives need the commitment of top management in order to be successful. Two of the three levels of integration described in Warnock and outlined here will be familiar to many teachers in schools where there has yet to be a philosophical shift towards the third level of total functional integration. The first two are not discrete but overlapping and represent progressive stages towards full functional integration.

The first level is referred to as LOCATIONAL integration and relates to the physical location of the special educational provision. Locational integration can be said to exist where a special school and an ordinary school share the same campus. It may represent a sharing of facilities and quite a high degree of interchange and cooperation between staff and pupils but it may be no more than 'parallel living'. Even if the contact between the two schools is minimal there will still be advantages. Children and their teachers may travel the same route to school in the mornings and some form of association is likely. From such small beginnings, tolerance and understanding can grow. For the parents of the special needs children much of the stigma attached to separate schools is removed. For children attending special units attached to ordinary schools the advantage in this respect is even greater. Children with a range of special needs attend the same school as the rest of the children in their street or in their locality. They get to know each other both in and out of school. They have the opportunity to observe their peers at school and model themselves on different types of behaviour. For the non-handicapped children, there will be opportunities to see and appreciate the difficulties which hamper the progress of so many children and the temptation to tease or ridicule will be reduced. This type of integration has been the model used in Sweden for many years where severely handicapped children are successfully educated alongside their peers.

The second form of integration is referred to by Warnock as SOCIAL and represents a greater degree of involvement than locational integration. At this level children attending a special unit or class attached to an ordinary school might share lunchtimes and breaktimes, attend a common assembly and take part in all school concerts or activities. Since young children seem to be able to accept individual differences more readily than older children, it is preferable that this type of association is introduced as early as possible. Indeed many more severe Down's Syndrome children are now being successfully integrated at nursery and infant level although we have yet to see how well they will be accepted in top juniors and secondary schools. Certainly many secondary schools do have classes for children and young people with moderate learning difficulties which operate along the lines described. Indeed, in one school known to the author, the young people in the special class are also made prefects when they reach the fifth year – thus sharing responsibility for the running of the school with their peers. Warnock notes that 'even for children with profound learning difficulties, the friendship and society of other children can effectively stimulate personal development'.

FUNCTIONAL integration is the third and fullest form which is achieved where locational and social association leads to participation in the classroom. It is therefore the most difficult to sustain as it makes the greatest demands on the teacher in terms of organization and teaching method which must ensure that all children benefit from the fully integrated classroom. Viewed dispassionately it can be seen that such a situation is the logical extension of mixed-ability teaching. It is accepted at infant and often at junior level as the norm. What is it then, that makes full functional integration such a startling prospect for many secondary school teachers? McCall (1983) says:

> Every class presents many levels of cognitive development, many levels of emotional maturity, many levels of educational attainment as well as varied types of attitudes to learning and styles of learning. Indeed, one of the most fascinating and at times frustrating aspects of the teacher's role is the need to plan and modify one's plans in the light of sure knowledge that one's class is seldom a static homogenous group of children who all learn at the same rate or in the same way even within one day, let alone from one day to the next.

For the teacher in the ordinary school who operates with this in mind, catering for a child or young person with special educational needs will merely be an extension of the process of meeting the educational needs of all the members of the class. For the teacher who operates on the assumption that a class is an homogenous group which will 'learn' the same material at the same rate, then meeting special needs will pose a problem. Such a basis of operation may well reflect an insensitivity and an inflexibility based on insecurity which will be bound to cause problems for many children. It points to an attempt to make all pupils fit the mould of the school rather than in looking at what the school can do for the pupil. It surely raises the question of what teaching is all about.

Provision within Secondary Schools

Figure 1.1 is offered as an aid to understanding the complexity of current provision in secondary schools. Provision in the bottom left-hand corner represents Warnock's first level of locational integration and it should be said that schools do perceive there to be many benefits in this system. Management is frequently able to relinquish decision-making to special needs staff and does not have to take the needs of the pupils into consideration when planning the timetable for the mainstream. The 'polyfiller' mentality of allocating whoever is free to take a few periods with 'the unit kids' is not uncommon. Also the existence of special classes with statemented children allows for extra (supernumerary) staffing which some schools fear may be lost if other arrangements are made. For the special needs staff, such limited integration often ensures virtual autonomy which they may not be eager to relinquish. They are able to plan to meet the needs of pupils as they deem best and are unlikely to be constrained by examination syllabuses. They are often able to communicate with parents and support agencies directly and generally provide a caring home base for their pupils. Special needs children

FUNCTIONAL

Phase 5
Integrated into mixed ability groups with NO SETTING but with
(a) extra help given in mainstream classes by support teachers* and/or
(b) withdrawal for extra help by SEN staff

Phase 4
Basics (English and Maths) taught by SEN staff. Integrated with other pupils (usually B Band) for some lessons taught by subject specialists

Basics taught by subject specialists as bottom set. Integrated into mixed ability. Withdrawn for extra help by SEN staff

Basics taught by subject specialists as bottom set. Integrated into mixed ability for other subjects. Withdrawn for extra help by SEN staff

Phase 3
Basics taught by SEN staff. Integrated into 'set' groups for other lessons (usually bottom set)

Basics taught by SEN staff. Integrated into 'set' groups for other lessons (usually bottom set)

Phase 2
Most lessons taught by SEN staff but some lessons taught by subject specialists – still as a discrete group

Basics taught by SEN staff. Other lessons taught by subject specialists – still as a discrete group

Phase 1
Taught as discrete group for all subjects by SEN staff

* Support teacher can be: subject specialist, technical specialist (as with hearing impaired pupils) or special educational needs teacher.

LOCATIONAL   SOCIAL

Model 1
Separate registration as remedial or special class

Model 2
Integrated registration/tutorial groups across lower band

Model 3
Integrated registration tutorial groups across year group or parallel band

Figure 1.1: Range of Integrated Provision in Secondary Schools

13

too frequently want the security which such a base offers and this is usually put forward as the main reason for perpetuating the system. Staff in the mainstream may view separate provision with relief. While it exists they are not required to teach the full ability range. Other pupils too may perceive such provision as being beneficial to them in that their 'progress is not being hindered'.

However, against such arguments in favour of locational integration with limited functional integration it must be remembered that there are other implications which may be less than healthy for the school as an institution, for the staff and for the children. The existence of a separate class or unit, often in poor accommodation, generally at the end of the queue for staffing and resources and rarely perceived to be worthy of mention, creates a two-class society within the school. Whilst management may be relieved of the day-to-day problems faced by the special class children, they still have to cope with the difficulties which arise when the pupils come into contact with those mainstream staff who are unprepared and unwilling to be flexible in their approach. It may be argued that such staff have been denied the opportunity of professional development by the very isolation of the special needs pupils. However, the 'hidden curriculum' of the school in the allocation of positions of responsibility subtly reinforces the belief of many mainstream staff that working with special needs children is not perceived to be important by senior management. The special needs staff are perhaps more aware of this than anyone and may further retreat into their isolated positions. Such isolation makes a difficult job even more stressful and is not of benefit to the pupils. In a time when schools are taking on board a host of new initiatives (see Chapter 18) special needs teachers need to be in touch with the mainstream so that they can secure the best for their pupils. The narrowness of the curricula and the over-emphasis on basics in many remedial departments has been highlighted by HMI (DES, 1984) and must not be ignored. Children with learning difficulties, whether they be low attainers or of limited ability, can all benefit from new courses being introduced into schools with extra funding and flexible approaches to curriculum content and teaching methods. Keeping them separate with palliatives in the form of 'alternative studies' and 'life and social skills' is not the answer. The dangers of offering courses with alternative certification need to be realistically examined by any school embarking on such a course. Pupils in the mainstream are not helped, either, by the differentiation of 'us' from 'them'. Such organization promotes a social distancing and encourages 'pecking-order' attitudes towards less able and low attaining pupils. Segregated provision removes the opportunity to foster cooperation and the egalitarian principles upon which comprehensive schools are founded.

Provision in the top right-hand corner of the diagram represents Warnock's level of full functional integration which can only be achieved by a whole-school approach. The advantages of this form of organization have been touched on here and are discussed in detail in the chapter by Tony Kloska (Chapter 4). It is worth noting, however, that a whole-school approach cannot be achieved without the full support of top management, and preferably needs a blocking of the timetable across either a year group or a parallel band. The latter allows for subject specialists to be released to act as support teachers in addition to special education teachers and technical specialists (as in the case of pupils with sensory impairments). Moving from one form of provision, for example, from a separate remedial department to a more integrated system of mixed tutor groups and withdrawals from some lessons may not go all the way to achieving equality of opportunity for special needs pupils but it is a move in the right direction. Mike Farrell describes a school in transition in Chapter 5: a school which is developing provision in order to achieve greater integration. Whilst advocating the benefits of an integrated school, it should not be assumed that this writer dismisses the idea that some children will need separate provision at certain times in their school career. Rather, such separate provision should exist based on the belief that its function is to reintegrate pupils as soon as possible and that the mainstream school should be ready and willing to accept them. Furthermore, the benefits of being taught by caring, empathetic teachers in a non-threatening environment should not be underestimated. Such conditions should, however, be encouraged in a more integrated situation for the benefit of staff and pupils alike.

The move from Phase 1 to Phase 5 of Figure 1.1. is a long one which requires commitment and careful planning. Whilst it may seem that changing the registration form or tutor group system may help integration, if this is accompanied by setting within a bottom band, or streaming and setting across a year group, the result is likely to be the creation of a 'sink set', with its well known accompanying features of disenchantment, disaffection, non-attendance and labelling. Thus a school operating Model 2 at Phase 3 is as likely to be creating problems for its pupils as a school operating Model 1 at Stage 1. It is therefore of vital importance, that not only the type of provision but the actual educational experience of a pupil with learning difficulties is examined when an 'integrated situation' is being discussed.

The secondary school which streams the intake will obviously not consider full functional integration except perhaps in the cases of children whose handicaps do not create or are not accompanied by learning difficulties. Such a case would be a young person confined to a wheelchair because of a physical disability but who is able to cope with the academic demands of mainstream. In a streamed or even a banded school setting, special needs children will usually be found together in a lump at the bottom – 'the dough which did not rise'. They form the core of the remedial classes along with the 'rejects'; children whom 'ordinary' teachers have not been able to cope with. They may attend games, craft and music with B Band classes although why such a distinction is made between these areas of the curriculum and others is rarely, if ever, justified by the school. For the most part, then, they are taught separately at the level of social integration. In some cases remedial department children often have an advantage over the integrated children who 'exist' in the class at the bottom of the band just above – the class which is most frequently moaned about in staffrooms, the class which nobody wants to teach. The question to ask here is, are these often 'disrupting' children fully integrated or have they subtly been identified as yet another segregated group? Perhaps, instead of being in one class, they are distributed amongst the other forms in the bottom band where they still perceive themselves to be failures but are not necessarily recognized as having special needs. Are they, in fact, functionally integrated and, if so, is it to their benefit? Many remedial department teachers would say that they would be better off within a special department in a caring environment. This is the crucial consideration and one which Warnock is at pains to bring attention to. Is the concept of streaming and banding contrary to the concept of total integration? What is certain is that some schools have begun to examine their own systems and to recognize the dangers inherent in an institution which selects on the basis of academic performance and penalizes those who do not 'make the grade'. Recognizing that some 20 per cent of children and maybe more will at any one time be needing extra support, skilful teaching and a relevant curriculum is pushing schools into trying new approaches which will ultimately lead to a realization of full functional integration.

The Education Reform Act

Although advances have been made in the last five years with regard to provision for children with special educational needs in secondary schools, the question which educators are now asking is, how will this Government's Education Reform Act affect the purposes and principles of the 1981 Act? Government has given assurance that it does not intend to repeal the 1981 Act, yet many of the measures outlined in the new Act will have an adverse effect on pupils with special needs if they go through in the present form. It is hardly surprising then if schools which are in the process of examining their organizational structure and designing INSET courses with a view to improving provision hesitate before making fundamental changes.

Professor Klaus Wedell in a paper prepared on behalf of a group of eminent special educators (1988) has examined how the provisions of the Act effect the main principles of the 1981 Act. Furthermore he has specified the amendments to individual clauses of the Act which are necessary if provision for children with special educational needs is to be protected. This paper has been submitted to Government and, at the time of writing, a response is awaited. The main principles of the 1981 Act affected by the new Act are summarized below:

(i) While the 1981 Act confirmed the Warnock contention that an estimated one in five pupils were likely to have special needs, the new Education Reform Act refers only to children having special educational needs if a statement has been issued to them. Whilst some LEAs do not statement at all, the variation in percentages of children with statements found in different LEAs confirms the fact that defining a need is often dependent on the level of existing provision and interpretation of the extent of the need. Many children (Warnock's 18 per cent) will therefore not be considered to have special needs under the new Act.

(ii) The idea of a National Curriculum which encourages a broad education is not antipathetic to developments in special education. The introduction, for example, of TVEI and CPVE across the full ability/attainment range has demonstrated that a broader view of education can be of benefit to all children. The Act does not, however, acknowledge the full breadth of curriculum objectives in terms of personal and social development which are important to many children with special needs.

(iii) Monitoring the age-related norms of attainment will be of benefit to children with special educational needs only if the information obtained is used to highlight the need for resources and allows for an examination of pedagogy and of the relevance and appropriateness of the curriculum. Oversimplification of test results are likely to produce unfavourable and unproductive comparisons between children and schools. Averaging of marks across a variety of tests may result in a child being labelled Level 1 (see the TGAT report, DES, 1988a) at 7 and remaining a 'Level 1 child' for the rest of his or her school career.

(iv) The 1981 Act recognized the right of parents to voice an opinion in the educational provision offered to their child. The new Act emphasizes the right of parents to 'opt out' of an LEA-controlled system. These two important principles are likely to create conflict:

(a) Parents of children with special educational needs will be, by definition, a minority of those concerned with any ordinary school. Their opinion is unlikely to carry weight when decisions about 'opting out' are made.

(b) Age-related assessment could lead to teachers becoming less concerned about the progress of children with special needs if performance is to be judged against norm-referenced criteria. If a school's provision for children with special needs is endangered, there is likely to be pressure on the LEA to statement more children.

(c) Where schools and colleges 'opt out', the links between them, special schools and other secondary schools are likely to be broken. School-college link courses will then be more difficult to provide for many pupils with special educational needs.

It is clear that without amendments to the Education Reform Act, the education of a large minority of pupils will be put in jeopardy. A whole-school approach to meeting special needs would be made more difficult to achieve. The modifications to particular clauses proposed by Professor Wedell would however acknowledge the full range of pupils' special educational needs and safeguard both present and proposed provision within ordinary schools.

In conclusion it may be helpful to remind ourselves that the Fish Report (ILEA, 1985) which reviewed special education provision in ILEA concluded:

> that integration in society is a process not a state... It is a process which requires continued and planned interaction with contemporaries and freedom to associate in different groups... The process of integration should be actively developed wherever the individual lives, learns, works and enjoys leisure activities... The process of integration should form an essential element in all education wherever it takes place.

The HMI report (DES, 1986) on the 'Lower Attaining Pupils Programme' (LAPP) which represents the attempts of thirteen LEAs to provide for all pupils' educational needs, also indicates that such programmes are virtually impossible to implement in isolation; they must be 'intimately and inescapably related to the curriculum and organization of the school as a whole'. Effective programmes which have been running for two years have resulted in a positive change in attitude towards school amongst the low achievers. The next step is seen to be building on the attitude change to achieve improved academic performance. Planning a 'whole-school' approach to meeting special educational needs must then surely be the aim of all caring and effective schools in the 1990s.

References

DAVIE, R., BUTLER, M. and GOLDSTEIN, H. (1972) *From Birth to Seven*, London, Longman.

DES (1978) *Special Educational Needs (The Warnock Report)*, London, HMSO.

DES (1984) *HMI Report: Slow learning and less successful pupils in secondary schools*, London, HMSO.

DES (1986) *HMI Report on the Lower Attaining Pupils Programme*, London, HMSO.

DES (1988a) *Report of the Task Group on Assessment and Testing*, London, HMSO.

DES (1988b) *The Education Reform Bill and the Implications for Children with Special Educational Needs of the National Curriculum, Grant Maintained Schools and Financial Delegation*, (Revised – April 1988), London, HMSO.

DOUGLAS, J.W.B. (1964) *The Home and the School*, London, MacGibbon and Kee.

DOUGLAS, J.W.B., ROSS, J.M. and SIMPSON, H.R. (1968) *All Our Future*, London, Davies.

GALLOWAY, D. (1985) *Schools and Persistent Absentees*, Oxford, Pergamon Press.

GALLOWAY, D. and GOODWIN, C. (1985) *Education of Disturbing Children*, London, Longman.

HEGARTY, S., POCKLINGTON, K. and LUCAS, D. (1981) *Educating Pupils with Special Needs in the Ordinary School*, Windsor, NFER-Nelson.

HOWE, P. (1985) *The attitudes of teachers towards children with special educational needs in comprehensive schools in an urban development area*, unpublished B.Ed. dissertation, University College, Cardiff.

ILEA (1985) *Equal Opportunities for All? (The Fish Report)*, London, ILEA.

MCCALL, C. (1983) *Classroom Grouping for Special Needs*, Stratford Upon Avon, NCSE.

POWER, M.J., BENN, R.T. and MORRIS, J. (1967) 'Delinquent Schools?' in *New Society*, Vol. 10, pp. 542–543.

REYNOLDS, D. (1982) 'The search for effective schools' in *School Organisation*, Vol. 2, No. 3, pp. 215–237.

RUTTER, M., MAUGHAN, B., MORTIMORE, P. and OUSTON, J. (1979) *Fifteen Thousand Hours*, London, Open Books.

SWANN, W. (1985) 'Is the integration of children with special needs happening? An analysis of recent statistics of pupils in special schools' in *Oxford Review of Education*, 11 (1), pp. 3–18.

WEDELL, K. (1988) 'The Education Reform Bill and provision for children and young people with special educational needs: a briefing paper' in *Association of Special Education Tutors Newsletter*, Spring 1988.

WEDGE, P. and PROSSER, H. (1973) *Born to Fail?*, London, Arrow.

Chapter 2

Teachers' Attitudes to Pupils with Learning Difficulties

Derek Phillips

How Attitudes may be Formed

Our view of people is filtered through the prism of our own wishes, desires, hopes and expectations. We see others' behaviours, and their apparent attitudes, through this refracting, psychological mechanism which has been constructed from the context of society in general and that part of it to which we perceive we belong: our sub-cultures. Through this process our own attitudes are developed, and they grow to be largely indivisible from the social milieu which gave rise to them and which helps to sustain them.

Our attitudes are, in one way or another, what we believe our experience to be.

This does not mean that attitudes are solely the result of what we have experienced to be true, nor does it imply that they reflect the reality of the object of our attention. For example, as a child, I need not have directly experienced the dubious delights of dentistry to have a level of antipathy to a forthcoming dental appointment. Attitudes may be formed vicariously. I may have been warned by callous friends – and I was, and with undisguised delight – that an imminent meeting with 'I. Pullem: Dentist' would be an agony of probes, picks, needles and drills. Even when I found the experience not half as bad as they had suggested, I would have been 'set' to wince as the innocuous little mirror on the long handle rattled against my teeth. Even the pink mouth-wash I treated like a poison.

Because I was (and still am) a child of my sub-culture, that is, I was influenced by, and reactive to, people's expectations of me, I probably passed on my attitudes to dentistry to some other naive child awaiting a first visit. And, as I expressed those attitudes, so I may have come to believe in them;

for, often, attitudes, based as they may be upon a learned emotion for or against an object or a person rather than upon some factual 'truth', may become firmly entrenched. The very articulation of such attitudes can lead to a formalizing of the attitudinal position, and to an apparent substantiation of them through the expression of them: 'If I've said it, it must be right'.

Because learning (and no less the learning of attitudes) is an interactive process, as some children develop through the process an antipathy towards dentistry (and caries because of it, possibly), so may the dentist develop an expectation of children's behaviour from wincing and whingeing children like me. Thus, the development of attitudes, while vicarious in some circumstances, may be empirically formed by others who are on the receiving end of certain behaviours. Such behaviours may be concomitants, or the results, of attitudes.

Attitude Formation in Schools

Teachers may build attitudes about pupils not necessarily as a direct result of their own interactions with them, but through an almost osmotic process which oozes from the experiences (real or imagined) of colleagues. So, too, will the pupils be constructing their own attitudes about school, and about teachers in particular, from reports of their friends' experiences (again, not necessarily 'real'), and from perceived behaviours of teachers.

This 'priming' of attitudes on both sides of the scholastic divide is a well-known phenomenon. We should not, therefore, be fooled into reacting to some pupils because of what other teachers may say about them, or how those teachers appear to behave towards them; yet we often do, for the steady drip of information and disinformation about pupils is likely to form stalagmite structures of attitudes which, once constructed, are extremely difficult to chip away.

This 'setting' of our expectations has been regarded by some social psychologists (for example, Allport, 1954) as determining what we will see or hear, think and do, when presented with the object of an attitude. However, attitudes may not be, entirely, triggers to an action. As a child, I would still have gone to the dentist, probably, even having been primed by my ghoulish friends, and whatever I would have said to a naive companion, I would still have returned. I may even have said 'Yes please' to the offer of a filling, and 'Thank you' at the end of the session.

Although attitudes may not dictate what we *do*, however, they probably form the templates against which we still *compare* the behaviours of others and from which we judge them. ('Teacher A is bad, but not as bad as teacher B.') At the same time, of course (and we often disregard this, from our egocentric eyrie) others are comparing and judging us against their own templates; this is the stuff of human interaction and there is no reason to suppose it occurs in schools to a lesser extent than in any other arena of our existence. As David Hargreaves (1972) has said, 'Interaction is not structured simply by the behaviour of two participants but by the ways in which the participants perceive each other'. This applies as much to schools as it does to the dentist's surgery. And, in this respect, our 'perception' of others may be beyond the senses; less upon the 'reality', more upon the expectations of the observer.

In *Fifteen Thousand Hours*, Rutter *et al.* (1979) reported not only that school characteristics (the 'ethos' of the school) tend to maximise the educational attainments of pupils, but also that teachers' attitudes to pupils are important ingredients: their expectations are likely to affect the ways in which pupils' behaviours and attitudes develop within and towards a school. So, one of the chief dynamic mechanisms working upon the development of pupils' attitudes and attainments may be that of a teacher's expectations regarding pupils' work.

The Relationship of Attitudes to Academic Attainments

There have been numerous studies which have indicated that attitudes of teachers to pupils, expressed by their expectations for those children, have a substantial effect upon academic attainments. This is not to say that the salient features of teachers' attitudes towards their pupils are always, or are solely, to do with the children's academic characteristics. They may also be directed at aspects of pupils' 'personalities'.

A number of people have addressed just that issue: do teachers categorize pupils in one dimension only, based upon characteristics of, for example, 'academic ability', or on 'personality'? Hallworth (1962) considered it possible that a favourable opinion of a pupil on one dimension could pass to other dimensions, but not necessarily with justifications. So, a pupil considered 'good' as far as general behaviour is concerned could also be regarded as being academically able.

In this study, Hallworth elicited the attitudes of male and female teachers in a variety of schools: grammar, secondary modern and comprehensive. He found all of them tended to regard their pupils in the same sort of way, irrespective of gender of teacher or of pupil, age of the child, and type of school. The attitudes Hallworth reported were formed, largely, from the teachers' perceptions of their pupils' apparent academic characteristics.

Taylor (1976) found the same. In an opening statement to his report, he said:

In teaching we know next to nothing of how teachers conceptualise their children and how different teachers may have varying preferences for certain types of information about their pupils (p. 25).

Taylor's aim was to 'chart the attributes which teachers use to explain and predict the activities and performances of the children in their classrooms', and he did an interesting job of it. Using George Kelly's repertory grid techniques, he found a clear preference on the part of the teachers in his sample for the pupil's academic performance. He also reported the broad measure of agreement between the attitudes of male and female teachers. To both of those groups, the academic industry and the attainments of their pupils were the most important characteristic features.

This concentration of teachers' attitudes upon the apparent academic ability of children had been forcefully commented upon earlier by Hargreaves (1967), who showed that there is a consistent link between 'streaming' and the frequently demonstrated expectations of teachers for pupils in those streams. He found that children who were placed in top streams were expected by their teachers to work hard, to behave well and to succeed academically: evidence of a 'halo' effect, where positive expectations in one dimension flow into others. Those children who found their way to the bottom streams, for whatever reasons, were not expected to work, were expected to misbehave and to truant, and to fail at school: evidence of negative attributes flowing from one dimension to others, sometimes called the 'horns' effect in these cases.

There is about Hargreaves' suggestion that feeling of expectancy so well described by Rosenthal and Jacobson (1968) in their famous 'Pygmalion' experiment, where pupils produced what was expected of them by their teachers. Their methodology, and their analysis of their results, have been severely questioned by many researchers, but the substance of their results fits with so many other findings from incursions into the field that it should not be rejected out of hand.

In their experiment, information about pupils was given to their teachers indicating that, predicted by IQ measures, some of the children would 'bloom' at a later time. Teachers reported that these pupils did, indeed, do well, but the original information fed to them was spurious. What Rosenthal and Jacobson did was to 'set' the teachers' expectations of good performances.

An opposing effect may operate. If children are marked ('labelled', if you like) as 'low achievers', but in fact do well, then there is strong indication that teachers may disregard the success and may react negatively against the pupils because they do not 'fit' the expectations held of them.

Information the teacher receives becomes part of that teacher's 'schema': part of the person's organization of past experiences and reactions. The possibility is that evidence is gathered to support that schema from whatever information seems to be available. It is filtered into an acceptable pattern by the teacher's understanding (his/her 'constructs') of the 'type' of child the information seems to suggest to the teacher. The pupil is then more firmly set into the system of classification as the teacher's attitudes crystallize around these constructs. This process has been recognised, and described, by David Hargreaves (1975) as one of Speculation, Elaboration and Stabilization. What seems to happen is that pupils judged by teachers in some way to be 'good' are given the benefit of the doubt even when they are not. Superior performances by pupils believed to be, in some way, 'bad', may be disregarded by teachers, or at least looked upon with scepticism.

While a number of studies have indicated that the salient features of pupil characteristics may be, for the teacher, academic ability, others have suggested different important dimensions; one of these has been that of social class.

Attitudes and Social Class

The issue of a relationship between learning difficulties and lower (rather than higher) social class has a relatively long research pedigree. (See Douglas, 1964; Douglas *et al.*, 1968; Davie *et al.*, 1972; and Wedge and Prosser, 1973, among others.) The essence of the argument is based, primarily, upon the cultural disadvantages which pertain, particularly, to the lower socio-economic groups: larger families, overcrowding, lower income, poor health, and language styles different from those which permeate the school environment, which erect linguistic barriers between teachers and disadvantaged pupils.

However, Barker Lunn (1970) suggested that an observed decline in the reading ability of children from lower social classes might be due, to a large extent, to their teachers' lower *expectations* of them: an attitudinal rather than an entirely cultural effect it would seem.

This supports Goodacre's (1968) study which showed that, rating their pupils' reading abilities at infant-school age, teachers rated more highly those children they believed to be from middle-class homes than those they thought came from a working-class background. The actual reading levels of the pupils, ascertained by standardized reading tests, did not reveal the degree of difference between the groups that was reported by the teachers. What is likely to be occurring in situations such as this is that the teachers are reporting their expectations of what standards pupils from differing social class backgrounds *should* attain: that is, pupils from middle-class families should attain 'higher' and those from working-class families should attain 'lower'.

One of the best-known studies of teachers' attitudes to their pupils' characteristics was carried out by Roy Nash (1973a and 1973b). He found personality characteristics of pupils were generally more important to teachers than apparent social class. However, he did hedge his bet a little by concluding:

> As regards social class it is almost certainly the case that some teachers are more sensitive to their pupils' social class than others (1973a);

which is to say that some do, and some don't. This qualification substantially undermines the idea that social class (or teachers' perception of it) is the single most important variable to teachers in building their constructs of their pupils.

What probably happens is that our own social backgrounds influence, to a degree, our expectations of others. Of course, if we are unaware of this possibility then our expectations are more firmly set. But this may be only one of the features of a child regarded as salient by the teacher, and it may not be the *most important* characteristic against which many of us measure other people because it is tempered by our own awareness of the potential influence that our own social background exerts upon our attitudes.

In my own research in this area (Phillips, 1986) while nearly 14 per cent of teachers' attitudinal statements, elicited by a repertory grid technique, about specific children referred to some aspects of their home backgrounds and their parents, only just over 1 per cent were statements directly related to social class. On the other hand, 44 per cent of the total statements given to me were to do with 'personality' characteristics; only 13 per cent of the total, however, were to do with 'academic' aspects of the pupils.

In addition, the teachers in my sample most frequently grouped characteristics of children they considered to have behaviour problems into a 'personality' dimension. However, they also linked some of these characteristics with statements of 'academic ability': for example, 'is dull', 'has a low-level of attainment', 'has learning difficulties', 'is remedial', 'finds the work difficult', and so on.

It was clear from my investigation that, although perceived social class was not the important characteristic others have found, there was an indication of the 'halo and horns' effects from 'personality' to 'academic' characteristics.

Teachers' Perceptions of Academic Failure

Leigh (1977) found that two dimensions were important to teachers: personality and 'academic ability'. Although these were separated for the sake of analysis, they often overlapped, indicating a measure – at least – of the halo effect mentioned earlier.

Blease (1978) was particularly interested in the expectancy effect in action with slow-learning children. Teachers' attitudes were elicited ·by asking the question 'If you were taking over a new class, which piece of information would you find most useful?' The replies fell into two categories: those related to 'personality' (these were in the majority) and those related to 'cognitive' attributes.

Allsop (1982) also looked at teachers' perceptions of children with learning difficulties. Narrowing her field of investigation to pupils with reading problems, she asked for teachers' attributions for those difficulties. Ravenette (1968) had already made a foray into this area and he had categorised the ways in which teachers attributed this type of failure into these broad groups:

Within child (that is, mental ability, physical ability, personality, attendance/migration);

Within home (that is, cultural background, encouragement at home);

Within school (that is, teaching methods, teachers' abilities and personality, classroom organization, materials).

Ravenette had found that the majority of the teachers in his sample (headteachers of schools in Kent and London) categorized reading problems in general mainly in terms of characteristics that lay 'within' the child. (It is interesting to note, however, that some six or seven years before the emergence of the 'schools make a difference' movement in Britain, Ravenette had recognized *some* statements of these teachers which directed attention at 'within school' factors for reading failure).

Using Ravenette's study as a benchmark for her own, Allsop looked at class-teachers' views of causative factors of reading difficulties (rather than more general views of headteachers), and in relation to the children they were actually in contact with. She found less emphasis was placed upon 'within child' causes and more upon 'within home' causes. When 'within child' factors were considered important, it was the 'personality' rather than the 'ability' of the child which was given more prominence.

The reason for teachers, in the studies of Ravenette and Allsop, seeing causes of reading problems residing within the child and within the home respectively, may have already been partly explained by Quirk (1967). He suggested that teachers see themselves significant, or not, in the school or a classroom according to whether they are faced with acceptable/satisfactory pupil-reactions to school and academic work, or problematic/troublesome ones. That is, when pupils behave and achieve well, teachers tend to see themselves as important influences. When the opposite occurs, teachers see themselves as not influential. In the latter situation, pupil-reactions are construed in terms of pupil-'pathologies' or of social determinants beyond the control of the teacher.

Good *et al.* (1969) had also investigated teachers' views of their pupils' poor academic performance. All the teachers in their sample invoked the 'innate idleness' and 'dimness' of their pupils or the parents to account for it. Only a small minority of the teachers also included themselves in their attribution of the pupils' poor attainments.

Whatever the primary focus of teachers' perceptions in regard to pupil-characteristics that lead to, or are concomitant with, academic failure, numerous studies have indicated that the attitudes of teachers expressed (not too subtly, sometimes) through their expectations of pupils have a substantial influence upon the academic attainments of their pupils. (For extensive reviews of these investigations, it would be helpful to see Pidgeon, 1970; Brophy and Good, 1974; and Nash, 1976).

It does appear that the teacher is likely to 'type' pupils upon some similarity with his or her existing schema (the 'template' I mentioned earlier). The teacher makes a tentative guess (not necessarily at a 'conscious' level) at what sort of pupil a child is likely to be as soon as they meet in class, or even before that when pupils are judged from prior reports. The possibility is that selective evidence is gathered to support the guess, from whatever source available, and filtered into a cohesive pattern to fit with the teacher's already formed constructs.

Using this sort of model, Leach (1977) has suggested that pupils who are perceived by their teachers as 'ideal' types are 'often rated highly on constructs such as lively, well-behaved, eager-to-learn, mature, stable, responsible, high IQ, good social background, stable family history'. Many of these constructs were not consistent with teachers' views of pupils with learning difficulties.

Because of the nature of our system of construing, it can happen that a teacher may perceive a child as having only a few of these factors; Leach suggested apparent high IQ, apparent higher rather than lower social class, an apparent high level of maturity. These perceptions may be based upon some discrete items of behaviour easily observable by the teacher; for example, neat work, polite speech, neat appearance, etc. After placing the child into the schema, Leach felt that other characteristics are 'assumed to cluster at similar positive (or negative) poles' by the teacher, as part of the 'halo' effect. In this way, some teachers, if they are naive regarding the formation of attitudes, may stereotype pupils into 'ideal', 'non-ideal' and 'intermediary' types.

What we seem to do, often, is 'judge the library by the titles of one or two books'.

The Effect of Attitudes upon Behaviour

There is not a great deal of evidence that attitudes lead directly to observable behaviour, but they may set up a situation where there is a predisposition to respond to the object of an attitude in a particular way. There are other determinants of behaviour besides attitudes. One of these may be the situation in which the holder of an attitude finds himself or herself. However, a number of studies have revealed that teachers tend to spend more time in the classroom interacting with pupils they believe to be 'bright' (Sharp and Green, 1975), and that there are often 'noticeable differences in [children's] academic and other *behaviour* [this writer's italics] depending upon whether the teacher liked them or not'. (Nash, 1973b).

The largest investigation in this area was carried out by Fry (1983). He set out to examine teacher-relationships with what he called 'problem' children, in terms of differences in measure of the teachers' classroom behaviours towards those two groups of pupils.

Fry's results indicated that 'problem' pupils received more 'negative effect' behaviours (verbal/non-verbal behaviours reflecting hostility or negative feelings) from teachers. They also obtained fewer social contacts with them and were asked less frequently to express their personal views and preferences. On the other hand, 'non-problem' pupils received a greater number of 'positive effect' behaviours (showing support or positive regard – such as smiling, joking, reinforcement and praise) from teachers and obtained more sustained feedback on their responses and task preferences.

Fry also concluded that there was, too,

> an apparent steady decline in teacher involvement with problem
> children [which was] accompanied by significantly greater passivity
> in children and a sharp incline in the incidence of problem children's
> serious misbehaviours (p. 85).

While, then, there may be equivocal evidence to support the contention that attitudes are springs to action on the part of the attitude-holder, it seems to be clearer that the behaviours of the pupil who is the attitude object is fundamentally affected by the existence and projection of the attitude by the teacher. Leach (1977) has said that not only are pupils' achievements affected by teacher-attitudes, but 'the recurring relationship of behaviour and low achievement generally found in schools ... highlights significant teacher-influences' (p. 189).

An Incomplete Equation

A serious limitation of this chapter is that it has (briefly) considered only one side of the attitudinal equation representing relationships between teachers and pupils: that is, the attitudes of teachers. The children, too, have their attitudes. They have their own constructs of 'good' and 'bad' teachers. They do not normally report them in school, at least not formally. But they may express their opinions (perhaps more eloquently) with their feet in the form of non-attendance, or directly at individual teachers by post-registration truancy. However, they are not usually asked to describe their attitudes to their teachers.

One of the earliest recognitions that an investigation of the other side of the equation is important was made by Ward (1926) when he said 'Surely one of the first steps towards the understanding of the young is to know how they regard us'. There are suggestions in more recent literature that a mutual understanding of reciprocal attitudes could lead to better school practice. For example, Reynolds (1982) said:

> It is likely that the key to successful modification of school practice
> lies in the mutual perceptions that govern teacher and pupil relations
> (p. 234).

At the heart of the educational process, it seems to me, are these centre-points of teachers' and pupils' reciprocal perceptions, formed from apparent attitudes and perceived behaviours (real, imaginary, or vicarious) and which lead to expectations of future behaviours. So often the behaviours of pupils and teachers are the result of the impact of the attitudes and behaviours of each upon the other. This develops a circularity. Perhaps it is only by breaking into the circle of mutual perception – expectation – reaction – mutual perception that an understanding of others' positions will be achieved. It is, often, only when the mirror of others' feelings to us is held up that we understand the influence of our views upon them.

For me, such an understanding is not a luxury in the educational process, but is a vital part of an unequivocal, equitable relationship between pupil and teacher. Salmon and Claire (1984) emphasized that:

Classroom communication, if it is to be effective, must depend upon mutual understanding; otherwise teachers' messages are not received as intended, nor ... are pupils' messages understood by teachers.

References

ALLPORT, G.W. (1954) 'Attitudes in the history of social psychology', in LINDSAY, G. (Ed) *Handbook of Social Psychology, Vol. II*, Cambridge, Mass., Addison–Wesley.

ALLSOP, NANCY (1982) *Exploring Teachers' Explanations for Reading Difficulties*, paper given at the British Conference on Personal Contruct Psychology, Manchester, Sept. 1982.

BARKER LUNN, JOAN C. (1970) *Streaming in the Primary School*, Slough, NFER.

BLEASE, D. (1978) 'Teachers' perceptions of slow-learning children: An ethnographic study', in *B. Educ. Res. J.*, 14, 1, pp. 39–42.

BROPHY, J.E. and GOOD, T.L. (1974) *Teacher-Student Relationship: Causes and Consequences*, New York, Holt, Rinehart and Winston.

DAVIE, R., BUTLER, M. and GOLDSTEIN, H. (1972) *From Birth to Seven*, London, Longman.

DOUGLAS, J.W.B. (1964) *The Home and The School*, London, MacGibbon and Kee.

DOUGLAS, J.W.B., ROSS, J.M. and SIMPSON, H.R. (1968) *All Our Future*, London, Davies.

FRY, P.S. (1983) 'Process measures of problem and non-problem children's classroom behaviour: The influence of teacher-behaviour variables', in *B.J. Educ. Psychol.*, 55, pp. 79–87.

GOOD, T.L. *et al.* (1969) *Listening to Teachers, Report Series 34*, Res. and Devel. Centre for Teachers Education, University of Texas at Austin.

GOODACRE, E. (1968) *Teachers and Their Pupils' Home Backgrounds*, Slough, NFER.

HALLWORTH, H.J. (1962) 'A teacher's perception of his pupils', in *Educ. Res.*, 14, 2, pp. 124–133.

HARGREAVES, D.H. (1967) *Social Relations in a Secondary School*, London, Routledge and Kegan Paul.

HARGREAVES, D.H. (1972) *Interpersonal Relations and Education*, London, Routledge and Kegan Paul.

HARGREAVES, D.H. (1975) *Deviance in Classrooms*, London, Routledge and Kegan Paul.

LEACH, D.J. (1977) 'Teachers' perceptions of "problem" pupils', in *Educ. Rev.*, 29, 3, pp. 188–203.

LEIGH, P.M. (1977) 'Greater Expectations: A consideration of the Self-fulfilling prophecy in the context of educability', in *Educ. Rev.*, 29, 4, pp. 317–324.

NASH, R. (1973a) 'Measuring teacher attitudes', in *Educ. Res.*, 14, 2, pp. 141–146.

NASH, R. (1973b) *Classrooms Observed*, London, Routledge and Kegan Paul.

NASH, R. (1976) *Teacher Expectation and Pupil Learning*, London, Routledge and Kegan Paul.

PHILLIPS, D.D. (1986) *Reciprocal Personal Constructs of Teachers and Pupils in Secondary Schools Elicited by Repertory Grid Techniques*, unpublished Ph.D. thesis, University of Wales.

PIDGEON, D.A. (1970) *Expectation and Pupil Performance*, Slough, NFER.

QUIRK, T. (1967) 'An experimental investigation of the teacher's attribution of the locus of causality of student performance', in *Dissertation Abstracts*, 28, 256, cited in LEACH, D.J. (1977) 'Teachers' perceptions of "problem" pupils', in *Educ. Rev.*, 29, 3, pp. 188–203.

RAVENETTE, A.T. (1968) *Dimensions of Reading Difficulties*, Oxford, Pergamon.

REYNOLDS, D. (1982) 'The search for effective schools', in *School Organisation*, 2, 3, pp. 215–237.

ROSENTHAL, R. and JACOBSON, L. (1968) *Pygmalion in the Classroom*, New York, Holt, Reinhart and Winston.

RUTTER, M., MAUGHAN, B., MORTIMORE, P. and OUSTON, J. (1979) *Fifteen Thousand Hours: Secondary Schools and Their Effects on Children*, London, Open Books.

SALMON, PHILLIDA, and CLAIRE, HILARY (1984) *Classroom Collaboration*, London, Routledge and Kegan Paul.

SHARP, R. and GREEN, A. (1975) *Education and Social Control*, London, Routledge and Kegan Paul.

TAYLOR, M.T. (1976) 'Teachers' perceptions of their pupils', in *Res. in Educ.*, 16, pp. 25–36.

WARD, J. (1926) *Psychology applied to education. Lectures given at Cambridge in 1880*, Cambridge, Cambridge University Press, cited in TAYLOR, P.H. (1962) 'Children's Evaluations of the Characteristics of the Good Teacher', in *B.J. Educ. Psychol.*, 32, pp. 258–266.

WEDGE, P. and PROSSER, H. (1973) *Born to Fail?*, London, Arrow.

Chapter 3

Special Educational Needs and Pastoral Care
David Galloway

Introduction

The Warnock Report (DES, 1978) and the 1981 Education Act have resulted in greater awareness that schools have a responsibility for a substantial minority of pupils with special educational needs. The widely publicized figure of 20 per cent may be criticized as a statistical artifact resulting from the way tests and behaviour screening instruments are developed. It may also be criticized as a political compromise, reflecting the committee's view that teachers should be entitled to expect extra help in teaching the most difficult or disturbing 20 per cent of pupils, rather than 10 or 30 per cent. There is much less doubt that teaching these children is always challenging and potentially stressful. This is scarcely surprising given the range of special needs in most ordinary schools, from sensory and physical disabilities to the many more children presenting learning and/or behavioural problems.

The Hargreaves Report on secondary education in London argued that many schools cater inadequately for pupils of below average ability (ILEA, 1984). It is implicit in the report that the pupils benefiting least from their schooling are those who might be regarded on Warnock's criteria as having special educational needs. Most teachers would probably agree on the importance of pastoral care for these pupils, even if they failed to agree on the definition, aims, scope and curriculum implications of pastoral care. It is argued in this chapter that the functions of pastoral care are educational and developmental, and should be incorporated into the timetable for all pupils. A more restrictive 'negative net' model is, however, still quite prevalent.

This involves heads of year and other senior staff with pastoral responsibilities in spending most of their time dealing with problems referred to them by colleagues. The problems may be of a 'welfare' nature, but are as likely to concern problems of discipline and classroom management. In one school the disciplinary functions of pastoral care staff had resulted in it being known in the staffroom as 'penal care'. To anyone familiar with this negative net model, there is a certain inevitability that pupils with special educational needs should, in many schools, monopolize the time and energy of pastoral staff. It is surprising, then, that there have been few attempts to establish conceptual links between the theory and practice of pastoral care and of provision for special educational needs.

This chapter assumes a commitment to educate children with special educational needs in ordinary schools, and identifies the implications for pastoral care. Pastoral care for pupils with special needs cannot be divorced from discussion of a school's overall pastoral policy and practice. Hence, it is necessary first to identify some underlying issues. These will lead to discussion of the specific pastoral issues concerning pupils with special needs, and of the educational implications of special needs for the school's pastoral programme.

Underlying Assumptions

For theoretical and practical reasons, schools are unable to cater effectively for their pupils with special needs if they do not also cater well for the majority of pupils. A central aim of special education is to equip pupils to live as normal a life as possible. In this respect, integration is merely a step towards the more radical goal of 'normalization' (Yesseldyne and Algozzine, 1982). Logically, this goal cannot be achieved if the mainstream of the school is not working well. The argument illustrates both the importance and the problems of a 'whole-school' approach to special educational needs. A 'whole-school' approach implies:

(a) a commitment to full functional integration for pupils with special needs, with a corresponding rejection of separate special classes and of withdrawal groups except, possibly, for specific, short-term purposes;

(b) a willingness to carry out a rigorous review of the school's organization, curriculum, teaching methods and pastoral care;

(c) a mutual expectation that specialist staff and colleagues in the mainstream will work together to ensure that pupils with special needs achieve recognition and success in the mainstream curriculum.

Curriculum initiatives for 'non-academic' pupils provide a good illustration of an obstacle to a whole-school policy. Whatever teachers intend, pupils of all ability levels are in no doubt about the second-class status of the alternative curricula. The message conveyed through the hidden curriculum is arguably as harmful for the examination candidates as for pupils with special needs (Hargreaves, 1983).

Just as effective teaching for pupils with special needs presupposes effective teaching for the majority, effective pastoral care for 'special' children presupposes effective pastoral care throughout the school. It is not in the interests of children with special needs that they should monopolise the 'pastoral' time of year heads. Nor is it in the interest of other pupils. Two questions arise from these considerations:

(1)   What are the implications for pastoral care of individual children with special needs?

(2)   How can pastoral care contribute to a 'whole-school' policy for special educational needs?

The Pastoral Programme

The principal components of pastoral care are personal, social, educational and vocational guidance. Thus, topics as diverse as personal and social education, sex education, study skills and careers guidance could all be seen as pastoral tasks. Obviously, these have curriculum implications, but it is worth distinguishing between

(1)   pastoral care: essentially an administrative concept, referring to how the school caters for the care and welfare of its pupils;

(2)   the pastoral curriculum: everything children need to learn in order (a) to make the best possible use of the school; (b) to promote their personal and social development; (c) to make informed choices, especially on subject options and on careers;

(3)   the pastoral programme: shows how the pastoral curriculum is to be taught, and at what stages in the pupils' career;

(4)   the tutorial programme: that part of the pastoral programme which is taught by form tutors (other parts may be covered by subject teachers, for example, aspects of health education in biology, home economics or PE).

In two seminal articles Marland (1980, 1983) has described the scope and content of the pastoral curriculum. The central point here is that the educational and developmental tasks which form the core of the pastoral curriculum are taught through the pastoral programme. It is a fallacy that pastoral activities consist mainly of individual case-work.

> *The paradox of actually delivering pastoral care is that you have to help individuals without giving individual help.* This means group work, and building up the work of tutors (Marland, 1983, p. 26; emphasis in original).

The Pastoral Team

The most frequent way of organizing pastoral care in secondary schools in Britain involves a horizontal network coordinated by a deputy head. Ideally, the deputy head would plan the pastoral curriculum with the team of year tutors (heads of year), in close cooperation with heads of relevant subject departments. This group would also produce an outline of each year's tutorial programme, but the details would be planned by each head of year as coordinator of a team of form tutors.

The head of year's responsibility as coordinator of a team of tutors is dictated not only by the need to plan the pastoral and tutorial programme, but also by practical considerations concerning pupils' welfare. It is clearly necessary

(a)   that every pupil in the school should be known well by at least one teacher;

(b)   that one teacher should be responsible for coordinating and disseminating information relevant to each pupil's progress or management;

(c)   that this teacher should also monitor each pupil's progress across the curriculum on a systematic basis.

In a primary school the class teacher undertakes these tasks as a matter of course. In secondary schools, where each pupil may be taught by ten teachers in the course of a week, they are just as necessary. Heads of year cannot realistically hope to undertake direct responsibility for the personal guidance of all pupils in their year, nor for oversight of their educational progress. Still less can deputy heads or counsellors. In practice the head of year must work through the team of tutors, in just the same way that the head of maths, or any other subject, has to work through teachers in that particular team.

Form tutors, then, have an essential role in pastoral care, extending beyond the tutorial programme to include more general responsibility for each pupil's personal and educational welfare. Just as an inexperienced subject teacher should expect a great deal of support from his head of department, so inexperienced form tutors should expect support and guidance from the head of year. Such guidance will be particularly necessary in the case of pupils with special needs. The head of year's task is to be aware of strengths and weaknesses of individual tutors and to provide or arrange in-service training when necessary. In the same way that the head of a subject department should not be judged by his or her own teaching ability, but by the quality of work throughout the department, so a head of year should be judged by the quality of pastoral care provided by the team of tutors.

Pastoral Tasks with Pupils with Special Educational Needs

Curriculum Coordination

Another of the fallacies of pastoral care refuted by Marland (1983) is its separation from the curriculum. In fact, maintaining oversight of a pupil's progress across the curriculum is one of the key pastoral tasks for form tutors.

Following assessment under the 1981 Act, the LEA produces a statement indicating the nature of the child's special needs and how they should be met. While overall responsibility for the curriculum of children with statements is likely to rest with the head of the special needs department, some of the needs identified will require the active involvement of staff with pastoral responsibilities. More important, it should be recognized that children with statements account for a very small proportion of the school's children with special needs. The tutors' responsibility for maintaining oversight of their pupils' progress across the curriculum places them in the front line in identifying special needs. Uneven performance in different subjects and deterioration in progress or motivation in one or all areas are just two obvious indications that further investigation is needed.

Dissemination of Information

Ensuring a reliable and smooth interchange of information is a traditional pastoral task, but still a necessary one. In the case of children with medical conditions such as petit mal, haemophilia or catarrhal deafness the need is obvious enough, though even here failures of communication seem to occur with extraordinary frequency. As important, and more difficult, is the need to exchange information relevant to the teaching and management of children whose needs are less obvious, less acute, yet in many ways more complex. The danger here is that on hearing information, for example about home problems that affect completion of homework, some teachers may expect less from the pupil, and thus inadvertently reduce the potential benefit of success and achievement at school. A more constructive response would, of course, be to make arrangements for pupils to complete *at school* the work they are unable to do at home.

Guidance in Specialist Areas

Some children require guidance of a more specialist nature than can be provided through the mainstream tutorial or pastoral programme. Obvious examples are study skills and careers guidance. Pastoral staff may not be able to offer such guidance themselves. They do, nevertheless, have a responsibility: (i) for identifying the need; (ii) for ensuring that it is met, if necessary by seeking support from agencies outside the school

Counselling

Few heads of year and even fewer form tutors have had formal training in counselling. They do, however, need some basic counselling skills to undertake their pastoral work effectively. This is evident if we consider common problems such as failure to complete homework. Possible reasons include: dislike of the subject; lack of understanding; dislike of the teacher; common or garden laziness; lack of facilities at home; incipient disaffection from school, perhaps associated with fringe membership of an anti-authority group of pupils; tension at home; and so on. Often, the explanation is obvious enough. Sometimes more detailed inquiry is needed, requiring patience, tact, ability to see the pupil's point of view in a non-judgmental manner and the ability to pursue a line of inquiry without arousing defensive anxiety in the pupil. Perhaps the most important skill for pastoral staff, though, is to recognize the limits to their own competence, knowing when to seek assistance from a more experienced member of staff or from a member of an appropriate agency outside the school.

Liaison with Support Services and other Agencies

Referral to one of the LEA support services is sometimes seen as a last resort, indicating that responsibility must now be passed to someone else. The unstated reason for referral here may be to initiate a process resulting in the pupil's transfer to a designated special school or centre, thus equating the School Psychological Service with the Special School Removals Service. More constructively, teachers can seek a partnership with support services, using their expertise to develop a clearer understanding of the pupil's needs, and of ways in which they may be met. This model assumes an equal partnership between teachers and members of the support services in which each shares experience and expertise with the other (Galloway, 1985a).

Liaison with Parents

Warnock's notion of parents as partners is a well known piece of educational rhetoric that is not always reflected in practice. Developing active, mutually cooperative links with parents is a fundamental pastoral task. In the case of pupils with special needs it becomes a necessary ingredient in any effective programme. Links with the parents of these pupils will not, however, be possible in the absence of similarly constructive links with parents of other pupils. A recent study in Wales has shown that such links can be established (Woods, 1984).

Special Needs and the Pastoral Programme

Personal and Social Education

The importance of personal and social skills has been emphasized in recent initiatives for education of the 14-19-year-old age group. Skills training, though, is merely one aspect of personal and social education. The Schools Council project on the overlapping topic of moral education appeared more concerned with cognitive and affective development, proposing a wide range of problems for class discussion (McPhail *et al.*, 1972). More recently Pring (1984) has provided a useful analysis from a more theoretical perspective.

The tutorial programmes of Button (1982) and Baldwin and Wells (1981) illustrate one way of introducing personal and social education into the tutorial programme. Their work may, however, unintentionally have fostered the view that personal and social education can safely be left in the backwater of the tutorial period, and hence that it has no implications for the wider curriculum. A further problem is that their materials are used very unevenly. Many schools have bought them, but many teachers feel uncomfortable with some of the activities proposed, and resist using them. The difficulty seems to be that these authors imply that tutorial work requires a new and different set of skills to those required in classroom teaching. It might have been more helpful to have started with the tutors' *existing* skills as subject teachers, and to have considered how these might be applied in the area of personal and social education.

The issues we need to consider here concern provision of personal and social education for all pupils, and provision for pupils with special needs. The usefulness of anything provided through the curriculum, though, depends on the social climate of the school. There is something more than faintly ridiculous in the spectacle of form tutor groups practising Button's 'trusting' activities in a school at which new entrants are regularly bullied by older pupils. The point is that behaviour in one context, in this instance the tutorial group, does not necessarily transfer to other situations. A practical example of this is the enormously varied ways in which the same pupils behave with different teachers. Nevertheless, acknowledging the importance of the school's social climate does not negate the desirability for personal and social education in the curriculum and/or in the tutorial programme. Developing pupils' awareness as thinking, contributing members of their peer group, school, family and wider community is an essential pastoral task. To succeed in this task it is essential that the climate of respect between teachers and pupils throughout the school should be consistent with the climate in the classroom.

Whether pupils with special educational needs have specific needs for personal and social education is more complex and more controversial. Certainly, these pupils frequently have poor relationships, both with other pupils and with adults. Social skills training has become a fashionable topic, attempting to teach more successful inter-personal skills. Unfortunately, in spite of the practitioners' enthusiasm, research on the usefulness of social skills training has yielded rather discouraging results, at least with delinquents (Hollin and Henderson, 1984). Again, a major problem is one of transfer; skills acquired in one situation do not necessarily transfer to others. A further problem is that groups for pupils with special needs may reinforce a separate identity, in which they see themselves as different from pupils in the rest of the school. Although empirical evidence is lacking, it seems probable on theoretical grounds that the most effective personal and social education for pupils with special needs will be provided in, and reinforced by, the school's mainstream. Separate groups are most likely to be useful if: (a) their aims are clear and limited; (b) they operate on a short-term basis; (c) opportunities are found to maintain new skills outside the group sessions.

Awareness of Disability

It is axiomatic from previous sections that effective pastoral care for pupils with special needs requires a climate throughout the school (a) which accepts and respects individual differences; (b) in which the achievements and efforts of the least able are valued as highly as those of the most able. It follows that the school should encourage all children to accept and respect exceptionality. As the Fish Report (ILEA, 1985) so clearly recognized, this has wide-ranging implications, requiring racial tolerance and respect for minority cultures as well as a constructively sympathetic approach to special educational needs. A pastoral programme has a central role to play here. It would include factual information about disability, and would seek to develop some understanding of related concepts. It would also aim to develop pupils' ability to recognise how they may help people with special needs, and to promote a willingness to do so.

Some topics that might be included in the pastoral programme are shown in Figure 3.1. Some of these are suitable for tutorial periods, while others could usefully be incorporated into the syllabus of different subjects. Naturally, the content will vary from school to school, depending on the interests, skills and priorities of staff. If awareness of disability is to be tackled by form tutors, the same principles apply as to any other aspect of the tutorial programme:

(1) members of the tutorial team should participate in preparation; if each tutor proposes an outline for one session and distributes this to all colleagues, no great expenditure of time is involved; moreover, this is an opportunity for tutors to learn from, and use, each other's skill and experience;

(2) content and structure should be clear, preferably with materials to use as guidelines in each period (many tutorial programmes flounder through lack of adequate preparation);

(3) the programme should not require knowledge or teaching techniques that some tutors may be unable or unwilling to acquire, but rather should build on and develop the existing strengths of members of the team.

Conclusions

Heads of year and form tutors can help to ensure that their pupils' special needs are recognized and met. The way teachers approach their pastoral responsibilities can create a climate which accepts and respects special needs, ensure that the achievements of children with special needs are valued, and create opportunities for them to contribute, and be seen to be contributing, to the school community. Conversely, as Best *et al.* (1983) demonstrate in

	CONCEPTS	FACTS	ATTITUDES	SKILLS
DISABILITY	Effect of treatment (e.g. wearing glasses prevents a defect from becoming a handicap). Historical figures with disabilities – effect on their behaviour. Can a physical disability sometimes be an advantage? Discrimination for and against disabled people: (a) in history; (b) in major world religions; (c) in literature; (d) in present-day society. The rights of disabled people: 'normalization'. Functions of helping organisations, e.g. Samaritans, AA, NSPCC.	Range of common disabilities in the class (e.g. shortsightedness, etc.). How the school caters for pupils/teachers with disabilities. Facilities (or lack of them) for the disabled: (a) in the school; (b) in public places in the locality. Common sources of confusion (e.g. deafness and intellectual handicap). Medical and welfare services for the disabled. Achievements of disabled people (e.g. paraplegic child olympics; public figures, mouth and toe paintings, etc). Side effects of some drugs (e.g. Thalidomide).	Attitudes towards children with disabilities: (a) in Middle Ages; (b) in nineteenth century; (c) today. Fear of disability; fear of the unknown. Disability in literature (e.g. Treasure Island). Social consequences of leprosy. Traditional employment of disabled people in circuses – changing attitudes. Acceptance of human variations (e.g., dwarfism, gigantism). Attitudes of major world religions to disability (e.g. in Bible, Koran).	Make survey of local provision for disabled people. Aids and equipment for disabled people and the elderly. Produce local maps for disabled. Produce braille map for the sight impaired. Make survey of locations of accidents to children (e.g., street intersections, danger spots in the home, etc.).

Figure 3.1: Topics Concerning Disability

their perceptive study of one school, pastoral care can also mask deficiencies both in climate and in organization. In other words it can operate to maintain an unsatisfactory status quo (Galloway, 1985b).

Children with special needs can reveal starkly any shortcomings in their school's curriculum, teaching methods and pastoral care. The challenge for everyone with pastoral responsibilities is to adapt and develop resources existing within the school to cater for the needs which are identified. This in itself would be a worthwhile exercise. Because provision of effective education for children with special needs is likely to improve the quality of education throughout the school, it becomes even more worthwhile.

References

BALDWIN, J. and WELLS, K. (1981) *Active Tutorial Work. 1. The First Year – 5. The fifth Year*, Oxford, Blackwell.

BEST, R., RIBBINS, P., JARVIS, C. with ODDY, D. (1983) *Education and Care*, London, Heinemann.

BUTTON, L. (1982) *Group Tutoring for the Form Tutor. 1. Lower Secondary School. 2. Upper Secondary School*, London, Hodder and Stoughton.

DES (1978) *Special Educational Needs (The Warnock Report)*, London, HMSO.

GALLOWAY, D. (1985a) *Schools and Persistent Absentees*, Oxford, Pergamon Press.

GALLOWAY, D. (1985b) *Schools, Pupils and Special Educational Needs*, London, Croom Helm.

HARGREAVES, D.H. (1983) *The Challenge for the Comprehensive School: Culture, Curriculum, Community*, London, Routledge and Kegan Paul.

HOLLIN, C.R. and HENDERSON, M. (1984) 'Social skills training with young offenders: false expectations and the "failure of treatments"', *Behavioural Psychotherapy*, 12, pp. 331–341.

ILEA (1984) *Improving Secondary Schools (The Hargreaves Report)*, London, ILEA.

ILEA (1985) *Equal Opportunities for All? (The Fish Report)*, London, ILEA.

McPHAIL, P., UNGOED-THOMAS, J.R. and CHAPMAN, H. (1972) *Moral Education in the Secondary School*, London, Longman.

MARLAND, M. (1980) 'The Pastoral Curriculum', in BEST, R., JARVIS, C. and RIBBINS, P. (Eds) *Perspectives in Pastoral Care*, London, Heinemann.

MARLAND, M. (1983) 'Preparing for promotion in pastoral care', in *Pastoral Care in Education*, 1, pp. 24–36.

PRING, R. (1984) *Personal and Social Education in the Curriculum: Concepts and Content*, London, Hodder and Stoughton.

WOODS, P. (1984) *Parents and School: A Report for Discussion on Liaison between Parents and Secondary Schools in Wales*, London, Schools Council Publications.

YESSELDYNE, J. and ALGOZZINE, B. (1982) *Critical Issues in Special and Remedial Education*, Boston, Houghton Miffin.

Chapter 4

Institutional Change — a Whole-School Approach
Tony Kloska

Despite Warnock, despite the 1981 Education Act, despite the great desire underpinning the work of many teachers involved with the special needs of pupils to promote a better understanding of their work, real change in many of our secondary schools will continue to remain an elusive objective. The reason is that these schools have a structure built into their organisational framework which is strong, traditional and ultimately defensive against any innovation which threatens to expose attitudes which are discriminatory, self-satisfied and narrow. It is this writer's intention to expose this structure for what it is but then to outline an approach which, if tackled in an honest, realistic and imaginative manner, could possibly change the very nature of some of our secondary schools. The basic philosophy of the approach is essentially simple. The consequences of its acceptance are complex and potentially exciting. Practice and theory will be discussed but the central thrust of the chapter is, in effect, a plea – to end the insularity that is sometimes sought, sometimes forced, sometimes produced by individuals and groups within these institutions. Many teachers will find some of the issues raised aggressive and demanding. It may well be useful to remember that most change is welcomed when it leads to benefits for those at whom the change is aimed. Therefore another plea is – be imaginative and open to the possibility of reappraisal of attitudes and practice.

In our secondary schools the principal restraining structure to significant and positive change is the division of the curriculum into subject areas. True, it has probably been handed down by our universities, either by shrewd calculation or by benign indifference, yet it is responsible for both pupils and teachers being unable to grasp the concept of wholeness, which, it can be argued, is a prerequisite for the interaction which is necessary to allow our schools to develop rather than to stagnate. The influence of this curriculum division is wide-reaching. It is to the provision made in schools for pupils with special educational needs that this writer would turn, in an effort to remove some of the negative effects that have been produced, whilst at the same time creating the opportunity for subject specialists to evaluate more aptly what they could offer to all pupils and to all teachers.

It is usually the case that in secondary schools Maths teachers teach Maths, English teachers teach English, Art teachers teach Art and so on. Each subject sub-group on the staff of a school regard themselves as the specialists for their particular block of the curriculum. Yet there is another sub-group of teachers who also regard themselves as specialists. They teach pupils with special educational needs. Herein lies an anomaly, for this last group gain their identifying specialist label not for *what* they teach (as in the case with the others) but for *whom* they teach. A whole-school approach to meeting the special needs of pupils would turn this anomaly on its head. A change in the nature of the institution would, logically, follow.

The term 'special educational needs' has essentially evolved post-Warnock. It would not be far from the mark to suggest however that in most secondary schools the term has merely become the latest label for what were formerly known as the remedial and possibly behavioural problems that certain pupils presented. If, however, a school is prepared to widen the special needs definition, the attempts made to work as effectively as possible to meet the requirements of the definition can expose a vast treasure-house of 'hidden' expertise and resources within any school. It must be noted that a radical shift in attitude by many teachers is a primary implication for a wider definition to be accepted. This ensues because acceptance of the definition challenges the status of teachers and of many pupils. Acceptance challenges the organization which subject areas have evolved. Acceptance challenges elements of the practice used to effect learning by individuals and groups of teachers.

A wider definition would consider the following to be pupils who have special needs, be they long-term or transitory:

Those pupils who have specific or general learning difficulties; who experience or present social, emotional or behavioural problems; who have a physical handicap; who are considered or assessed to be seriously underachieving *whatever* their ability level; who are considered or assessed to be specifically or generally most able. (Definition produced by a small group of cross-professionals on a Suffolk Educational Working Party sub group).

There are, or can possibly be deduced, enough elements in this definition to forecast that any pupil, at some point in her/his school life, could have a special educational need.

Acceptance of this definition has major consequences for all teachers in a school. To begin with, the special needs staff will have to adopt a radically different role from the present one, which in most instances sees them being regarded as almost sole providers of the expertise and resources on offer to a relatively small number of pupils. The nature of this different role will be detailed at a further point. For all other teachers a far greater degree of responsibility to identify, assess and meet the special needs of pupils has to be accepted. The whole school will, of necessity, have to look to external agencies and resources in its immediate community and sometimes further afield.

Various questions are possibly being formulated at this point. Why should the definition be widened? Why is there implicit criticism of the current practice designed to meet the special needs of students? Why are specialist teachers, so often the victims of other initiatives, to be asked to increase their workload? The answers to all these questions have a common base. It is as a result of the curriculum division in secondary schools that current practice and attitudes discriminate against an identified minority of pupils whilst making dangerously generalized assumptions about the majority.

It is not this writer's intention to denigrate the mantle of specialism worn by subject teachers. Rather it is to call for their expertise to be evidenced and made available to all pupils. As importantly, it is a call for subject specialists to open themselves to the influence of the other teachers across the curriculum, so that a *whole* response to the needs of pupils can be generated.

Prior to examining the wider definition of special needs in greater detail, it would be appropriate to outline the role of the special needs teachers resulting from a whole-school approach.

Role of Special Educational Needs Coordinators

The prime task would be to coordinate the development of strategies which are identified by the whole staff in the identification of a response to the special educational needs of pupils in the school. Many of these strategies will, as it were, be released onto the open market through the developing awareness that all other staff will gain of their responsibilities towards pupils with special needs. There will be a clear necessity to instigate appropriate in-service training to enable this process to become more refined and sophisticated. These coordinators will have to provide a range of information concerning the resources which exist in the school, local community and Education Authority as a whole. They will have to instigate programmes which lead to the development of appropriate assessment methods, parental involvement and the support of external agencies. There would be a responsibility to foster analysis of the curriculum and the teaching practice and materials used to deliver the curriculum in the school. They would assist in creating the structures necessary to allow contact between the school, other schools and support professionals. Their baseline would therefore be one which allowed them to enable the whole school to respond to the special educational needs of pupils in a flexible and dynamic fashion.

What then, with reference to the wider definition, is the current state of practice, and what are the implications and new directions practice will have to take? Particular schools may have already developed reasonably progressive practice but for the majority the generalizations concerning current provision probably hold good.

Pupils with Specific or General Learning Difficulties

Such pupils are often an identified group taught by remedial teachers for subjects like English, Mathematics and Humanities. This can take the form of full-time extraction from these subjects or part-time extraction from mainstream classes but they are still taught separately from their peers. Occasionally there is in-class support within these areas of the curriculum but the constant factor is that these pupils are readily identifiable by their peers as being, in some way, different. The pupil with a specific learning difficulty is often, in a sense, processed to the point where he/she is treated in a very similar fashion to pupils who are generally regarded as having low ability. The needs of this group of children in other areas of the curriculum are often not met and structural arrangements exist within some subject areas to allow the creation of 'sink' groups so that the majority of pupils are not 'held back' by their less able peers. Curriculum content is often watered down to the level where there is little resemblance to the concepts being tackled by the rest of the ability range.

A whole-school approach would lay a great deal of responsibility on *every* department in a secondary school to adapt its curriculum so that such pupils are given every chance to become exposed to the concepts their more able peers are tackling in that subject. Subject specialists would be responsible for teaching these pupils within whichever organizational framework the department felt appropriate. Each department could call for support from the special needs coordinators in the production of resources and teaching methods.

Pupils Experiencing or Presenting Social, Emotional or Behavioural Difficulties

The range of strategies developed by schools in this country is enormous, with the proliferation of labels used to describe pupils stemming from the in-vogue theory of the moment. In secondary schools a pupil who has or presents problems of this nature is entering into a merry-go-round system which almost exclusively focuses all attention on the pupil. Class teachers seek help, advice or sanctions from Heads of Department; form tutors go directly to senior pastoral staff when they are unable to resolve a situation. The idiosyncratic nature of teaching is at its most pronounced level when it comes to the nature of official interventions with these pupils. On-site units, off-site units, sanctuaries, time-out rooms, behaviour modification, active tutorial work, home systems, horizontal arrangements (year groups) – the list could go on for a page. The use of external agencies such as Educational Welfare Officers, Social Services and Educational Psychologists makes this an even more confused area of practice than it has any right to be. When the difficulties are perceived to be reasonably serious any one of the previously mentioned strategies or professionals could become involved. Sadly it is in the nature of schools to be more concerned with those pupils who present their difficulties in an overt and aggressive manner and a lot of time is directed towards them. Before anyone levels the accusation that the writer is playing down the level of seriousness of this situation it would be fair to point out that he taught in an on-site unit for a number of years. The point is, however, that somehow the system is expected to *deal with* these pupils and the writer would propose that by adopting a whole-school approach a school should, initially at least, critically examine what role *it* has to play in the instigation of the difficulties presented by pupils. In no way does this deny that some pupils can be extremely disturbed or disturbing. Issues such as classroom management, pupil-teacher interaction and pupil and teacher survival strategies need to be identified and sometimes resolved in favour of the pupil. Also a level of concern needs to be reached so that some of the more idiosyncratic elements in meeting the needs of these pupils are rationalized and the pupils needs are *met* and not *dealt* with.

Pupils with Physical Handicaps

Quite rightly, more physically handicapped pupils are coming into ordinary schools. Local authorities are providing more resources which allow schools to meet the needs which arise. Sadly, it is at the point where physical resource meets physical need that many LEAs and schools feel their obligation has been fulfilled. A whole-school approach could allow vital work to start on examining the attitudes of all individuals in the schools towards handicap. Such work would benefit the handicapped and non-handicapped pupil alike.

Underachievement of Pupils whatever their Ability Level

The term 'low achiever' is usually synonymous with children of low ability. Efforts are made to provide opportunities for these pupils to improve. It is within the scope of a whole-school approach to examine the methods used by teachers across the curriculum to motivate the underachievers of whatever ability level and to disseminate proven good practice throughout the school. There is of course a realization that teachers are often under great pressures from syllabus and lack of resources/time but there are clear grounds to support the contention that the underachieving pupil has a special educational need.

Generally or Specifically most able Pupils

This is a politically and educationally fraught area of discussion. Some see no need to allocate extra time or resources to such pupils, others do, and individual schools, departments and authorities have made movements to meet the special needs of these pupils. The provision ranges from curriculum extension work to the establishment of high-flier groups. Each school will of course make its own decision but this writer does believe that such pupils do have a special need and their inclusion within the definition is morally justified. A whole-school approach would allow identification of attitudes and practice over this issue and if a scheme or philosophy were to be adopted then the school would be better positioned to tap into the external resources that are available.

The gulf between present and possible practice is wide. A principal reason is that, at the moment, there exists a fundamental abrogation of responsibility by many teachers, parents and Local Education Authorities towards the special educational needs of a minority pupil grouping. There is a fundamental difference between the philosophy which calls for these pupils to be *dealt* with and the philosophy of the whole-school approach which requests an overall acceptance of the responsibility an institution has to *meet* the needs of any pupil at any point in their school life. To continue to follow current practice devalues the skills of all concerned and can only lead to the burgeoning expansion of 'the professional groups whose very job depends on their identifying problems' (Tutt, 1983).

The Whole-school Approach

> At this point in our history we must enter once again into the debate that preceded mass schooling over a century ago, namely: what kind of society do we want to create and how can the education system help us to realize such a society? The answers we reach will determine the relation between education and society into the twenty-first century (Hargreaves, 1982).

A whole-school approach is not a cost-cutter in terms of time, physical or human resources. The approach does not deny the obvious areas of skill, expertise, good practice and integrity which exist today in our secondary schools. It does not imply a revolutionary overthrow of the organization and management systems developed in schools. The approach has as its basic assumption the awareness that schools are full of good practice and caring and positive attitudes towards the social and academic development of pupils. At the moment many of these elements are locked into subject areas and individual classrooms. They are not widely available and that situation cannot be justified. Neither can current practice which allows discrimination (whatever the good intention which underlies it) against or for, a minority of pupils. Schools also have elements of bad practice and negative attitudes (amongst teachers and pupils) which need to be exposed and challenged. A whole-school approach is capable of taking the previously mentioned, but lengthy definition of special education needs to its logical conclusion which is that a special educational need is 'an individual need that may occur at any point in the educational process which cannot automatically be met by existing practice'.

How then can a whole-school approach meet this definition? The school will need to embark upon an on-going process of self-analysis. Questions concerning the aims and objectives of the school should be raised to evaluate the difference, if any, between their representation on paper and the reality of how they are achieved. Analysis can be instigated across the curriculum into how teachers actually teach and how subject departments work. How do pupils learn? How do they cope with points in their school life such as transition from one school to another? How do they cope with the subject choices that are made at 14? How do both pupils and teachers respond to and assess failure and success? How does a school respond to crisis? What are the effects of timetable, buildings, fabric, resources and external pressures on the atmosphere and ethos of a school? How do pupil and teacher motivations, expectations and strategies relate to each other? What is the status of the school in the community, in the eyes of parents and the LEA?

Implications of a Whole-school Approach for Teachers and Subject Divisions

Teachers in each area of the curriculum have to set in motion a process which allows them to assess the criteria by which the definition is met. Potentially their target group is every pupil they teach. The pastoral teams have a similar task but both groups need to acknowledge that the whole school needs the opportunity to be positively critical and that good practice and resources are in common ownership. Central themes in the process will include extensive self-evaluation in cooperation with all colleagues in a subject department. Departments would need to assess their in-service training requirements, which could be serviced initially by the special needs coordinators and staff from other areas in the school. The ideal objective would be a situation wherein all teachers in each subject area valued their personal and group skills so highly that they were eager to share their knowledge and commitment with the whole school. The situation at the moment, in this writer's opinion, is that individual teachers and subject areas are defensively aggressive. It is likely that the status concept is the root cause of such an attitude but if a school can convince itself that it is not threatened by its 'parts' or from external influences then it will grow to a position of strength. The approach looks for a situation where critical comments can be made openly, *understood* and acted upon. The process will not be without problems as traditional concepts will have to be systematically examined and, if needs be, abandoned. For instance classroom doors will have to open so that colleagues can observe and learn from each other. The invisible walls which schools sometimes build around themselves will have to be removed in order to improve the present level of school/community interchange. Importantly, the schools population, led most often by its staff, can sound a more positive note than the one made by Hopkins when he wrote

> Against this scenario is one of pervasive and rampant social change. The implication of this for schools is that, as society's major agent of socialization there is pressure on them to reflect the changes and to be able to relate teaching methods, classroom climate, and curricula to changing societal norms. At the same time they have a responsibility

to the communities they serve, for school is the major societal institution intervening in most people's lives. Potentially ... schools can significantly reduce the sense of alienation and anomie individuals and communities increasingly feel. Unfortunately this is rarely the case. (Hopkins and Wideen, 1984).

A whole-school approach does challenge the power, autonomy and privacy experienced by many teachers but it does not imply that all teachers are somehow going to turn into clones. It would be undesirable, and impossible, to destabilize the highly personalized and idiosyncratic nature of the job of teaching.

Implications for Practice

Resources

Each area of the curriculum would have to consider carefully the concepts and skills they were presenting to pupils. Resources would need to be structured in such a way that the whole ability range, in a particular group, have an opportunity to undertake and respond to the content of set tasks. It is perfectly possible to set the same question at a number of readability levels, each level requiring an increasingly more in-depth answer. Books which have an inappropriate reading level will require an additional 'in-fill' resource to allow them to be accessible to the whole range. For less able pupils various practical resources will require additional information to enable them to understand fully the reasons for use.

Teachers are the greatest resource to learning. It is this writer's observation that a proportion of teachers sometimes use language at inappropriate levels for the ability range they are teaching, often without any realization that they are doing so. Observation by colleagues could enable this issue to be remedied.

Information

Teachers would be expected to share their analyses of a pupil's attitudes towards learning, and levels of achievement. It is a strange thought that often the only teacher who sees reports on a particular pupil is the form tutor, and then at lengthy intervals. The whole-school approach would require the special needs coordinators, department representatives and pastoral staff to develop a system which encouraged a greater exchange of information on all pupils. This would enable all the teachers of an individual pupil to build a complete picture of that pupil.

Classroom Management and Pastoral Interventions

One of the drawbacks to the manner in which educational institutions have coped with the assessment of the appropriate social behaviour of pupils is that they focus a disproportionate amount of time and effort on those pupils who present problems. This situation is eminently understandable but it discriminates against the greater number of pupils who, in most part, behave appropriately. However, the time spent on the former possibly prevents the needs of the latter being identified and met. A whole-school approach would set in motion the necessary training to allow teachers to help teachers, through observation and discussion, assess the impact of their behaviour on the behaviours of pupils. Gross discrepancies between the approaches of particular Home or Year pastoral teams can be rationalized through the cooperative measures and exchanges set up by a whole-school approach.

As can be deduced, the special needs coordinators take on a very different role through such an approach, one which enables the whole school to meet the needs of all pupils. They will work with teachers, in and out of classrooms, with the different levels of management in a school and with external agencies. Most importantly, they will be working with and for all pupils. They will have an overview of the transitory and long-term needs of pupils and can facilitate a range of strategies at the request of any pupil or teacher or parent.

Implications for Special Needs Staffing Levels

Obviously the number of special needs staff will vary from school to school but the number cannot be tied to many of the formula used to assess staffing levels at present. A reasonable starting point would be one member of staff for each half-year group. A whole-school approach needs great flexibility. An approach which requires in-class support, withdrawal groups, opportunities for teacher observation, liaison with other schools and external agencies, providing in-service training, preparation of appropriate resources with other specialist teachers, extending existing practice and so on requires adequate staffing. It cannot be done in a piecemeal manner. Local Education Authorities which back such an approach have to accept the resource implications. An individual school cannot be expected to weaken the provision within subject areas to put more pressure on the teaching staff.

Philosophical Implications and Conclusion

Decisions made about educational methods do not rest upon some kind of empirical evidence but are clearly rooted in political judgments and concepts of what constitutes a good person and a desirable society (Whiteside, 1978).

It is not the objective of instigating a whole-school approach towards pupils with special educational needs to cause institutional change, but it is possible to forecast how such change would be effected by the approach and why it would be desirable. In this final section the writer takes the opportunity to broadly present issues which have relevance.

Schools, and institutions, encourage labels and categories to be employed. 'Special Needs' is one such. An examination of the language used in schools and the reasons for its use is useful at this point.

> For example, the categories by which we differentiate 'smart' children from 'stupid'; 'academic' areas from 'non-academic'; 'play' activity from 'learning' or 'work activity' and even 'students' from 'teachers' are all common sense constructions which grow out of the nature of existing institutions (Apple, 1979).

Apple continues by asserting that such categories should not be seen as absolutes because in effect they are really only historically treated data. He says, and this writer agrees, that as such they are not always wrong but we should realise that they are 'categories that develop out of specific social and historical situations which conform to a specific framework of assumptions and institutions' (Apple, 1979). The categories which are promoted by institutional organization, whether they be specific or general, are probably generated to be helpful but there are serious implications which have been discussed in this chapter.

A whole-school approach can examine the institutional context because it has a philosophical base that all pupils have needs and to each pupil (and certainly to their parents), their needs are special. The needs should be recognized as individual to the individual. A whole-school approach can allow pupils to be given a radically different message from the one they receive at the moment – that within the mainstream flow of school their needs will be met by a framework which is prepared to change as the perceptions and attitudes of the population of these institutions become more refined. Teachers and pupils who are new to the school will be agents of change and not consigned to existing and traditional categories.

A whole-school approach can be seen as threatening and capable of provoking anxiety. The remodelling of rules, functions, status and work load will affect the 'status quo'. The interventions and strategies necessary to introduce a whole-school approach require sensitivity, care and time. The aim is to develop the skills and qualities of pupils and staff with the support of parents, governors, external bodies, institutions and agencies.

It is not a matter of dropping all structure – that produces chaos – but of getting the structure carefully shaped to serve young people's needs within the actual perspectives of the contemporary world. The sort of qualities needed today, the sort of qualities needed in the future, are qualities of personal wholeness ... to be attained ... by the nourishment of individual uniqueness, and motivation (Hemming, 1980).

References

APPLE, M.W. (1979) *Ideology and the Curriculum*, London, Routledge and Kegan Paul.

HARGREAVES, D.H. (1982) *The Challenge for the Comprehensive School Culture Curriculum and Community*, London, Routledge and Kegan Paul.

HEMMING, J. (1980) *The Betrayal of Youth*, London, Marion Boyers.

HOPKINS, D. and WIDEEN, M. (1984) *Alternative perspectives on School Improvement*, Lewes, Falmer Press.

TUTT, N. (1983) 'Maladjustment — A sociological perspective', in *AWMC Journal, Autumn 1983.*

WHITESIDE, T. (1978) *The Sociology of Education Innovation*, London, Methuen.

Further Reading

BARTON, L. and WALKER, S. (Eds) (1985) *Education and Social Change*, Beckenham, Croom Helm.

KING, R. (1983) *The Sociology of Schools Organisation*, London, Methuen.

Chapter 5

Meeting Special Needs: A School in Transition
Mike Farrell

Introduction

The aim of this chapter is to describe one school's attempt to promote organizational changes in order to break free from its conventional banding arrangement. The transformation is the result of a growing awarenes, by the headteacher and teachers at the school, that perhaps the needs of pupils would more appropriately be met by replacing the banding structure with a system of mixed–ability. Also, the changes have followed in the wake of the Warnock Report and the Education Act 1981 which have changed the artificial and traditional dichotomy between mainstream education and special education.

The initiative discussed below is not, in itself, particularly innovative, since similar schemes can be observed in various stages of evolution and in many permutations in schools throughout England and Wales (Hodgson *et al.*, 1984). However, in a geographical area which has a recent history of categorization of pupils either at the point of entry to secondary school, or very soon afterwards, the changes are radical.

Each secondary school is unique in terms of the interaction that exists between its pupils and teachers, the attitudes that prevail, the ethos of the school and the nature and extent of learning difficulties. It is difficult, therefore, to provide a prescriptive, definitive model of an organizational system to cater for children with special educational needs in all schools. No such prescription is attempted here. Rather, an explanation is given of one method of offering a balanced and appropriate curriculum for pupils who are frequently placed in 'remedial' departments or at the lower end of 'B' and 'C' bands in secondary schools.

The Past

The school became comprehensive in 1971 with the amalgamation of a grammar school and a secondary modern school. A brief examination of the school's banding structure during the past ten years will give an insight into the remarkable evolution which has occurred. For instance, in the academic year of 1977-78 five bands existed – A, B, C, a 'buffer' class, and a remedial class. A reduction in the number of pupils, an appraisal of the curriculum, a desire to create more examination opportunities for low achievers, and a recognition that the 'C' band and buffer class often contained groups of disaffected pupils, all combined to suggest to the headteacher that the needs of the pupils would best be met by dispensing with the 'C' band and buffer class. By 1983-84 the bands were eventually reduced to two plus a remedial class.

Following a series of discussions the headteacher decided to eliminate the banding system and implement a mixed-ability structure in September 1985. Initially, however, it was thought appropriate to retain a separate remedial class. As head of special education I feared the dangers of such a policy of segregation. I maintained that there was little educational or social justification for not including children with learning difficulties in what was to be a fundamental reorganization. Subsequently consultations took place with the local authority special education adviser, senior staff and departmental heads, and the headteacher agreed to modify his original proposals and announced that all pupils would be involved in the new scheme.

Obviously, it would have benefited neither pupils nor teachers to suddenly be confronted with children who have special educational needs without receiving support. Thus, I proposed an initiative which is often referred to as the 'withdrawal system'. To support my assertions several points were made to highlight the advantages of incorporating the withdrawal scheme into the mixed-ability situation. I postulated that:

(1) the present banding arrangement gives a false and dangerous impression that special educational needs are confined to the remedial class but do not exist outside it;

(2) by sharing the same curriculum as the rest of the school, children with special needs are offered the same opportunities as other pupils during early adolescence. It would also result in social and academic integration;

(3) the withdrawal system of provision allows periods to be set aside for individual and small group work. It also grants the special education teacher more time to support mainstream colleagues;

(4) registration in an ordinary form provides social integration. Pupils with special needs consider it more socially acceptable to identify with a registration form rather than a 'remedial' class, with its attendant stigma and susceptibility to produce labels and stereotypes;

(5) under the present system the timetable which the pupils in the remedial department receive is entirely fortuitous. It depends less on careful planning than on where on the timetable lessons can be filled in. Such a situation would not arise if all pupils with special needs began with the same timetable as their age peers;

(6) the withdrawal system can be mutually beneficial for mainstream pupils and those with special educational needs. At its most basic level it provides an escape-valve when pressure becomes too great in some mixed-ability classes. Also, teaching pupils with special needs in the mainstream gives teachers the chance to re-examine the curriculum and tailor it to meet the needs of a diverse group of pupils. The withdrawal system also affords greater opportunities for liaison between subject teachers and the special education teacher.

The Present

Rationale

The withdrawal system of provision refers to a situation in which pupils identified as requiring support in basic skills or in specific subjects are withdrawn from the mainstream for periods of individual or small group teaching.

The scheme involves having no remedial or special class or unit on entry to the school. All pupils are assigned to a registration class where, initially, they receive a common timetable. The special education teacher appointed to teach first-year pupils receives a blank timetable. This teacher inspects the school's general timetable and decides, on the basis of a variety of information (primary school records, norm and criterion referenced tests, advice from external agencies, progress in class, etc.), which children to withdraw and when to withdraw them.

Organization

Prior to transfer I visited the feeder primary schools to discover the incidence and nature of any special educational needs which existed within each school.

The remedial advisory service and the district educational psychologist were also consulted so that a thorough picture was drawn of any pupil who might require special support.

The teacher in charge of year one administration sorted the whole intake into mixed-ability form groups. Following her discussions with the head-teachers and teachers from the feeder primary schools, she divided between each mixed-ability form, as equally as possible, the pupils with the greatest learning difficulties. Thus, in order to minimize the pressure on mainstream teachers, approximately three pupils with the most complex and severe learning difficulties were allocated to each class.

In this way the necessary information was acquired which enabled me to begin the task of providing modified individual timetables for pupils who needed them. During the first two weeks I contacted those pupils whom I considered needed to be withdrawn. They were individually interviewed and provided with an adapted timetable. Care was taken to ensure that each pupil understood the adjustments by arranging several subsequent meetings.

The amount of time pupils are withdrawn varies according to their needs. For example, a pupil who has moderate learning difficulties may need to be withdrawn from English, mathematics, the humanities and science.[1] He or she would return to a mainstream class for music, drama, art, crafts and physical education. On the other hand, a pupil who has mild learning difficulties may be withdrawn infrequently, for a short period of time and for very few subjects. A child with a specific learning difficulty, in spelling for example, may be withdrawn for only one or two periods a week. Another pupil, with poor numeracy skills perhaps, may need to be withdrawn from mathematics only. It can be seen that this type of organization recognizes and caters for a continuum rather than a category or special educational need.

There is a reluctance, to begin with, to withdraw pupils from French and Welsh since it can create problems, arguably greater than those found in most other subjects, if and when children return to the mainstream. However, the heads of the language departments have been asked to identify, during the first terms, those pupils with extremely poor language skills who would probably derive greater benefit from being withdrawn in order to receive extra teaching in basic subjects.[2]

Assessment

During the first half term about forty pupils, which is just over twenty per cent of the intake, were assessed for strengths and weaknesses. Assessment consisted of a combination of classroom observation, criterion-referenced checklists and diagnostic tests. The results were recorded in individual record books which were designed to form the basis of teaching programmes. Regular appraisal was carried out to evaluate pupil progress and, where necessary, modifications were made to the teaching programme.

For the remainder of the academic year several pupils not originally identified as requiring extra support were referred because a mainstream teacher considered they were not coping with a particular subject. At the same time, however, pupils also returned to full-time mainstream education. At the end of the year the progress of the children who had been withdrawn, and the progress of the pupils who returned to the mainstream, was reviewed. Subsequently, a list was produced indicating those pupils who would continue to require support.

Teaching

At present, two main forms of teaching procedure are employed. For children with the most serious learning difficulties, such as those with little or no reading ability, a developmental approach is operated to meet the particular needs of the pupils. Much of the work is based upon the objectives method advocated by Ainscow and Tweddle (1979). Realistically, it must be accepted that many of these pupils are likely to go on needing additional assistance throughout their school careers.

A different technique is used for those children on the 'borderline' who might, in time, return to the mainstream for the majority of the curriculum. Within the constraints that exist within a secondary school, links are maintained with subject teachers to expedite the return of these pupils to the mainstream.

Evaluation

Some colleagues have suggested that it would make little difference if pupils with special educational needs were placed, at the outset, into a remedial band and moved to the mainstream when appropriate. However, there are important educational and psychological grounds for placing such pupils in the mainstream to begin with. In this way the child with special needs becomes the responsibility of all who teach him or her. This has tremendous implications for the way the pupils are viewed by subject teachers and for the quality of education those pupils receive. The formidable task of one special education teacher being responsible for providing the majority of the curricular experience for children with special needs no longer exists. Also, subject teachers generally would consider it more favourable if pupils were withdrawn from their classes rather than vice versa.

If it is accepted, then, that the withdrawal system is appropriate for a school's procedure for meeting the needs of pupils with learning difficulties, how can its effectiveness be evaluated? One method which has been used is to conduct efficacy studies comparing one form of organization with another. However, the majority of these studies have been inconclusive or produced conflicting results.

Perhaps a more profitable course of action would involve monitoring individual schemes for social and academic benefits using sociometric and statistical techniques combined with systematic classroom observation. The limited amount of research which has been applied to this particular scheme has indicated both academic and social success, although it has to be admitted that the research and the scheme itself are at a very early stage.

The Future

In this school the withdrawal scheme has now entered its second year. Whether it continues in its present form and follows a natural progression through the school's system depends on a number of factors, including the availability and willingness of teachers, the attitudes of the headteacher and senior staff and the way in which the school is organized. If constraints can be circumvented it would be encouraging to see an expansion of the scheme which would eventually contribute towards the adoption of a whole-school policy for children with special educational needs.

Regardless of the arrangements a school makes for its low achievers, I believe there are several significant features which should be considered. They are especially pertinent to the withdrawal scheme discussed earlier and I have outlined them below in the hope that they will assist those who desire to see children with special educational needs receive a balanced and appropriate curriculum.

(1) Curriculum development is a crucial factor. Pupils with specific needs can often benefit from a mainstream curriculum provided that teachers are willing to adapt it to suit the children's needs. If pupils with special educational needs are to be appropriately educated in the mainstream then it is essential that teaching methods are adapted to suit a wider range of ability than they are at present.
Special education teachers also have a contribution to make by ensuring that the mainstream curriculum is made more accessible to children with special needs. Expertise can be provided in a number of ways, including advice on the readability levels of books and worksheets, adapting the conceptual level of certain topics, suggesting alternative

teaching methods, and generally supporting pupil and teacher within the mainstream.

(2) It appears that any positive and enduring reform in the fortunes of low achievers in the secondary school cannot be effected from the position of head of department. Some local education authorities have established, within comprehensive schools, senior posts with specific responsibility for the coordination of special education. It is only at senior teacher level, or above, that a whole-school policy for children with special needs can be implemented.

(3) To increase educational opportunities for low achievers, secondary schools should be prepared to accept new initiatives. Team teaching is a prime example. It should not be regarded as an alien concept but should be viewed as an extension of mixed-ability teaching. Team teaching is particularly beneficial to pupils with mild or moderate learning difficulties in the secondary school. For instance, there is often a dilemma when withdrawing children temporarily from certain lessons since they inevitably miss the work that their age peers complete during those lessons. If pupils with special needs can be supported within the mainstream the dilemma can be resolved. Apart from the discontinuity in children's work, the stigma and isolation, which is often a consequence of being withdrawn from lessons, can be eliminated in a well-planned team-teaching situation.

In practice, three main types of team teaching have been discovered in secondary schools in England and Wales (Hegarty *et al.*, 1981). The special education teacher works exclusively with the pupil with special needs, predominantly supports that pupil while simultaneously helping other pupils, or works with a small group of pupils which would usually, but not always, include the pupil with special needs. It is important to realize that the mainstream teacher retains the ultimate responsibility for subject content and remains in charge of the class. The role of the special education teacher is advisory and supportive.

(4) In any attempt to successfully meet the needs of pupils with learning difficulties the importance of in-service training cannot be underestimated. Some teachers understandably feel that their training has not prepared them to teach children with special needs. Unfortunately this often leads to a tendency for some teachers to view these children as the responsibility of someone else. All courses of initial teacher training are now required to contain an element on special educational needs. This is a welcome development but it should be combined with enthusiastic efforts to increase in-service training through school-based and local authority courses.

(5) Finally, but perhaps most importantly, a whole-school approach to special educational needs is vital. This approach should influence the major elements in our education system – the curriculum, school organization, staff development, resources, and pupil and parental involvement.

Conclusion

This particular secondary school has made a courageous attempt to increase the participation of children with special educational needs in the educational and social activities it makes available for all its pupils. Admittedly, emphasis has been placed upon the physical and organizational aspects of integration. What is required now is to put greater effort into achieving diversification and extension of the curriculum so that functional integration can be realized.

A school which strives to modify its structure to broaden and extend the education of its low achievers should be supported and congratulated, since it can be a demanding business. However, given positive attitudes by all, an appropriate curriculum, carefully designed instructional objectives, and a flexible school organization, a great deal can be accomplished.

Editor's Notes

1 Advocacy for this type of withdrawal should be seen in the context of a school in transition and not as part of a whole-school approach.
2 For a different view, see Chapter 10.

References

AINSCOW, M. and TWEDDLE, D.A. (1979) *Preventing Classroom Failure*, Chichester, Wiley.

HEGARTY, S., POCKLINGTON, K. and LUCAS, D. (1981) *Educating Pupils with Special Needs in the Ordinary School*, Windsor, NFER-Nelson.

HODGSON, A., CLUNIES-ROSS, L. and HEGARTY, S. (1984) *Learning Together: Teaching Pupils with Special Educational Needs in the Ordinary School*, Windsor, NFER-Nelson.

Chapter 6

Effective Schooling for Children with Special Educational Needs: Research and its Implications
David Reynolds

Introduction

In the last decade an increasing amount of attention has been given to how the individual school can be an important factor determining whether children develop their academic and social potential. In the past it was usually the family or the individual child that was seen as responsible for any deficiency in academic progress or social adjustment and a vast array of research literature was produced that confirmed that view (e.g. Davie *et al.*, 1972; Douglas *et al.*, 1968). In the area of truancy from school, for example, one authoritative review of the evidence listed over fifteen times more studies that looked at family or individual causes than those which had looked at schools themselves as possible causes of such disaffection (Carroll, 1977). In the field of behaviour problems, another review concluded that the role of the school 'had scarcely been considered' (Upton, 1982) as a possible cause of pupils' problems.

The major influence determining that research was more individual or family background orientated rather than school orientated was perhaps the nature of the inter-relationship between educational research and the broader traditions of psychology. What seems to have happened is that educational research, conscious of its youth, its insecurity and its general lack of any agreed theoretical and methodological guidelines, grasped at psychology as a source discipline of secure and trusted theoretical and methodological approaches. In entering into a close relationship with psychology, however, educational research entered into a relationship with a discipline that was essentially family obsessed. Whether because of the importance of the family environment in the explanations advanced by psychologists like Freud or

whether because of the influence of the early experience thesis that saw early
– inevitably family – influences as determining later experience (Clarke and
Clarke, 1976), psychological explanations usually emphasized the primary
importance of the family. One recent psychology textbook for teachers
(Fontana, 1983, p. 7) argued that:

> [the child's] closest relationships are usually formed within the home
> ... not surprisingly therefore the influence of the home is of critical
> importance in a child's psychological development generally and in
> particular in the use he makes of his abilities, in the formation of his
> attitudes and opinions, and in the development of his motivation
> towards school and towards a future career.

A set of beliefs was created, then, by the late 1960s and early 1970s which
had a self perpetuating effect. The basic tenets of this – the importance of the
family and the unimportance of the school – were rarely questioned.
Educational researchers as liberals, middle class and closely related to the
State education enterprise shared the view of the system as basically
beneficial. As former teachers, many researchers were already using
'individualized' explanations of pupil problems in any case. School-focused
research work was difficult to investigate, beset with conceptual and
methodological problems and enormously time-consuming, involving the
collection of data on pupils, schools, communities *and* families simply to
judge if there were any school effects on pupil progress in the first place. If
we define a 'paradigm' as a model of enquiry that guides scientific work and
provides a conceptual framework for understanding the phenomena to be
studied, then it must be clear in this case that the initial belief that families
and individuals were important determinants of educability generated
research which, by its concentration upon families and individuals and its
neglect of their school, reinforced the initial paradigm that had created the
research in the first place.

Even when evidence existed which directly contradicted the importance
of family background, this evidence was either ignored or occasionally
'massaged' to look less threatening to the basic tenets of the paradigm. In the
case of the National Child Development Study of 1958 (Davie *et al.*, 1972),
although great emphasis was put in the study publications upon the *dependence*
of the child upon the wider social environment, the excellent reading
performance of Scottish children from an area with the worst housing
conditions in Europe shows clearly the partial *independence* of pupils from their
environment, a point taken up by Rutter and Madge (1976). Independence was
not emphasized in the report, which emphasized dependency.

In the further case of Mia Kellmer Pringle's personal writing, the
statement was made that 'it is the early years of life which are particularly

vital to later development' (1974, p. 15), yet her own NCDS cohort study findings show clearly that this is not the case, since:

> ... although overall the early years are important as a foundation... these findings suggest that adverse circumstances, whether enduring such as poor housing or traumatic such as the loss of a parent are of equal importance for a child's development whether experienced early (that is in this context before the age of 7) or later in childhood (Fogelman, 1983, p. 354).

It would seem from both these examples that, as Clarke and Clarke (1976, p. 3) note, 'we thus build models of phenomena or events against which new experiences are compared ... such integration may require distortions of phenomena without which they cannot easily be accommodated'.

In recent years, however, dissatisfaction with these traditional individualized or family-based explanations has grown. There is not space here to consider the deficiencies in this viewpoint in detail (see Reynolds, 1985, 1987) but, in brief, it was the absence of any predictive power by the theories that most seemed to discredit them. To take delinquency as an example, the detailed survey of delinquent behaviour amongst boys from the Cambridge Institute of Criminology generated five major factors of individual character or family background that were said to cause delinquency, namely low family income, large family size, 'unsatisfactory' child-rearing, parental criminality and the child having a low IQ score. However, of the high-risk group that was identified because they possessed many of these adversities, half of the pupils were *not* delinquent – also, large numbers of delinquents came from families that did not score highly in terms of family/individual risk factors (West, 1983).

Increasingly from the 1960s onwards, then, children's behaviour and development became increasingly seen as *independent* of basic individual/family factors. The immediate situation that a person was in, the opportunity structure of the immediate environment and the characteristics of various social institutions like schools and communities all became areas of interest as attention shifted away from family and individual factors (see Rutter, 1980, and Reynolds, 1987, for further details).

What Makes an Effective School?

Whilst the past has been noticeable for *family*-based explanations of pupils' educational problems, then, more recently research has accumulated in many countries which shows the impact by contrast of individual *schools* on their pupils' levels of needs and difficulties. In Britain, the evidence has come mainly from academic researchers (Rutter *et al.*, 1979; Reynolds, 1976, 1985), whilst in the United States school practitioners and policy-makers have contributed much more of the research literature (see the reviews in Edmunds, 1979, and Anderson, 1982). Other research has been undertaken in Australia (Caldwell and Spinks, 1988; Ramsay *et al.*, 1982), in Canada (Renihan and Renihan, 1984) and in Third World countries (Vulliamy, 1987; Heyneman and Loxley, 1983). Put together, this literature is usually described as being about 'school effects' or most likely about 'school effectiveness'.

It is important to realize that we know from this research at present far more about what factors are associated with academic effectiveness than those factors which are associated with more social outcomes. Rutter *et al.* (1979) can identify over thirty factors associated with academic effectiveness, yet can only identify seven factors associated with social effectiveness as measured by a school's possession of a low delinquency rate. The recent study by Mortimore *et al.* (1988) could find only six school factors associated with behavioural effectiveness (such as low rates of misbehaviour) yet could identify thirteen school factors associated with effectiveness in terms of good reading scores, even though the schools' effects were of the same size in the two different areas. Our relative ignorance of the factors making for *social* effectiveness is also unlikely to be remedied by work from abroad, since virtually all the American studies (with the notable exception of Brookover *et al.*, 1979) look only at *academic* effectiveness (see reviews in Purkey and Smith, 1983).

Although we have much work on the general area of school effectiveness (e.g. Gray *et al.*, 1986; Galloway, 1985), it is also important to note that we have in Britain only three studies which have been able to systematically collect data on the school *processes* of effective and ineffective organizations, two on processes in secondary schools (Rutter *et al.*, 1979; Reynolds, 1976, 1982) and one on primary school processes (Mortimore *et al.*, 1988).

The Rutter study finds that certain factors are *not* associated with overall school effectiveness, amongst them class size, formal academic or pastoral care organization, school size and administrative arrangements (i.e. whether a school was split-site or not), and the age and size of the school buildings. The important within-school factors making for high effectiveness were argued by Rutter (1980) to be:

(1) The balance of intellectually able and less able children in the school, since, when a preponderance of pupils in the school were likely to be

unable to meet the expectations of scholastic success, peer–group cultures with an anti–academic or anti–authority emphasis may have formed.

(2) The system of rewards and punishments – ample use of rewards, praise and appreciation being associated with favourable outcomes.

(3) School environment – good working conditions, responsiveness to pupil needs and good care and decoration of buildings were associated with better outcomes.

(4) Ample opportunities for children to take responsibility and participate in the running of their school lives appeared conducive to favourable outcomes.

(5) Successful schools tended to make good use of homework, to set clear academic goals and to have an atmosphere of confidence as to their pupil capacities.

(6) Outcomes were better where teachers provided good models of behaviour by means of good time–keeping and willingness to deal with pupil problems.

(7) Findings upon group management in the classroom suggested the importance of preparing lessons in advance, of keeping the attention of the whole class, of unobtrusive discipline, of a focus on rewarding good behaviour and of swift action to deal with disruption.

(8) Outcomes were more favourable when there was a combination of firm leadership together with a decision–making process in which all teachers felt that their views were represented.

Our own Welsh research paints a picture of the high effectiveness school organization (Reynolds, 1982; Reynolds *et al.*, 1988) that is in some ways similar to that of the above London study. Effectiveness in our work was associated with small class size, small school size, a low rate of staff turnover and a school situation that was in old and traditional buildings. In terms of organizational processes, effective schools had balanced rule enforcement, low levels of physical punishment, heads who devolved power, close school/ parent relations, staff with positive expectations of their pupils and organizational forms which involved pupils academically and socially in the organization of the school. High effectiveness schools we argued to be 'incorporative' of their pupils, rather than 'coercive' of them (Reynolds and Sullivan, 1979).

The characteristics of effective primary school organization have recently been extensively described (Mortimore *et al.*, 1988) and twelve factors have been identified that are associated with high performance in cognitive areas such as reading and writing and in non-cognitive areas such as truancy levels:

(1) Purposeful leadership of the staff by the head. This occurs where the head understands the school's needs, is actively involved in it but is good at sharing power with the staff. He or she does not exert total control over teachers but consults them, especially in decision-making such as spending plans and curriculum guidelies.

(2) Involvement of the deputy head. The deputy head can have a crucial role in whether a school is effective or not. Where the deputy was usually involved in policy decisions, pupil progress increased.

(3) Involvement of teachers. In successful schools, the teachers were involved in curriculum planning and played a major role in developing their own curriculum guidelines. As with the deputy head, teacher involvement in decisions concerning which classes they were to teach was important. Similarly, consultation with teachers about decisions on spending was important.

(4) Consistency among teachers. Continuity of staffing had positive effects but pupils also performed better when the approach to teaching was consistent.

(5) A structured day. Children performed better when their school day was structured in some way. In effective schools, pupils' work was organized by the teacher who ensured there was plenty for them to do, yet allowed them some freedom within the structure.
Negative effects were noted when children were given unlimited responsibility for a long list of tasks.

(6) Intellectually challenging teaching. Not surprisingly, pupil progress was greater where teachers were stimulating and enthusiastic. The incidence of 'higher order' questions and statements was seen to be vital – that is where teachers frequently made children use powers of problem-solving.

(7) A work-centred environment. This was characterized by a high level of pupil industry, with children enjoying their work and being eager to start new tasks. The noise level was low, and movement around the class was usually work-related and not excessive.

(8) A limited focus within sessions. Children progressed when teachers devoted their energies to one particular subject area and sometimes two. Pupil progress was marred when three or more subjects were running concurrently in a classroom.

(9)   Maximum communication between teachers and pupils. Children performed better the more communication they had with their teacher about the content of their work. Most teachers devoted most of their time to individuals, so each child could expect only a small number of contacts a day. Teachers who used opportunities to talk to the whole class by, for example, reading a story or asking a question were more effective.

(10)   Thorough record-keeping. The value of monitoring pupil progress was important in the head's role, but it was also an important aspect of teachers' planning and assessment.

(11)   Parental involvement. Schools with an informal open-door policy which encouraged parents to get involved in reading at home, helping in the classroom and on educational visits, tended to be more effective.

(12)   A positive climate. An effective school has a positive ethos. Overall, the atmosphere was more pleasant in the effective schools, for a variety of reasons.
There was less emphasis on punishment and criticism and more emphasis on rewarding pupils. Classroom management was seen to be firm but fair in the effective schools.

Whilst there are obviously differences between the three studies in their respective findings, the degree of communality in the findings on organizational effectiveness is also quite impressive. Also impressive is the extent to which American research into school organizational effectiveness suggests similar factors to be responsible in their elementary and high schools. Comprehensive reviews of this literature are available elsewhere as we noted above and all we can do here is to take one 'meta-analysis' of all the American findings conducted by two Canadians (Renihan and Renihan, 1984) that show a similarity with British findings. They found that the following factors were important in creating an effective organization in the studies they reviewed:

(1)   **Leadership**
This point is reinforced in studies which highlight several key leadership qualities. These include assertive administrative and instructional leadership, assumption of responsibility, high standards, personal vision, expertise, and force of character.

(2)   **Conscious attention to climate**
In effective schools specific attention is given to the creation and maintenance of a climate which is conducive to learning. In short, very

specific rules, regulations, and guidelines are laid down and they are clearly understood by everyone.

(3) **Academic focus**

Several authorities identify a marked emphasis on basic academic skills as a common characteristic of effective schools. Further, the importance placed upon basic skills is reflected in the major portion of school time allocated to them.

(4) **Great Expectations**

Central to the notion of positive ethos in the school is the duality of high expectations for student performance on the one hand and high expectations that students can achieve on the other.

In effective schools, performance is monitored to ensure that students meet pre-established standards which are made well known to them.

(5) **Sense of mission**

Successful schools project a consistent philosophy and a sense of mission which are always shared by teachers, pupils and administration. Such a focus on mission is reflected in the following characteristics:

– shared norms and consistency throughout the school;
– agreed-upon ways of doing things;
– clearly stated goals known to all;
– a high degree of acceptance of the importance of goals;
– joint planning.

Central to this notion is the critical element of ownership, for when staff, students, and community are involved in charting a direction they become committed to its success.

(6) **Positive motivational strategies**

Studies at both the school and the classroom levels of analysis have repeatedly indicated that in successful schools there is a greater conscious reliance on praise rather than blame. In addition, successful schools evidence strategies which are designed to enhance their students' self-image and to foster a friendly and supportive atmosphere.

(7) **Feedback on academic performance**

Effective schools provide consistent and continuous feedback to students on their academic achievement. Furthermore, student evaluation is tied to monitoring of teaching performance and the appropriateness of curriculum level objectives. More specifically effective schools use the results of standardised (preferably criterion-referenced) achievement tests to make significant decisions regarding programmes and modes of instructional delivery.

It is important not to over-emphasize the extent of the agreement between the various British studies and between these studies and the American literature. Rutter *et al.* (1979), for example, find that high levels of staff turnover are associated with *effectiveness*, a completely counter-intuitive finding that is not in agreement with the Reynolds (1976, 1982) findings of an association between high levels of staff turnover and *ineffectiveness*. Similarly, the consistent American findings on the link between frequent monitoring of pupil progress and effectiveness is not in agreement with the recent findings of Mortimore *et al.* (1988) that frequent testing of children is a characteristic of ineffective primary schools.

Nevertheless, in the area of school processes linked with effectiveness there seems to be emerging broad agreement on many issues as the results of the second and third 'waves' of school effectiveness research are known.

Changing Educational Policies

All this recent work into the characteristics of effective schools has clear implications for educational policies about children with special educational needs, since there was a close relationship in the past between research that 'individualized' the treatment of pupil problems and policies that were targeted at remediation of individuals rather than at remediation of their schools. Before outlining what the implications of the recent research are in policy terms, it is useful to consider in some detail the ineffectiveness and inefficiency of the range of individualistic educational policies that were encouraged by the old psychologically-based research into educational needs and problems.

The first example of such policies is that of inter-professional communication between different groups involved with the education and care of children with special needs. A pioneering Welsh action research project in this area (DHSS, 1975) concluded with a whole series of recommendations involving better record-keeping, better communication between professionals and common in-service training. However, whether the educational system itself should have been readjusted to help the child and whether the system and its personnel were causing children's problems was not discussed in this document nor in the other flurry of publications on this subject which followed its selection as the theme for the 1980 meeting of the Association of Directors of Social Services.

Precisely the same 'individualizing' of problematic behaviour arises with a second policy example, the appointment of school counsellors to schools. Most presentations of counselling theory emphasized its developmental purpose: Hamblin (1974), for example, stated that it should encourage:

(1)   the growth of self-acceptance in pupils;

(2)   the development of controls from inside the pupil rather than continuing a reliance upon external influences and pressures; and

(3)   the learning of relevant and competent coping strategies and of problem-solving techniques which are both realistic and viable for the pupils

Hamblin emphasized that school counselling as an activity was client-centred and not school-centred. However, research showed that schools did not expect client-centredness of their counsellors, whom they wished to resocialise their deviants and minimise their pupil wastage (Murgatroyd, 1976). The pupils saw counsellors as those who checked the attendance registers, reported truants, found lost property and 'told you how to behave'. The counsellors themselves saw their role as that of promoting agency, rather than individual, needs which may have led them merely to become agents of social control within the school.

Truancy provides a classic example of the use of school counsellors as part of an institutional 'soft machine', for although truancy may be the rational reaction of a psychologically normal child to an institution which is not using his or her other talents (Reynolds and Murgatroyd, 1977), most counsellors tended merely to attempt to get truants to attend, rather than attempting to see if the child was being misused by the institution (Murgatroyd, 1975). The theory of counselling as a client-based activity is difficult to square with its use to minimize pupil deviance within schools and it appeared to be simply a school-based, school-centred attempt to solve school problems by individualizing their treatment.

These two policies of inter-professional cooperation and the use of school counsellors are but two examples of the range of conventional policies that attempted to deal with the individual special needs pupil rather than with his or her school. Other examples are the screening mechanisms that can detect 'at risk' children (Davie, 1975), the increase in the provision of educational psychologists and child guidance clinics, the growth of off-site therapeutic units and the use of home tuition (Blagg and Yule, 1984). A full description of these and other attempted remediation policies is given by Topping (1983). In a sense, the special schools themselves have also been merely an individually targeted solution to special educational needs.

Lest it be thought that this analysis is simply a personal hobby-horse, an acknowledged expert on special educational needs recently went so far as to argue that:

Most of professional time, effort and money currently spent in identifying and meeting these pupils' needs is (a) based on a false premise (b) counter productive. The false premise is that professional efforts should be directed at helping the child adjust to the demands of school ... The effect has been to individualize problems, locating causes in the child and the child's family, and evaluating the outcome of treatment programmes in terms of the child's adjustment to the school (Galloway, 1985, p. 3).

As well as encouraging the development of certain forms of educational policy and offering a rationale for action that individualized the explanation of the educational system's difficulties, there are some suggestions (Gillham, 1981) that the past research also had a major impact in confirming the 'common sense' or 'taken for granted' explanations of their problems given by practitioners within the educational system. We know from many studies that teachers and other educational practitioners operate with individualized explanations of pupil behaviour in America (Cicourel and Kitsuse, 1963), in Britain (Sharp and Green, 1975) and in their general discourse within schools (Woods, 1979).

A list of seven so-called explanations of truancy given by a head teacher at a conference on truancy in Hertfordshire illustrates these professional perceptions rather eloquently (from Reynolds, 1984 – italics added in original):

1. 5th form boy. *Very lazy*, appalling attendance now for two years, *frequent truancy admitted by parents* who pretend to want to do something about it. *Father has endless supply of plausible explanations.* Mother rang up (at 10.30) on one occasion to say he (the boy) is still in bed and I can't get him up. Three full days in school so far this term (A.T.C. Camp last term).

2. 3rd form girl, sister of No. 1. Quite an able girl. Truants to avoid P.E. and games. She has a skin rash about which she is embarrassed and she appears to have made an effort lately. Nevertheless, *she could easily go the same way as her brother.*

3. 5th year girl. *Bone idle*, above average ability: lives some way from school and the journey is not easy. Has rarely had a complete week at school, none since September 1982. Hardly ever in complete uniform. *Parents always defend her by saying there are others.* We have had trouble over uniform since she was in the 2nd form *(and with her older brother* before that). Absence notes appear sometimes, rarely punctually. On Thursday, 1st February we had a note explaining two days absence which said she wasn't really well but the 5th year is so important ... The girl had by then had 22 absences out of 40 possible sessions.

4. 5th year girl. Hasn't managed a full week's schooling since September. Has learned the truancy pattern *from her older sister* who is now at home, out of work, and writes many of her sister's absence notes. *Difficult to know who is in charge of whom in this family. Parents are divorced but share the same house and bed (one works days: one works nights!)* I think mother has custody. *She will always back up explanations of absence through a variety of minor ailments.*

5. 3rd year girl. Another case where it has proved almost impossible to contact parents. *Mother has broken three appointments to see Mrs Bradshaw* about daughter's reluctance to take part in P.E. and consequent truancy. Very long periods of absence attributed to illness. Another appointment arranged for today with E.W.O.'s help but daughter is away again.

6. 5th year girl. A case where *mother condones blatant truancy*. There is always some plausible excuse for why the girl has been seen out when away from school, e.g. yesterday morning after a week's absence we telephoned and were told by an older sister that she was on her way to school. She didn't arrive. Today she came with a note from mother saying that she has been away for a week because mother was unwell and had been to the dentist yesterday!

7. 5th year girl. *There are grave problems of control versus independence in this family.* The truancy is, I think, because the girl needs to be away from all pressures. She attempted suicide last term and was briefly taken into care. Attendance became perfect and class participation positive and encouraging. She is now back home and it has all started again.

Special Educational Needs and Organizational Development

The old individualized explanations of pupils' special needs or problems were directly related to a set of policies and to teacher beliefs that were concerned with action targeted at individuals rather than at their schools. However, the clear message of the literature on effective schools that we reviewed earlier is that the old sets of educational policies are inappropriate if the *school* is itself the 'problem' rather than the problem *child* or the child with special educational needs. What is appropriate in present circumstances are policies aimed at school change.

All the existing recipes for school change involve a whole-school approach that attempts to improve or 'jack up' the performance of *all* pupils in a school, not just those who may be in lower streams or who may have specific educational needs of various kinds. Such an approach is widely recommended in the United States (e.g. Fullan, 1982) and in Britain (e.g. Holly, 1986) as being the only practical way of attempting school change, since change attempts that focus only upon small sectors of the school such as the department or the year group run the risk of being swamped in their effects by the large, unchanged remainder of the school system and its personnel. The chance of obtaining the reinforcement in terms of improved pupil behaviour, attendance and attainment that would help maintain the organizational changes themselves is also clearly greater when the whole organization is attempting the change. Also, it is clear that if perhaps 20 per cent of the pupils in schools will have special educational needs at some time in their careers (DES, 1978), then anything which falls short of an approach that is targeted at *all* pupils stands a severe risk of being highly ineffective.

It is important to realize, though, that the whole-school change strategy of the kind being adopted in many different education systems may be particularly important in improving the performance of children with special educational needs. There is recent evidence from Scottish research (Cuttance, 1988) that more disadvantaged pupils may be significantly more affected by the general quality of their school environment than their more advantaged counterparts – Cuttance's statistical modelling gives an estimate of 7.72 per cent of pupil variation in examination attainments as due to school quality in the case of a disadvantaged pupil, compared to only 5.03 per cent for an average pupil.

There is also evidence from studies of truancy (Galloway, 1985) and examination performance (Gray, 1981) that more socially and academically disadvantaged pupils may be exactly those who tend to be served by the more ineffective schools. Figure 6.1 shows clearly that a large group of schools where there are 'poor' intakes in terms of pupil ability are performing in many cases well below the levels that would have been expected of them. These schools are highly likely – given the nature of their intakes and catchment areas – to have high proportions of pupils with special educational needs.

It is clear, then, that attempts to improve overall school effectiveness will have disproportionately large effects on the more disadvantaged and lower ability pupils who are likely to make up the majority of pupils defined as having special educational needs. What are the blocks that stand in the way of this improvement for special educational needs pupils?

From our own work in Wales it is clear that the underperforming or ineffective school is not simply possessed of the organizational structures and internal processes that we have noted throughout this chapter. It also has a 'culture' or set of expectations amongst its teachers that can effectively act as a block upon change. There are the fantasies – that change is someone else's

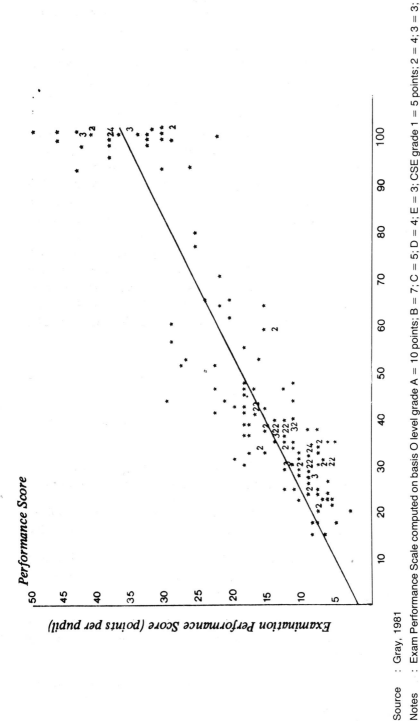

Source : Gray, 1981

Notes : Exam Performance Scale computed on basis O level grade A = 10 points; B = 7; C = 5; D = 4; E = 3; CSE grade 1 = 5 points; 2 = 4; 3 = 3; 4 = 2; 5 = 1.

% of intake with High Verbal Reasoning Scores defined as % of Band 1 pupils + .35 of Band 2 pupils in intake. The numbers 2, 3, etc. indicate almost identical positions for two or more schools.

Figure 6.1: Relationship of School Fifth Year Examination Performance to Balance of Intake

job. There are the 'cling-ons' of past practice – 'we've always done it this way'. There is the 'safety in numbers' block – individuals wanting or needing to change are held back by the large number of other teachers they are linked with who are resistant to change. There is fear of failure – all change in schools involves risk, yet many teachers are reluctant to risk the potential improvement that change could bring to their schools because of the fear that the changes may fail. The schools also employ scapegoats successfully – their own problems are seen as due to the pupils, the parents, the catchment area or 'the state of society'. The schools are also knowledge-deficient – about alternative ways of organizing, about the outputs of their existing practices and about the processes required to get changes in the school organization. The schools are also used to closed leadership, where power resides in a small number of hands – solutions are expected from those in authority rather than being seen as potentially lying in the hands of others within the organization.

Changing such schools is likely therefore to be a very complex process. From reviews of the North American (Fullan, 1982), Australian (Caldwell and Spinks, 1988) and British (Gray, 1982) literature and from our own work in attempting to change such ineffective schools into effective ones (Murgatroyd and Reynolds, 1984, 1985; Reynolds, 1988), the following principles seem basic to any attempt to get organizational development (OD) in schools:

(1) OD should focus on the school, rather than on the work of the individual teacher in the classroom.

(2) OD should focus upon the solution of problems, rather than being concerned with normal long-term school development.

(3) OD should encourage changes in actual *behaviour*, rather than merely being concerned with changing the attitudes of group members.

(4) The OD process should as far as possible be 'owned' by the staff of schools, rather than being something imposed on them by outsiders.

(5) Within schools, the process of OD must be 'bottom-up' rather than 'top-down' in orientation, with school staff actively participating in the process of change and development.

(6) OD requires constant procedures of evaluation of its effects and the feedback of this data to school staff, so that the effectiveness of the change attempts can be judged.

(7) The time scale of OD should be long-term, unlike short-term courses or the usual INSET provision.

77

(8)   OD needs to be concerned not just with the formal organization of schools, and with school processes, but also with the relationships that exist between organizational members.

Conclusions

It should be clear from all our preceding discussion that a body of knowledge now exists that has direct implications for educational practice in the area of special educational needs. Certain areas within this body of knowledge are of course in the process of development – we are still partly unsure of some of the characteristics of the effective school, and whether such a school is effective in all types of catchment area is still a matter for some debate. The detailed, insightful descriptions of within-school life that are needed to help practitioners with the practical implementation of school effectiveness work are still not available.

These gaps in our knowledge are unlikely to be filled by further academic research, however, since the number of researchers working in the field remains quite small. It will only be by individual head teachers and teachers themselves attempting their own 'action research' that our knowledge of what makes an effective school will increase, since by trying out the existing 'recipes' of effective schools within their schools we will gain an idea of which findings about school processes are truly valid across different school contexts. The long-term gain in research terms of practitioners undertaking OD work within their own schools will be paralleled by a likely shorter-term gain for pupils with special educational needs as their immediate school environments are improved. For both research and practice, then, new school-based educational policies would seem to be an urgent necessity.

References

ANDERSON, C.A. (1982) 'The search for school climate: a review of the research', in *Review of Educational Research*, Vol. 52, No. 3, pp. 368–420.

BLAGG, N. and YULE, W. (1984) 'The behavioural treatment of school refusal: a comparative study', in *Behaviour, Research and Therapy*, Vol. 22, pp. 119–127.

BROOKOVER, W.B., BEADY, C., FLOOD, P., SCHWEITZER, J. and WISENBAKER, J. (1979) *School Social Systems and Student Achievement*, New York, Praeger.

CALDWELL, B. and SPINKS, J. (1988) *The Self Managing School*, Lewes, Falmer Press.

CARROLL, H.C.M. (Ed) (1977) *Absenteeism in South Wales*, Swansea, Faculty of Education.

CICOUREL, J.V. and KITSUSE, J.I. (1963) *The Educational Decision Makers*, New York, Bobbs Merrill.

CLARKE, A.M. and CLARKE, A.D.B. (Eds) (1976) *Early Experience: Myth and Evidence*, London, Open Books.

CUTTANCE, P. (1988) 'Assessing the effectiveness of schools', in REYNOLDS, D. and CUTTANCE, P. (Eds) *School Environments and Child Development*, (in press).

DAVIE, R. (1975) *Children and Families with Special Needs (An Inaugural Lecture)*, Cardiff, University College Press.

DAVIE, R., BUTLER, M. and GOLDSTEIN, H. (1972) *From Birth to Seven*, London, Longman.

DES (1978) *Special Educational Needs (The Warnock Report)*, London, HMSO.

DHSS/WELSH OFFICE (1975) *Working together for Children and their Families*, London, HMSO.

DOUGLAS, J.W.B., ROSS, J.M. and SIMPSON, H.R. (1968) *All Our Future*, London, Davies.

EDMUNDS, R.R. (1979) 'Effective schools for the urban poor', in *Educational Leadership*, Vol. 37, pp. 20-24.

FOGELMAN, K. (ED) (1983) *Growing up in Great Britain*, London, Macmillan.

FONTANA, D. (1983) *Psychology for Teachers*, London, Macmillan.

FULLAN, M. (1982) *The Meaning of Educational Change*, New York, Teachers College Press.

GALLOWAY, D. (1985) *Schools and Persistent Absentees*, Oxford, Pergamon Press.

GILLHAM, W.E.C. (ED) (1981) *Problem Behaviour in the Secondary School*, London, Croom Helm.

GRAY, H. (Ed) (1982) *The Management of Educational Institutions: Theory, Research and Consultancy*, Lewes, Falmer Press.

GRAY, J. (1981) 'A competitive edge: examination results and the probable limits of secondary school effectiveness', in *Educational Review*, Vol. 33, No. 1, pp. 25–35.

GRAY, J., JESSON, D. and JONES, B. (1986) 'The search for a fairer way of comparing schools' examination results', in *Research Papers in Education*, Vol. 11, No. 2, pp. 91-122.

HAMBLIN, D. (1974) *The Teacher and Counselling*, London, Basil Blackwell.

HEYNEMAN, S. and LOXLEY, W.A. (1983) 'The effect of primary school quality on academic achievement across twenty-nine high and low income countries', in *American Journal of Sociology*, Vol. 88, pp. 1162–1194.

HOLLY, P. (1986) 'Soaring like turkeys: the impossible dream', in *School Organisation*, Vol. 6, No. 3, pp. 346-364.

KELLMER PRINGLE, M. (1974) *The Needs of Children*, London, Hutchinson.

MORTIMORE, P., SAMMONS, P., ECOB, R. and STOLL, L. (1988) *School Matters: The Junior Years*, Salisbury, Open Books.

MURGATROYD, S.J. (1975) 'School centred counselling', in *New Era*, Vol. 56, No. 4, pp. 90–91

MURGATROYD, S.J. (1976) 'Ethical Issues in Secondary School Counselling', in *Journal of Moral Education*, Vol. 4, No. 1, pp. 27–37.

MURGATROYD, S.J. and REYNOLDS, D. (1984) 'Leadership and the teacher', in HARLING, P. (Ed) *New Directions in Educational Leadership*, Lewes, Falmer Press.

MURGATROYD, S.J. and REYNOLDS, D. (1985) 'The creative consultant', in *School Organisation*, Vol. 4, No. 3, pp. 321–335.

PURKEY, S. and SMITH, M. (1983) 'Effective schools: A review', in *Elementary School Journal*, Vol. 83, pp. 427–452.

RAMSAY, P.D.K., SNEDDON, D.G., GRENFELL, J. and FORD, I. (1982) 'Successful or unsuccessful schools: A South Auckland study', in *Australia and New Zealand Journal of Sociology*, Vol. 19, No. 1.

RENIHAN, F.I. and RENIHAN, P.J. (1984) 'Effective schools, effective administrations and effective leadership', in *The Canadian Administrator*, Vol. 24, No. 3, pp. 1–6.

REYNOLDS, D. (1976) 'The delinquent school', in WOODS, P. (Ed) *The Process of Schooling*, London, Routledge and Kegan Paul.

REYNOLDS, D. (1982) 'The search for effective schools', in *School Organisation*, Vol. 2, No. 3, pp. 215–237.

REYNOLDS, D. (1984) 'Creative conflict: The implications of recent educational research for those concerned with children', in *Maladjustment and Therapeutic Education*, Spring 1984, pp. 14–23.

REYNOLDS, D. (Ed) (1985) *Studying School Effectiveness*, Lewes, Falmer Press.

REYNOLDS, D. (1987) 'The Effective School', in *Educational Psychology in Practice*, October.

REYNOLDS, D. (1988) 'British school improvement research: the contribution of qualitative studies' in *International Journal of Qualitative Studies in Education*, Vol. 1, No. 2.

REYNOLDS, D. and MURGATROYD, S.J. (1977) 'The sociology of schooling and the absent pupil', in CARROLL, H.C.M. (Ed) *Absenteeism in South Wales*, Swansea, Faculty of Education.

REYNOLDS, D. and SULLIVAN, M. (1979) 'Bringing schools back in', in BARTON, L. (Ed) *Schools, Pupils and Deviance*, Driffield, Nafferton.

REYNOLDS, D. (1988) *Bringing Schools Back In* (in preparation).

RUTTER, M. (1980) *Changing Youth in a Changing Society*, Oxford, Nuffield Provincial Hospitals Trust.

RUTTER, M. and MADGE, N. (1976) *Cycles of Disadvantage*, London, Heinemann.

RUTTER, M., MAUGHAN, B., MORTIMORE, P. and OUSTON, J. (1979) *Fifteen Thousand Hours*, London, Open Books.

SHARP, R. and GREEN, A. (1975) *Education and Social Control*, London, Routledge and Kegan Paul.

TOPPING, K. (1983) *Educational Systems and Disruptive Adolescents*, London, Croom Helm.

UPTON, G. (1983) *Educating Children with Behaviour Problems*, Cardiff, University College Faculty of Education.

VULLIAMY, G. (1987) 'School effectiveness research in Papua New Guinea', in *Comparative Education*, Vol. 23, No. 2, pp. 209–223.

WEST, D.J. (1983) *Delinquency*, London, Heinemann.

WOODS, P. (1979) *The Divided School*, London, Routledge and Kegan Paul.

SECTION II:
MEETING THE NEEDS OF LOW ACHIEVERS ACROSS THE CURRICULUM

Introduction

Once a teacher is committed to the notion of integration with all its implications for classroom teaching, there is often still a need to bridge the gap between theory and practice. Many newly qualified teachers do enter the profession with enthusiasm and good intent, only to succumb to more traditional views and teaching practices simply because they lack support and guidance. This section provides such guidance. In a variety of curriculum areas, teacher educators, all with recent and relevant experience in schools, highlight good practice and tackle assumptions about low-attaining pupils which have been allowed to flourish for too long.

Mike Newman's chapter 'Special Needs in Science' opens the section because so much of what he says is applicable to all areas of the curriculum. It addresses, bluntly and honestly, questions which many teachers have found themselves asking at some time in their careers. 'How can we contain 3C in periods 7 and 8 of a wet Thursday afternoon?' Furthermore it takes the lid off some of our more deeply held traditional views on examinable curriculum content and instead looks at science as a way of *doing* things. It points the way forward for all pupils. This chapter is accompanied by a list of useful publications and resources in science compiled by Colin Johnson.

Glyn Johns' chapter on mathematics, which follows, discusses the spread of attainments of children entering secondary school and reviews the recommendations of the Cockroft Report. The case for a more relevant syllabus is cogently argued and suggestions are made regarding course work and resources.

The chapter on English by Barry Johnson encourages enthusiasm in teaching the four skills of listening, talking, reading and writing. It is full of suggestions of what to do and draws clear attention to what not to do. This chapter is recommended to all teachers regardless of their subject, as literacy is the very foundation of our education system. Mark Fowler's chapter, being specifically focused on the teaching of modern languages, serves to dismiss long-held assumptions about who should and who should not be allowed access to this area of the curriculum. The benefits to pupils with special needs who are taught a second language can no longer be ignored in any school which believes in equal opportunity. For language teachers who are experiencing problems regarding the ways and means, this chapter will prove invaluable.

'Meeting the Needs of Low Attainers in Music' by William Salaman takes us back to our school days to examine our own experiences and ask ourselves whether we were low attainers in music and, if so, why? The suggestion is made that the syllabus was such that it created failures and that the way to achieve success is to build in practical musical activities at all levels. The curricular implications of this 'new thinking' are explained and each of the facets of involvement in music examined. The aim of the new approach to music teaching is to allow all pupils to attain success through the creative arts.

The final chapter in this section on the curriculum is by Dilys Price and focuses on all aspects of physical education. It is often the case that pupils with special educational needs are integrated with other classes for PE activities although, as is pointed out elsewhere, there is rarely an educational case made for this and their problems are often disregarded. Dilys Price, whilst supporting integrated teaching situations, highlights the difficulties which many children experience in PE and calls for an awareness of causation and sensitivity in helping them to overcome their fears and problems. To ignore such problems will often compound the disadvantages of ill health, lack of fitness, lack of confidence and low self-esteem, which many pupils with learning difficulties at school take on with them into adult life. This chapter gives clear guidance to teachers as to how to help prevent the formation or maintenance of negative attitudes to physical education and physical activities in both able-bodied and disabled-bodied pupils. The message of this last chapter is applicable to all subjects – 'A sense of individual failure should not be an objective in our lesson structure – instead getting the youngster motivated to do his or her individual best, to work with the concept of excellence as the aim should be what we want to bring into a young person's world. Excellence can be achieved at every level and every child can gain the self-confidence which striving and reaching towards excellence can bring'.

Chapter 7

Special Needs in Science
Mike Newman

It would be rather nice to have a clear idea of what 'Science' is.

There are many activities that go on when X appears on the timetable as teaching SCIENCE in Lab Y. Some of these activities are very interesting; some, instructive; some broaden young minds; some are distinctly minority pursuits. Some, it must be admitted, contribute little to the sum total of human happiness and erudition.

Teachers continually face the problem of selecting aspects of their discipline that suit particular slices of the school population. Often this is with the sharp formulation – 'how can we contain 3C in periods 7 and 8 of a wet Thursday afternoon?'

Since it is clearly and demonstrably the case that some bits of SCIENCE do not suit 3C at all, it would be helpful to be convinced that what we give them is an honest and worthwhile sample of something that really does deserve the name of 'science'.

This is *the* prior question. There is no use in giving tips on how to sell the 'less able' on something that we do not ourselves value. If teachers despise what they are doing, then, whatever else they communicate, they will effectively pass on that contempt. And 3C will respond, perfectly reasonably, in kind.

Thus no one gets pleasure when 'less able' pupils are presented with a dull grind through factual material that is either beyond them or is so watered-down as to be both unsatisfying and unintelligible.

This is, in fact, a general rather than a 'special' problem. The very phrases with which we describe 3C are meaningless, from the cumbersome 'less academically motivated' to the shorter and less polite terms to which their teachers sometimes resort. Every child is 'less able' at something than someone, and 'more able' than somebody else at something else.

What we really mean is that most children cannot get to grips with that traditional slice of our discipline that we have become accustomed to presenting, in a very particular, even peculiar, way, as a sacrifice on the altars of the public examinations boards. And since the job of the boards has been to select the top 20 per cent, it should not surprise us that the other 80 per cent are, in this sense, 'less able'.

The question does not end here. Just because the sheep are capable of jumping over hurdles, does not, unfortunately, validate those hurdles. It most certainly does not follow that sheep science is worthwhile, because it has high status, and all we have to do is find something to occupy the goats.

We need some criterion of the scienciness of SCIENCE that will help us to find activities that can be conducted with profit by all children. It cannot be established in advance whether these activities will be the same for all or 'differentiated', to use the DES's current cant. There may be activities that are meaningful to a minority and nonetheless worthwhile for those who can cope. This may be so, but we should not unthinkingly assume that because such activities are for the elite they are thereby, and solely thereby, worthwhile.

There may be other activities that all could engage in, bringing to them a bewildering range of interests and expertise, taking away an equal or wider range of profitable experience. The key here, of course, is in the word 'activity'. No possible passive experience could suit all, or even most (or possibly any). Listening to a dictator's drone fulfills neither special nor general needs. Conducting stereotyped 'experiments' from a recipe book to predictable 'conclusions' may not either.

Can we say what Science is?

This is not such an easy question. One major distinction often drawn is that between 'content' and 'process'. Content is usually taken to mean the explanatory concepts that have so far been elaborated by generations of practising scientists. Process refers to the act of investigation and, hopefully, discovery. The two facets of science can be summed up as shown in Figure 7.1.

The essential point about this analysis is the constant interplay between the previous contributions to science (CONTENT) and the continuing acts of investigation (PROCESS). Interplay works two ways. Previous contributions determine what is regarded as a problem, as well as the instrumentation and methodology available to tackle it. Current investigatory effort not only adds to content but gives it a special nature. The products of science are different from those of any other aspect of human culture: they are tentative,

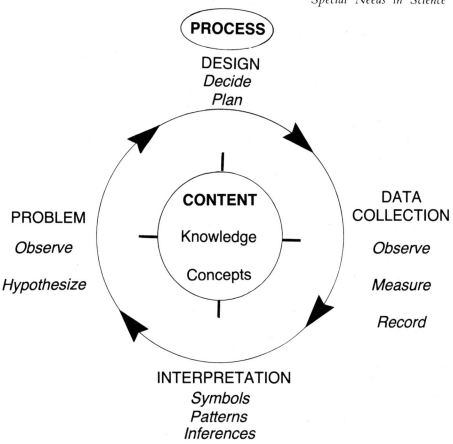

Figure 7.1: The Two Facets of Science

subject to continual evaluation and modification. A scientific theory is our current best attempt to explain how some bit of the world works. No more. No less.

The Assessment of Performance Unit drew some conclusions from their national surveys of children at 11, 13 and 15. It is clear from the weight they put on process categories that they regard this as a neglected aspect of school science. This opinion is now received wisdom:

> There is wide agreement that many 'O' level science syllabuses are overloaded, out of date and narrow, paying little regard to the relevance of science to industry or to adult life, and concentrating on abstract concepts from too early a stage ... Most 'O' level and CSE examinations place undue emphasis on the recall of facts, concepts and theories ... It is very rare for such a science examination to test pupils' ability to use their science in solving realistic problems or in applying it to practical situations (DES, 1982, p. 3).

The APU reports demonstrate that this stress on the abstract, the verbal and the non-practical is playing pointedly to the weaknesses of most children:

> In general the written form of a question as opposed to a practical one, and a written response compared to an action response, depress pupils performance... (p. 21)

> Looking at the results across investigations it is clear that most 13 year olds are successful in setting up investigations to solve problems; they show enthusiasm and an unexpected diversity of approach. (p. 15)

> They are much more likely to adopt 'scientific' solutions in the practical context; the opportunity for practically working through a problem results in a more realistic and successful path to the solution being adopted (DES, 1984, p. 15)

This conclusion — that pupils do less well in a passive abstract context, better in concrete activity runs through all the survey reports. It results in two of their major prescriptions for improvement:

> The need for the explicit inclusion of science process, including practical problem solving, as an integral part of the science curriculum in order to present all pupils with a broad view of science within which *the majority of them can demonstrate success* ... A reduction of the concept loading of the curriculum for most pupils in order to create time for the development of scientific processes and also to allow children more time to become familiar with the concepts they do meet, and to use them in a variety of situations (DES, 1985, p. 40)

The point hardly needs to be stressed. If these are general conclusions for science teaching, they apply a thousand times more strongly when considering pupils with special educational needs.

Success in Science

There remains an important stumbling block. It is not clear from the previous discussion just what it is that enables us to say that a piece of 'process' has been successful or that a given explanation is worthy of inclusion in 'content'.

This is an educational point of some importance. We are looking for activities that children can do. They must be able to recognise success when they meet it. Doing more practical work, even if enforced by GCSE assessment criteria, is of no earthly value if its results are unintelligible to the children.

Unfortunately it is at this point that the philosophers are in confusion. There is no agreement on how to recognize success in science. Even worse, some of the proposed methods are profoundly abstract and most unlikely to be understood by more than a tiny minority. There are three main trends that may be explored for their educational relevance:

Science as Logic

Many people see the test of success in science as logic. They may be called logical empiricists or positivists. They view theories as universal statements bound together by intricate reasoning, from which can be deduced predictive statements about the world. There is a great deal of controversy about how the system works. 'Verificationalists' believe that the universals can be built up by 'inductive' reasoning from a succession of experiences or experiments. 'conventionalists' believe that it is meaningless to inquire whether the universals are true, that the most we can say is that they are convenient as conventions. 'falsificationists' believe that we cannot prove the universals, we must treat them as conjectures and then try to refute them. Those who are interested in such disputations can read further (for example in Losee, 1980).

Teachers, on the other hand, should be worried at this point. If these philosophers are right, then there is something about science that puts it out of reach of most people.

Many research workers have studied children's use of logic. Piaget was convinced that the use of logic – in the sophisticated sense necessary to evaluate the validity of a deduction – is confined to what he called 'formal operations' (see, for example, Inhelder and Piaget, 1970). Recent national surveys have indicated that the use of formal operations is much rarer than Piaget thought, perhaps less than 20 per cent of 16-year-olds (see Shayer and Adey, 1981).

It must not be thought that children cannot reason at all. An excellent set of examples of what children *can* do is set out in the objectives of the Schools Council 5-13 project. But there can be no sense in taking an over-logical view of science, when we know perfectly well that we are going to create an additional experience of failure for most pupils. The fact that most school science write-ups end with 'conclusions' underlines the approach that has been taken in the past. There are at least three reasons to stop doing this:

(1)   It is not established that the logical empirists are correct in their view of science. There are alternative views, as we shall see.

(2)   Even if they are, it is not established that this is the most sensible emphasis, given pupils' obvious difficulty in this area. How often do teachers have to resort to dictating the conclusions?

(3)   In strict logic, few school experiments result in enough evidence to justify any valid conclusion. Much of the time we are telling lies to children (see, for example, Wright, 1981).

Science as Personal Knowledge

Many writers have rejected the impersonal element in logical views of science. Those who may be called relativists believe that a bit of science is successful when enough people decide to accept it.

Thomas Kuhn (1970) highlighted the fact that many real scientists are not so bound by logic as to discount their theories when the first experimental result falsifies them (or appears to do so). He speaks of periods of 'normal science' during which theories are taken for granted and scientists work on minor puzzles. At rare intervals of 'revolutionary science' there is much more questioning and scientists have to decide whether to switch from one set of theories to another. Kuhn sees such 'paradigm switching' as more akin to a change of religion than a process of logical thought.

Writers in this trend speak of either individuals or groups (in institutions like scientific societies) making up their minds, influenced by many factors – including tradition or the hope of advancement – in a very personal way.

The implications for science teaching are not so clear. Should we base ourselves on the uncritical 'normal science' which tends to stress an unquestioning, even dogmatic attitude? It may well be that this is a fair description of much science and much school science. But should it be so?

In any event, if success is the same as acceptance then how can we separate science from all sorts of irrational but widely held beliefs? The logical flaw at the heart of relativism is that it provides no rational basis for choice between one set of ideas and another.

This too is a central point for education. Research workers over the past ten years (e.g. Driver, 1982) have become much more conscious that children are not empty vessels waiting passively to be filled up with whatever content we choose to pour in. Well before they enter school, children are actively exploring the world, building up their own 'mini-theories' about how it works. They also watch television and films, listen to trusted adults and assimilate all sorts of ideas, bearing on science, but possibly at odds with the received version. These 'alternative frameworks' (sometimes referred to as 'gut science' and 'lay science' respectively) are persistent. They have been taught over a longer period, and possibly much more effectively, than school science. We reach three further conclusions:

(1)   Teachers need to know where the children are starting from. Mini-theories are likely to result in incorrect predictions on many occasions but unlikely to be as powerful as adult science.
If we believe they have accepted our view, because their predictions are sometimes right, then we and they will be disappointed and frustrated at the sudden unexpected divergence. Yet another experience of failure! In order to know what children think – it is necessary to listen to them.

(2)   If we are serious about teaching science, we will be wanting to change their framework to the currently accepted scientific view. Relativists have no authority to do so. If one belief system is as good as another, what can teachers appeal to other than their position of power?

(3)   If we wish to change chidren's views, and feel we have the authority to do so, we must still find the method. If we cannot appeal to logic, and if we cannot appeal to the majority, we must find some way of *showing* the increased power of our explanations.

Science as a Way of Doing Things

There are some philosophers ('realists' or 'materialists') who believe that there is a sense in which we can speak of the 'truth' of a scientific theory. Rom Harré (1986) refers to scientific theories as 'candidates for reality'. Many people who read about the philosophy of science are amazed to learn that this is a minority viewpoint – and indeed, in some ways, hardly respectable.

Yet it suits many practising scientists and it seems natural to children. There is no absolute measure of 'truth', of course, and scientific theories remain tentative. We do not find out all of the truth at once. But there is a good measure of the truth of a scientific theory – our explanation hits off at least some aspects of reality *if it enables us to do something we could not do before.* This view of science was well expressed by J.D. Bernal, himself a practising scientist:

> Science is not a matter of thought alone, but of thought continually carried into practice and continually refreshed by practice. That is why science cannot be studied separately from technique. In the history of science we shall repeatedly see new aspects of science arising out of practice and new developments in science giving rise to new branches of practice (Bernal, 1954, p. 17).

An even better description of scientific method makes clear its links with those of ordinary life, particularly the manual trades:

> ... first you have a look at the job and then you try something and see if it will work... (*ibid.*, p. 11)

Having a look at the job is dignified in scientific language as 'making observations'. Trying something sounds better as 'hypothesizing'. But the reader will have spotted the link with the APU conclusion that children do better in the practical context. We now have a distinguished scientist, a Nobel prize winner, telling us that the practical context is the real context in which science works. Attempts to mystify it, to reserve it for the elite, to speak in high-flown abstract terms not only lead to pupil failure but also lead away from the springs of success in real science in the real world. On the other hand here we have the authority to challenge pupils' mini-theories. If they can make things work – well and good. If they cannot, they can, through activity, feel the need to change.

Three conclusions flow from this:

(1) We must find a way of teaching science in which children know they have succeeded because they have made something or done something that works.

(2) In real science the final test that something works is that it works for other people. The piece of technique can be incorporated into social labour. Ultimate success for a child in school science must be to share ideas with others in such a way that they can make or do something too.

(3) Technique affects people's lives. All citizens have the right to understand so that they can control. Through being shown something that works – inside or outside school – children can begin to decide for themselves whether or how we should use it.

What Shall we Teach 3C?

The reader may think that this chapter has gone too deeply into science and ignored the children; that there has been too much philosophy and not enough practical hints. The reason for this approach should be clear to anyone who knows science and knows science teachers. 'SCIENCE' is a high status subject. High status subjects are dangerous, because they tempt teachers into exclusive attitudes. They breed failure. 'I shall make my subject so hard that you can't do it. And then I shall blame you, because you can't'.

In reality teachers have no motive to continue with this attitude. Because pupils, given experience of failure, turn nasty. We are then involved in the self-destructive spiral of lack of self-esteem, problems in control, mutual contempt and a boring time all round.

This chapter has tried to show that teachers need not feed their self-image by destroying that of the child.

The essence of science lies not in logic nor in complex concepts. School science must be demystified. All children can make something work. They have a lifetime's experience of doing so outside the classroom.

How will this work in practice? Many of the 'less able' science courses, created under the impact of the raising of the school leaving age in the 1970s, have been moving in this direction. An annotated list is to be found at the end of the chapter. These courses are practically based. They often involve making things. They often cover non-traditional and exciting areas of science. They still largely fail for two reasons:

(1) The pupils have a long previous history of failure which colours their attitude to school work of any sort.

(2) The pupils know that their 'successful' colleagues are doing work of a different character. They therefore undervalue their own courses – even though these may be the best of what is offered in school science.

There is only one answer to this. The differentiation between high status abstract conceptual science and practical science must end. Practical science must be for all.

Postscript

The method of science teaching advocated here is based on:

(1) Finding out where the children are at by listening to them.

(2) Putting emphasis on social interaction by group work and group discussion.

(3) Seeking success through making things that work.

The reader may fairly ask if this method works. The author must answer that some people have made it work. It all depends on your relationship with the children – which is personal and cannot be taught. It also depends on how long and how bad has been their experience of failure. A radical change of method with fifth-form toughies is less likely to succeed than a consistent policy starting in the first year (preferably in consultation with feeder primary schools).

Since teaching, like science, can only be learned in practice the beginner should see two people in action:

(1)   A primary teacher, working with a cross-disciplinary science course such as Schools Council 5–13.

(2)   A CDT teacher, working with a project-based technology course (the WJEC GCSE Technology is 60 per cent based on things the children have made or done themselves).

Once you have seen what can be done, you will know, at least, that it is not impossible.

References

BERNAL, J.D. (1954) *'Science in History'*, 3rd ed., London, Watts.
DES (1982) *Science Education in Schools*. A consultative document, London, HMSO.
DES (1984) *Science at age 13*. Science Report for Teachers, No. 3 (APU) London, HMSO.
DES (1985) *Science at age 15*. Science Report for Teachers, No. 5 (APU) London, HMSO.
DRIVER, R. (1982) *The Pupil as Scientist*, Oxford, Oxford University Press.
HARRE, R. (1986) *Varieties of Realism: a Rationale for the Natural Sciences*, Oxford, Basil Blackwell.
INHELDER, B. and PIAGET, J. (1970) *Growth of Logical Thinking from Childhood to Adolescence: An Essay on the Construction of Formal Operational Structures*, London, Basic Books.
KUHN, T.S. (1970) *The Structure of Scientific Revolutions*, 2nd ed., Chicago, University of Chicago Press.
LOSEE, J. (1980) *A Historical Introduction to the Philosophy of Science*, 2nd ed., Oxford, Oxford University Press.
SCHOOLS COUNCIL (1973) *Science 5–13 series*, London, Macdonald Educational.
SHAYER, M. and ADEY, P. (1981) *Towards a Science of Science Teaching: Cognitive Development and Curriculum Demand*, London, Heinemann Educational.
WRIGHT, P.G. (1981) 'Evidence and Non-evidence for the Existence of Atoms and Molecules', in *Education in Chemistry*, 18:13, p. 74.

Appendix: Science Materials for Pupils with Learning Difficulties
Colin Johnson

Courses and Resources 11–13

(a) Pupil Material with Practical Work

ACCESS TO SCIENCE (G. Mitchell and G. Snape)
Six pupils' books, each with teachers' notes: Measurement; Separating substances; Water; Air; Classification; Reproduction (Nelson/Harrap, 1981)

BASIC SKILLS IN SCIENCE (J. Merrigan and P. Herbert)
Skills book with thirty-eight pupil activities, 'each teaching one basic skill'; corresponding book of Test Sheets, and Teachers' Book. (Hart-Davis, 1979)

CENTRE SCIENCE (eds. C. Terry, T. Gibson and T. Loosmore)
Twenty short units, with two teachers' guides and a 'Measuring Guide': Beginning science; Separating Colours; Acids and alkalis; Measuring; Separating things; Magnetism and Electricity; Classification; Keys; Units of Life; Measuring temperature; More Measuring; Air; Heating things; Forces; Small things; Invertebrates; Measuring Time; Senses; Materials; Patterns and Variation. (Granada/Hart-Davis, 1981)

ESSENTIAL SKILLS IN SCIENCE
Photocopiable worksheets for 11-14-year-olds. (Hobsons, 1986)

SCIENCE IN PROCESS
Ten themes: Be Scientific; Air; Chemicals; Communication; Time; Energy; Environment; Growing; Liquids; Structure and Forces. Available as two

books of five themes or singly, with the themes providing the vehicle for the development of process skills. Also two Teachers' Resources Packs. (Heinemann/ILEA, 1987–8)

SCIENCE WATCH (P. Butler, D. Carrington and P. Ellis)
Science Skills 1 and 2, and Teachers' Packs with worksheets. (Cambridge, 1986)

SCIENTIFIC EYE (A. Hart-Davis)
Lively Yorkshire TV series with 'textbook', teachers' guides and practical worksheets, intended for the 9–13 age range. Likely to motivate almost anyone! (Bell and Hyman, 1985)

THIS IS SCIENCE (K. Dobson)
Teachers' guide and two pupils' books, for average ability and below. Similar content to many 11–13 courses, but gently paced and much good sense in the teachers' book. (Macmillan, 1979)

WARWICK PROCESS SCIENCE (P. Screen)
Five-year course: seven 'content-free' modules for developing process skills in year 1; thirty units for years 2 and 3; more to come for years 4 and 5. (Ashford Press, 1987)

(b) Readers

DATABANK (D. Crystal and J.L. Foster)
Thirty readers and some worksheets, specifically for slow learners: Heat; Light; Sound; Air; Food; Electricity; Computers. (Edward Arnold, 1985)

READING ABOUT SCIENCE (Ed. S. Kellington)
Five readers, intended as adjuncts to the Scottish Integrated Science course, but containing graded topics suitable for a wide range of ability: Units, living things and energy; Substances, solutions, cells and seeds; Heat, electricity and electromagnetism; Gases, acids and the earth; Senses, force and transport in living things. (Heinemann, 1982)

Courses and Resources 14–16

(a) Pupil Material with Practical Work

FOUNDATION SCIENCE (K.A. McInlay and J.M. Braidwood)
Pupil text and four workbooks, with assessment guide and teachers' guide,

originally written for Scottish Standard Grade: Healthy bodies; Energy; Materials; The environment. (Longmans/Oliver and Boyd, 1984)

GRIFFIN TECHNICAL STUDIES
Kits with associated booklets (separately available, and originally published by Mills and Boon, now part of Bell and Hyman), including: Cosmetics; Pond life; Polymers; Minerals and ores; Fossils; Dyes and dyeing; Enamelling; Glass-making; Lapidary; Corrosion; Plant hormones; Astronomy; Weather; Earth studies; Human chemistry; Surfaces; Flow; Homecraft; Detergents; Fibres; Crime detection; Colour in nature; Microscopy; Colourful chemistry; Human mechanics; Printing; Batik. (Griffin/Mills and Boon, 1970)

KEEP BRITAIN TIDY GROUP SCIENCE PROJECT
Technologically orientated packs for 12-16-year-olds, containing teachers' guides, work card masters, film strip and pupil reader. Five units: Paper, Glass, Metals, Plastics, Waste Management and Resources. (KBTG, 1981–5)

LAMP PROJECT (ASE)
Materials for a modular science course for 'less academically motivated pupils'. Two teachers' guides: Guide to the project; Modular course organization. Fifteen topic briefs, containing pupil material: Fuels; Heating and lighting a home; Pollution; Materials; Photography; Gardening; Health and hygiene; Space and space travel; Paints and dyes; Flight; Science and food; Science and the motor car; Problem solving; Fibres and fabrics; Electronics. Also LAMP Energy studies. (Association for Science Education, 1976)

MODULAR SECONDARY SCIENCE RESOURCES (MSSR)
Three spiral-bound books of photocopiable resource material, usable in many different ways. Topics: Energy Sources; Materials; Waves; Colour and Perception; Particles; Keeping Warm and Keeping Cool; Light; Science from the Environment; Chemicals and Chemical Reactions; Classification (John Murray, 1987)

NUFFIELD SECONDARY SCIENCE (Ed. H. Misselbrook)
Eight themes, arising from 'Science for the Young School Leaver' (Schools Council Working Paper No. 1): Interdependence of living things; Continuity of Life; Biology of man; Harnessing energy; Extension of sense perception; Movement; Using materials; The earth and its place in the universe. Teachers' guides, apparatus and assessment guides. (Longmans, 1969)

OPEN SCIENCE (Schools Council 'Science for the Less Able' Project)
Thirteen units and a teachers' guide: Life spotting; Snaps and circuits;

Electricity in the Home; Starting and stopping; Find out about machines; Science at home; Fire; Keeping going; Structures; Safe Eating; Pollution; Machines on the move; Grow your own. (Collins/Hart-Davis/Hutchinson, 1980)

SCIENCE AT WORK (Dir. J. Taylor)

Eighteen modules with strong practical emphasis, each with teachers' notes: Body maintenance; Building science; Cosmetics; Domestic electricity; Dyes and dyeing; Earth science; Electronics; Energy; Fibres and fabrics; Flight; Food and microbes; Forensic science; Gears and gearing; Photography; Plant science; Pollution; Science of the motor car; You and your mind. Also Extension material, sold as copymasters, and a Technology series covering: Electronics; Microcomputers; Telecommunication; Microelectronics; Computers and computing; Biotechnology. (originally Addison-Wesley, now Longmans, 1979)
Extension work for the more able. (1983)

SCIENCE AT WORK: TECHNOLOGY

Extension to the above material. (Longman, 1987)

SCIENCE FOR THE INDIVIDUAL

Embryonic series from the Avon Resources for Learning Development Unit. Sample material on Microbes at work; Explosions and flames; Have a heart; Cement and concrete. (Avon RLDU, 1986)

(b) Readers and Textbooks

ASPECTS OF SCIENCE (Ed. D. Foster)

Fifteen topic books with ideas for practical work: Chemicals at home; Disease; Food; Fuels; H_2O; How animals move; Into space; Metals and alloys;
Naming things; Optics; Speed; The senses; Useful Gases; Using electricity; Weather (Longmans/Addison-Wesley, 1982)

BASIC SKILLS: SCIENCE (P. Leckstein)

Forthcoming (John Murray, 1988)

CORE SCIENCE (Ed. S. Kellington)

Four readers with assignments and activities: Energy; Healthy bodies; Materials; Environments. (Heinemann, 1984)

LIVING WITH SCIENCE (Ed. J. Bowers)

Five readers: Photography; Modern materials; Heating and lighting a home; Fibres and fabrics; Health and hygiene. (Cambridge U.P., 1984)

MODULAR SCIENCE (Eds. R.W. Fairbrother, E.W. Jenkins and P.J. Scott)
Seventeen pupils' books, with teachers' notes 'with language and presentation ... for pupils in the lower part of the ability range': You and your
ancestors; Conserve or ...?; Plastics everywhere; The atmosphere; The
commonest compound; Energy; Electronics; Music and noise; Atoms,
molecules and crystals; Heat and insulation; Food science; Man and other
animals; Metals; Plant science; Space science; Plants and man; Getting
around. (Blackie, 1979)

NUFFIELD WORKING WITH SCIENCE
Originally a major scheme for the 'non-academic sixth former', now re-
issued as source materials for CPVE. Topics: Brewing; Crime Detection;
Efficiency; Enterprise; Fire; Football; Hair; Pottery; Psychology; Questioning
Prejudice and Superstition; Study of a Local Industry. (Longman, new
edition 1987)

SCIENCE AND TECHNICAL READERS (Various authors)
Twelve readers introducing 'technical and scientific subjects through
controlled use of language': Energy: Electricity; Nuclear energy; Astronomy;
The engine; Auto transmission; Industrial safety; Preventive medicine;
Petroleum upstream; Petroleum downstream, Flight; Computers. (Heine-
mann, 1980)

SCIENCE FOR LIFE (K. Bishop, D. Maddocks and W. Scott)
Course book with emphasis on 'relevant and balanced understanding of the
world' and four books of worksheet Copymasters. (Collins)

SCIENCE IN ACTION series (Eds. R.W. Thomas and R.S. Lowrie)
Six topic books for background and reference: 'Science and ... the armed
services, the railways, crime detection, the weatherman, firefighting,
farming'. (A. Wheaton & Co., 1977)

SCIENCE YOU NEED (A.R. Ferguson)
Single volume on 'basic scientific prin iples in the context of everyday life'
(Nelson, 1979)

Science for Pupils with Learning Difficulties: A Reading List

Assessment and Monitoring

AINLEY, D. and LAZONBY, J.N., 'Observation as a means of evaluation of science
    courses for less able children — a case study', *School Science Review*, 1981, 62
    (221), pp. 631–641.

BRYCE, T.D.K., *TAPS I & II* (Techniques for the Assessment of Practical Skills in Foundation Science), Heinemann, 1983 and 1988.

DES, *APU Science Reports for Teachers 1–11*, ASE, 1984–8.

HARLEN, W., *Guides to Assessment: Science*, Macmillan, 1983.

HODSON, D. and BREWSTER, J., 'Towards science profiles', *School Science Review*, 1985, 67 (239), pp. 231–240.

KEMPA, R., *Assessment in Science*, Cambridge University Press, 1986.

Communication

BARLEX, D. and CARRE, C., *Visual Communication in Science*, Cambridge University Press, 1985.

BOOTH, V., *Communicating in Science: Writing and Speaking*, Cambridge University Press, 1985.

BULMAN, L., *Teaching Language and Study Skills in Secondary Science*, Heinemann, 1984.

CARRE, C., *Language teaching and learning: Science*, Ward Lock Educational, 1981.

DAVIES, F. and GREEN, T., *Reading for Learning in the Sciences*, Schools Council/Oliver and Boyd, 1984.

PERERA, K., 'Some linguistic difficulties in school subjects', in GILLHAM, B. (Ed.), *The Language of School Subjects*, Heinemann, 1986.

PRESTT, B. (Ed.), *Language in Science*, ASE Study Series No. 16, Association for Science Education, 1980.

SUTTON, C. (Ed.), *Communicating in the Classroom*, Hodder and Stoughton, 1981.

Curriculum Planning

BLACKBAND, M., 'Steps towards integrated science', *Support for Learning*, 1987, 2 (1), pp. 32–35.

CLEGG, A.S. and MORLEY, M., 'Applied science – a course for pupils of low educational achievement', *School Science Review*, 1980, 61 (216), pp. 454–463.

DALE TUNNICLIFFE, S., 'Science materials for special needs', *British Journal of Special Education*, 1987, 14 (2), pp. 73–75.

DES, *A Survey of Science in Special Education*, HMSO, 1986.

DITCHFIELD C., 'Reviewing developments in science education for young people with learning difficulties', *Support for Learning*, 1987, 2 (1), pp. 36–40.

HEGARTY, S., *et al.*, *Recent Curriculum Development in Special Education*, Longman for Schools Council, 1982 (see Sections 3 and 5).

KERSHAW, I. and SCOTT, P.J., 'Science for pupils of low educational attainment', *School Science Review*, 1975, 56 (196), pp. 449–463.

KITE, J., 'Developing a scientific approach in children with special needs in the junior school', *Support for Learning*, 1987, 2 (1), pp. 26–31.

PECK, M.J. and WILLIAMS, J.P., 'Science for the least able pupils leading to a CSE qualification', *School Science Review*, 1978, 60 (211), pp. 353–357.

REID, D.J. and HODSON, D., *Special Needs in Ordinary Schools: Science for All*, Cassell, 1987.

TOWNSEND, I.J., 'Science for the Special Child, Parts 1 & 2', *School Science Review*, 1971, 52 (181), pp. 768–771 and 1972, 53 (184), pp. 475–496.

WILKINSON, D. and BOWERS, J., *LAMP Project, Teachers' Guides I & II*, ASE, 1976.

General Teaching Guides

ARNOLD R., *et al.*, *Me? Teach Science?*, (Some suggestions for starting to teach science to children with special educational needs), Hampshire LEA, 1987.

BOWKER, M.K., *et al.*, *Problem Solving for the Less Able*, Hereford and Worcester LEA, 1986.

COUNTY OF AVON, *Science for Pupils with Special Educational Needs*, Avon LEA, 1985.

COUNTY OF CHESHIRE, *CHASSIS Teachers' Handbook*, (Cheshire Achievement of Scientific Skills in School), Cheshire LEA, 1986.

DITCHFIELD, C., *Better Science: For young people with special educational needs*, Secondary Science Curriculum Review 'Curriculum Guide 8', Heinemann, 1987.

FOSTER, D., *Teaching Pupils of Low Scientific Attainment*, RLDU, Bristol, 1984.

KINCAID, D., *Science for Children with Learning Difficulties*, Schools Council/ Macdonald, 1983.

JONES, A.V. 'Students with special needs', Chapter 7a in NELLIST, J. and NICHOLL, B., *The ASE Science Teacher's Handbook*, Hutchinson/ASE, 1986.

JONES, A.V. (Ed.) *Science Education for Children with Special Educational Needs*, Physical Science Dept., Trent Polytechnic, 1986.

TRAVERS, N., *The Teaching of Science to Pupils of Low Scientific Attainment*, Northumberland LEA, 1984.

The Demands of Science

AINLEY, D., 'Some strategies for teaching electronics to less able pupils', *School Science Review*, 1985, 66 (234), pp. 31–39.

CLIS, *CLIS in the Classroom – Approaches to Teaching*, Children's Learning in Science Project, Centre for Studies in Science and Mathematics Education, University of Leeds.

DRIVER, R., *The Pupil as Scientist?*, Open University Press, 1983.

HMI, *Slow Learning and Less Successful Pupils in Secondary Schools: some evidence from HMI visits*, HMSO, 1984.

JENKINS, E.W. (Ed.), *The Teaching of Science to Pupils of Low Scientific Attainment*, Centre for Studies in Science and Mathematics Education, University of Leeds.

OSBORNE, R. and FREYBERG, P., *Learning in Science: The Implications of Children's Science*, Heinemann, 1985.

SHAYER, M. and ADEY, P., *Towards a Science of Science Teaching*, Heinemann, 1981.

SMITH, V., 'Teaching science to the slow learner', *School Science Review*, 1983, 65 (230), pp. 138–140.

Handicapped Pupils and Science

AYRES, D.G. and HINTON, R.A.L., 'Meeting the needs of visually handicapped pupils in ecology', *School Science Review*, 1985, 67 (238), pp. 18–26.

COLEMAN, D.A., 'Technology with the young disabled', *School Technology*, September 1981, p. 2.

JONES, A.V., *Science for Handicapped Children*, Souvenir Press, 1983.

JONES, A.V. and BARNETT, A., 'Science for the physically handicapped', *Special Education: Forward Trends*, 1980, 7 (3), p. 25.

LEACH G., 'Making science more accessible', *Special Education: Forward Trends*, 1982, 9 (1), pp. 13–15.

LEACH, G., 'Practical examination science and physically handicapped pupils', *School Science Review*, 1985, 66 (236), pp. 436–446.

STEPHENSON, S.C., *The Teaching of Science and Maths to the Blind*, RNIB, 1980.

Chapter 8

The Low Attainer in Mathematics at Secondary School

Glyn Johns

The Mathematical Attainment Profile

The 'Mathematical Attainment Profile' illustrated in the Cockcroft Report (1982) (Fig. 5, para. 190) draws attention to several important facts relating to the expectations of pupils on entry to a comprehensive school. In an average entry (say 200 pupils), only one pupil will eventually start a degree course in Mathematics. About twelve of these pupils can expect to receive an 'A' level in the subject, a quarter will attain an 'O' level or its equivalent qualification, whereas 68 per cent of the pupils will receive some external qualification. A large proportion (32 per cent), however, can expect little from their school mathematics, and they will leave school with no qualification in the subject.

Throughout the course of its investigation, the Cockcroft Committee became increasingly aware of the differences of attainment which existed within age groups of children. At 11 years, they suggested, there was a 7-year difference in attainment, which means that some children at this age have a greater understanding of mathematics than many pupils who leave school at 16 years. In its discussion of this range of attainment, the Cockcroft Committee identified three factors which need to be considered as a starting point for a discussion of secondary school mathematics. They are: (i) the level of attainment at the beginning of the course, (ii) the pupil's speed of learning and a need to ensure that sufficient understanding has been attained before proceeding to another topic, and (iii) the nature and the content of the mathematics at secondary stage.

As part of the review of the secondary school curriculum, the Cockcroft Committee examined the end product of the system at 16 years and considered, in particular, the implications of the examination system. The Committee then identified problems which had occurred as a consequence of the changes brought about by the introduction of comprehensive education where schools offered both the 'O' level and CSE examinations to 16-year-olds. It noted that the content of CSE examinations had been increased especially to include topics of an algebraic kind. Furthermore, up to 80 per cent of the pupils in secondary school followed courses which were demonstrably too difficult for them, and the 'O' level syllabus then was shown to exert an enormous influence on the mathematics curriculum. Consequently, those pupils whose attainment is average or below, according to the Cockcroft Committee, have been greatly disadvantaged (para. 442).

'We cannot believe that it can in any way be educationally desirable that a pupil of average ability should, for the purpose of obtaining a school-leaving certificate, be required to attempt an examination paper on which he is able to obtain only about one-third of the possible marks' (para. 444) is the conclusion reached by the Cockcroft Committee. Such a system, it suggests, leads many pupils into feelings of inadequacy and failure. As a consequence, teaching, instead of developing understanding, concentrates on drilling routines in preparation for external examinations. Admittedly as is noted in the Report, some schools devised limited grade CSE examinations under Mode 3 procedures which allowed the content of the examination syllabus to be suitably matched to the needs of the pupil. However, very many secondary schools are following mathematics syllabuses whose content is too extensive and not suited to the level of attainment of the pupils. It remains to be seen to what extent the GCSE courses will alter this situation.

The Foundation List

Cockcroft's decision to set out a foundation list of mathematical topics is possibly one of its most important recommendations. In making this recommendation, the Committee were well aware that they were running contrary to the present practice where the syllabus which is primarily designed for the most able pupil is considered to be the starting point for curriculum development, and the rest of the school pupils are usually given a watered-down version in which particular topics may be deleted or modified in their depth of mathematical treatment. In contrast to this approach, Cockcroft recommended that 'the development should be from the bottom upwards' by considering the range of 'work which is appropriate for lower attaining pupils and extending this range as the level of attainment of pupils increases'.

The Foundation List (para. 458) is intended as the basic curriculum for pupils in the lowest 40 per cent of the range of attainment in mathematics or those pupils who are expected to have minimal or no success with external examinations. The list has been specifically designed to be relevant to the requirements of everyday life, and no topic is included unless it can be developed sufficiently for 'it to be applied in ways which pupils can understand'. Thus formal algebra is not considered to be appropriate to be included in the list.

In drawing up this list, the Cockcroft Committee were acutely aware that many pupils were leaving school with little understanding of the mathematical content of the courses at secondary level. To support this conclusion, they drew attention to the fact that the pupil of average ability was able to obtain a Grade 5 CSE pass with as little as 30 per cent of the total marks. Furthermore, they reported that even pupils at the higher level of ability said that much of mathematics learned at school was 'very often not about anything' but simply an 'excessive preoccupation with a sequence of skills'.

A 'differentiated curriculum' was proposed to cater for the wide differences of ability and attainment which occur within the normal year entry to a secondary school. It was suggested, then, that all pupils cover the topics in the Foundation List and they all received a variety of teaching approaches. Differences will occur in the depth of content, in the methods of assessment and the emphasis given to different aims, but in no way should the Foundation List be seen as 'limiting the range of work which should be attempted by pupils whose attainment is higher' (para. 457).

The Foundation List contains ten topics: number, money, percentages, use of calculators, time, measurement, graphs and pictorial representation, spatial concepts, ratio and proportion, and statistical ideas. These topics, naturally, are not intended to be covered as separate units; number work, for example, will be applied throughout, and the calculator will be used at all times. Details are provided for each topic and comments are added which suggest approaches to the teaching presentation. It is expected that pupils will read, write and talk about mathematics, carry out calculations in a variety of ways and be able to associate calculation and measurement with appropriate units.

Each topic is presented in terms of performance objectives, teaching aims and teaching comments. Thus, in the topic 'percentages', there are specific performance objectives when pupils are expected to be able to calculate a percentage of a sum of money and to increase or decrease a sum of money by a given percentage. More generally, the pupil is expected to appreciate the use made of percentages in everyday life and this may be considered as a teaching aim. Finally, in dealing with the topic 'percentage', it is recommended that the teaching should be based upon the idea that '1%' means '1p in every pound' or 'one in every hundred', and not on the use of particular formulae.

The presentation of a syllabus in terms of specific topics is a particularly commendable feature of the Foundation List. When these topics are drawn up in a systematic fashion pupils are given a preview of forthcoming work showing the integration of topics within the subject. Moreover, such a syllabus allows teachers within a mathematics department to consider the needs of all the pupils. The aim is to develop mathematical skills and understanding for adult life and employment, to use special skills which are needed in science and other school subjects, as well as developing an awareness that mathematics provides a powerful and useful means of communication.

Clearly, the syllabus should be specifically designed for the particular school, and take into account the abilities of the children and the requirements of the teaching staff. An outline syllabus could include such topics as the core content topics as number, money, measurement and spatial relations, whereas other core topics may be included later in the broader scheme of work. It is suggested that algebra, at this stage, should be treated informally giving more attention to generalizations rather than emphasizing symbolizations. This approach is suggested by the text *Algebra of a Sort: Mathematics for the Majority* (Schools Council, 1973), and it provides an effective introduction to problem-solving methods.

A project could be included as part of this core curriculum and in the broader topic list. This development is partly suggested by the Cockcroft Report (para. 460) when it recommends that additional topics may be included in the Foundation List, particularly when they arise from school or leisure time activities. The special features of a project at this stage are to develop the particular interests of the pupils and to reinforce their mathematical understanding. All too frequently, school mathematics is criticized because it lacks relevance both to everyday life and, surprisingly, to other school subjects (DES, 1979).

The inclusion of the project as an assessed component of the GCSE examination is a new venture, although this provision has been available for some forms of CSE examinations for a long time. Project work provides special challenges for the teacher especially with regard to the preparatory work required for the individual schemes, and for its eventual assessment. In this respect, *Foundation Mathematics* (Brown, 1984), a textbook series for the early years at secondary school, provides excellent resource materials. Developed from these exercises, project work should add a new and exciting dimension to mathematics at secondary school.

Applications of Mathematics

One of the characteristic features of the Foundation List is the attention that is given to the use of mathematics in everyday life. Thus, in number work –

'The emphasis should always be on the use of number skills in everyday situations'. Referring to the topic 'money', it is suggested that the teaching should be on the use of money in everyday situations such as shopping, leisure activities, 'do-it-yourself', budgeting and household accounts. Again, in dealing with percentages, the aim is to appreciate their use in everyday life. Naturally, the topics 'time' and 'measurement' are very much linked to their everyday use. In teaching 'graphical representation', good use should be made of published information especially advertising; whereas in 'spatial relations', use should be made of models, dress patterns, scale drawings, photographs and maps. The concept of ratio and proportion is linked to such ideas as 'best buy', craft work, cookery and model-making, and statistical ideas include the use of averages in newspaper reports.

In constructing the Foundation List, the Cockcroft Committee have very clearly made a bold attempt to ensure that mathematics should be relevant to the requirements of everyday life. However, they acknowledge that this aim is easier to state than to achieve, and they quote evidence from the National Secondary Survey (DES, 1979) which says that schemes of work frequently referred to the need to relate mathematics to everyday situations, but in practice 'the convincing realisation of this aim was much more rare'.

There are several reasons why the applications of mathematics should be considered as an appropriate approach to teaching the subject. The first and obvious reason is that mathematics is used extensively both in ordinary everyday situations and in a wide range of practical applications (Lighthill, 1980). Secondly, mathematics is used in other subject disciplines as a means of communication and it has a special place in science, geography and aspects of social science. Thirdly, the applications of mathematics may be used both to introduce a teaching topic and to strengthen the pupil's understanding of the underlying mathematics.

A considerable amount of work has been undertaken recently to promote the use of applications in solving real problems. The work of the Spode Group (1983) has been exploring the teaching of mathematics to all pupils in the range 14-16 years through the consideration of real problems. Likewise, the Shell Centre for Mathematical Education has specialized in this area and Burkhardt's book (1982) *The Real World of Mathematics* has produced some positive approaches toward making use of everyday situations. Ormell's Work in the Seventies (Schools Council, 1975) also provided a vast amount of material for use at 'O' and 'A' levels. In the United States, the National Council of Teachers of Mathematics has produced a Source Book of Applications of School mathematics (NCCT, 1980). This publication lists hundreds of relevant applications as well as producing information which may be used to develop project work.

According to Fitzgerald (1982) in a review of the role of applications for pupils of low attainment, there is considerable evidence that 'many young people have never mastered many of the processes inflicted upon them in school mathematics'. Sadly, it would seem that these pupils would benefit most from a less abstract but more relevant approach. Certainly, there are textbook series which endeavour to make the subject more practical and consequently more interesting. Unfortunately, these days, for reasons especially of economy, teachers make less use of a standard textbook and resort to worksheets which may simply be a list of practice examples. Indeed, local HMIs, commenting on this situation, lament that the work in children's exercise books contains little written language work, and a vast amount of computation.

Resources for Teaching the Low Attainer in Mathematics

Many terms have been used to describe pupils who have difficulty with their schoolwork. They include 'remedial', 'less able', 'under-achievers' and 'disadvantaged'. The term 'low attainer' is used in this context because 'it describes the observable performance of pupils without implying a cause' (Denver *et al.*, 1982). About one-third of the total school population may be included in this banding, although this proportion will vary and depends upon the school circumstances. Schools situated in the more affluent areas will usually have a smaller proportion of their enrolment designated as low attainers.

Since most secondary schools stream their pupils before they reach the third year, low-attaining pupils are generally firmly fixed in the bottom stream. These pupils are clearly well aware of their limitations in the subject and many, unfortunately, seem to derive little benefit from the years spent learning mathematics at secondary level. Low levels of motivation are evident by the third year with girls tending to 'opt out' in greater numbers than boys.

A variety of reasons are put forward to account for low attainment. For convenience, the causes are usually grouped as: factors which lie within the control of the school, for example, teaching methods and use of materials; and factors which are outside the control of the school, for example, physical characteristics and home background. Although low achievers in mathematics invariably attract much attention and much has been done to improve their lot, it must be acknowledged that as a group they present a considerable problem even for experienced teachers of mathematics. Mathematics is used to communicate information concisely and precisely, and it relies heavily on the use of symbolic notation, thus, for this and other reasons, it is a difficult subject both to learn and to teach. Most pupils seem to have difficulties with learning mathematics at school; clearly, low attainers have their own special problems. What then is the best policy for teaching low attainers?

A policy for low attainers must first be seen as a part of the overall school policy for these pupils, and secondly it must form an essential part of the plan for the school mathematics department. According to the Cockcroft Report, the syllabus should be developed from 'the bottom upwards', so that the curriculum for the low attainer should form the foundation studies from which the rest of school mathematics should be developed. Teachers need to work together in developing this policy and a cooperative effort should take in to account both the needs of the pupil and the resources of the department. Regrettably, in some schools, teachers work in isolation having only a weak link with the collective work of the department.

A variety of answers may be given to the question 'Why teach mathematics to the low attainer?' These include:

(1) To acquire the basic skills necessary for everyday life.

(2) To provide a range of interesting mathematics so that the individual enjoys and appreciates at least some aspects of the subject.

(3) To equip pupils with work skills so that they can make themselves available for job opportunities when these arise.

For the most part, these reasons, as shown, are related to the need to use mathematics in daily life, and, in this respect, these skills, although limited, are vital and fundamental. Generally, job requirements are specific in their demands for mathematical skills, but they can vary even over a short period of time. Above all, the skills need to keep pace with the changing technological scene (Fitzgerald, 1985).

A wide range of activities are available for teaching mathematics to the low attainer. These include written materials, apparatus, audio-visual aids and electronic devices. Without a doubt, the textbook is a central resource for the teaching of mathematics. Fortunately, these days a wide range of texts have been written with the low attainer in mind, and, in this context, Lumb (1978) has provided a most useful list of books showing their suitability for levels of ability within the age-range 14 to 16 years. Recent books include *Maths You Need* (Ferguson, 1979), *Championship Mathematics* (Cornah, 1979), *Numbers at Work* (Gillespie, 1980) and the *Integrated Mathematics Scheme* (Kaner, 1983-85). Kaner's texts, in particular, provide a substantial scheme of work for pupils in the age range 14 to 16 years. They are beautifully produced with clear diagrams and many coloured photographs. Real-life situations are used to promote mathematical ideas, and, as a whole, the series aims to stimulate interest for those pupils taking a foundation course. Mathematical ideas are cleverly integrated into a background of everyday applications, and incidental material is introduced at every opportunity, thus meeting Cockcroft's criticism that a secondary mathematics course, for the most part, contains little incidental information. Possibly, many teachers will adapt the ideas provided by these texts to meet their particular needs, and consequently produce their own worksheets. It is a pity, then, that teachers don't share these resources, especially as computer systems are available (for example, *Microsoft Windows* used with Nimbus Research Machines) which provide an easy and versatile means of representing and amending the work, and, at the same time, allow easy storage of information.

Apparatus can serve several purposes within the mathematics lesson, and is particularly useful in promoting understanding and consolidation of learning. Even the most simple piece of apparatus can act as a physical model for some abstract mathematical idea, whereas more sophisticated equipment, such as Dienes Blocks, enable different number systems to be seen in physical terms. Current school practice suggests that secondary school teachers make very little use of apparatus, in contrast to their colleagues in the primary schools. This course of action seems to be unfortunate and has undesirable consequences, particularly for the low-attaining pupils. Apparatus, however modest in construction, can be employed at all times. For example, addition of positive and negative temperatures may be successfully demonstrated with the use of wooden rods, and coloured blocks are seen to have relevant use for the teaching of the elementary ideas of probability.

A large number of facilities are now available for audio-visual work with low attainers in mathematics. Such presentations are flexible and take into account the reading difficulties experienced by many of these pupils. Individual work is possible using tape-recorders, and class participation is heightened using such television programmes as *Everyday Maths* produced by the BBC. Video-recorders, when available, are a most effective resource for pupils, especially if they experience difficulty with written work.

The ability to use a four-function calculator is often suggested as a basic definition for numeracy. Calculators, by removing the drudgery of written calculations, allow pupils to become more confident with arithmetic and, at the same time, to have some experience of the more realistic applications of mathematics. For all pupils, they act as support systems, but they are particularly useful for those pupils with very real and apparent difficulties in learning even the most elementary ideas in mathematics. Generally, developments with calculators in school have run parallel with innovations occurring with the use of the microcomputer. In this respect, the *Microsmile* programs developed by teachers at the SMILE Centre in London (ILEA, 1985) form the basis for excellent resource materials. Unfortunately, although computers are widely used in the primary school at all ages and at all levels of ability, their use in the secondary school is much less apparent.

The resources, then, which are available for teaching the low attainer in mathematics are wide and varied, and take in account the need to recognise the difficulties these pupils have with normal school work. Essentially, the curriculum should be based upon the Foundation List and the work should be closely related to mathematics in everyday life, so that pupils leave school well equipped to handle the skills they need both as a consumer and as a potential employee.

References

BROWN, J. (1984) *Foundation Maths Books 1 and 2*, Edinburgh, Oliver and Boyd.

BURKHARDT, H. (1982) *The Real World of Mathematics*, Glasgow, Blackie and Son.

COCKCROFT, W.H. (1982) *Mathematics Counts: Report of the Committee of Inquiry into the Teaching of Mathematics*, London, HMSO.

CONNAH, P. (1979) *Championship Maths*, London, Macmillan.

DENVER, B., STOLZ, C. and BROWN, M. (1982) *Low Attainers in Mathematics: 5–16*, London, Methuen.

DES (1979) *Aspects of Secondary Education*, London, HMSO.

FERGUSON, A.R. (1979) *Maths You Need*, Surrey, Nelson.

FITZGERALD, A. (1982) *New Technology and Mathematics in Employment*, Birmingham, Faculty of Education.

FITZGERALD, A. (1985) 'Applications of Mathematics for Pupils of Low Attainment in Mathematics', in *Teaching Mathematics and Its Applications*, Vol. 1, No. 1.

GILLESPIE, J. (1980) *Numbers at Work*, Cambridge, National Extension College.

ILEA (1985) *Microsmile*, London, SMILE Centre.

KANER, P. (1983–85) *Integrated Mathematics Scheme, Books L1, L2 and L3*, London, Bell and Hyman.

LIGHTHILL, J. (Ed.) (1980) *Newer Uses of Mathematics*, London, Penguin.

LUMB, D. (1978) 'Mathematics for the Less Gifted', in *Mathematics in School*, Vol. 7, No. 2.

NCCT (1980) *A Sourcebook of Applications of Mathematics*, Virginia, NCCT.

SCHOOLS COUNCIL (1973) *Algebra of a Sort: Mathematics for the Majority*, London, Chatto and Windus Educational.

SCHOOLS COUNCIL (1975) *Mathematics Applicable: Introductory Probability*, London, Heinemann Educational.

SCHOOLS COUNCIL (1978) *Algebra with Applications*, London, Heinemann.

SPODE GROUP (1983) *Solving Real Problems with CSE Mathematics*, Bedford, Cranfield Press.

Chapter 9

Teaching English to Low Achievers
Barry Johnson

As a teacher of English to low achievers, you have a lot going for you. First, you see each class regularly for a substantial part of the week. Second, the subject matter is relatively wide open, even allowing for the literature set for exams. Taken together, these two factors form an important basis for the essential elements in teaching the low achiever: good relationships and interesting material. In educational terms, such pupils are far more likely to be motivated by affective considerations than instrumental ones. But a good relationship is not an end in itself. In all English classrooms pupils should explore what language is, what it does, and above all, the joys of language; they do so through the four skills of listening, talking, reading and writing, encouraged as far as possible by the environment of the classroom as well as the personality of the teacher.

Which of these language skills should have the highest priority, and within each of them what are the priorities for low achievers? How should we go about meeting these priorities? The following three sections will attempt to tackle these important questions, though in practice, of course, the skills will be combined with each other in varying proportions.

Oracy

The skills of listening and talking are best dealt with together, and before the other skills. With slower pupils, oracy takes on a higher priority, increasing in extent as one considers younger pupils and those who are close to the mainstream/special education division, which still exists in many schools. For such children, the skills of oracy are and will remain far and away their main means of communicating with others, and for a substantial minority, oracy will always be the sole means of communicating. Educational systems in general have never really faced up to this fact, and the British systems are no exception. Although the implications stretch right across the curriculum, the English teacher has a particular responsibility in the development of oracy, a responsibility now recognised in the new GCSE examination.

In terms of oracy, what should our pupils be able to do when they leave school? They should:

> be able to talk clearly and confidently to another person or a small group, in semi-formal as well as casual contexts. Some will be able to address larger groups, and participate in more formal exchanges, but these will be a small minority, and these skills will not loom large for low achievers in a mixed ability classroom.

> be able to understand, carry out, and give simple oral instructions.

> appreciate the social role of language, have something interesting to say in informal conversations, and the ability to express themselves in an interesting way and to respond to other people's contributions in a way which shows interest.

Their main aid in achieving all this is likely to be a model set for them by their English teacher. Show enthusiasm; tell them about your interests, and take an interest in theirs. Many children need constant encouragement if they are to make useful contributions, or even any contribution, to the classroom talk. We need to take what they say seriously, and show respect for their views. This can sometimes be extremely difficult, particularly when, for example, racist views are expressed. Responses will vary according to the circumstances: if the intention was to shock, it's better to dismiss or ignore the remark; if to hurt or insult someone present, this is much more serious, and should be dealt with by you immediately in line with the school's disciplinary procedure. If, however, the remark was a genuine expression of opinion, it should be taken seriously and made the subject of discussion, though not necessarily involving the whole class. Show dislike of the opinion, but not the opinion-holder. At the end of a tiring day or a hard week, this counsel of perfection may seem particularly unattainable, but squashing opinions in a heavy-handed way is not likely to encourage the opening out of the serious talk that you want.

Neither is a preoccupation with 'correctness' of accent, dialect and style likely to produce a free exchange of views in the classroom. An attack on someone's language is very much an attack on that person's identity, and a devaluing of important group loyalties. The distinction between spoken and written language is important here; while Standard English is the normal dialect for the written language, regional dialects are capable of expressing just as much or even more of a range of meaning and feeling orally, while the changing of a regional accent should be no part of any teacher's job. Diversity of dialect is a resource in the classroom, not a problem, and children should be encouraged to discover, think about, and document differences between Standard English, their own dialect, and those of television personalities, for example. West Indian Creole is particularly interesting, revealing as it does historical links with West African languages, and British English of the eighteenth and nineteenth centuries.

Dialect usage is related to style, of course, and here again is a starting-point for discussion, arising from role-play. 'Was it right saying that in such a situation? What could have been said? Why would that have sounded better?' Questions such as these are more useful than a bald 'Don't say that, say – '. (See Harris, Chapter 16, for further discussion of dialect).

When planning oral work, coverage of the whole range of uses, and of the strategies within each use, should be kept in mind. The classification suggested by Tough (1982) lists six main uses, each with its own range of strategies: directing, self maintaining, reporting, reasoning, predicting, and projecting, with a seventh use, imagining, possible in conjunction with any of the others. Within reporting, for example, strategies range from simple labelling of the components of a scene ('There's a bus, a car, and some children'), to recognizing the central meaning and relating it to one's own experience ('There's been an accident. I nearly got run over by a bus once'). It is useful to bear these uses and strategies in mind, as they can help in formulating questions which will extend a pupil's oral (and written) capability, towards more explicitness and variety. In particular, listening out for and encouraging the higher uses of reasoning, predicting and projecting will help to develop the talk that takes place in oral sessions.

Most productive talk is likely to take place during group work. The ideal group size is five, and children should be directed into them, not allowed to choose for themselves. The composition of groups should be determined by the particular occasion and task. Obviously, compatibility is always a factor, but a drama session may call for a 'shy' group and/or a loud group; a task which requires some reading or a written final report may well suggest mixed ability; discussion of boys' and girls' comics could be carried out in single-sex groups. Where a variety of topics are being discussed at the same time, interest groupings will result. As far as possible, and within the limitations imposed by group size and classroom furniture, the groupings should be natural and task-related in a way that is clear to the pupils. The task itself, the time allowed, and the required end-product should also be clear from the start. For widespread, genuine talk, the interest level should be high, and so flexibility of topic choice is essential. The photocopying machine and the computer have a lot more to offer here than the class textbook or reader. A controversial issue from the letters column of a local newspaper, for example, is likely to be a more promising starting-point than an item dreamt up years ago by a textbook writer living in a completely different part of the country. Abler pupils will do what the textbook suggests because they want to do well in English, but you can't rely on all children feeling that way. Smaller groupings of two or three children working through an appropriate microcomputer program may well benefit from the planning talk and decision-making discussions it involves. The variety of programs now on the market, and the ease with which these can be loaded from a disk drive, means that English teachers now have a highly motivating aid to participation in discussion for nearly all children.

A special application of group work is the drama lesson. Whether or not drama 'comes under' English in your school, it should be a part of the classroom repertoire of all English teachers. Here, the starting-points are endless, and the value to the low achiever is enormous. Photographs, music, a video clip, a taped sound effect: all these can give rise to improvised pieces which can be polished and recorded, with selected good examples written down, or they can be used to prompt mime sequences. Non-verbal communication is important in its own right, but can be crucial to the introverted, who may hardly ever communicate with anyone in school. If their confidence can be built up by praise and a non-threatening environment, such as membership of the 'shy' group in a cut-off corner of the room, they may become less reluctant to express themselves in a small group discussion. High motivation and a small appreciative audience are also more likely to lead to clearer speech, which for many children has to be the top priority in oracy.

Reading

Here the priorities are:

> the ability to understand simple instructions;
>
> the ability to search for, discover and act upon information from a wide range of sources;
>
> the enjoyment of reading as a leisure activity.

Traditionally, 'reading' in the English classroom meant class textbooks, covering language exercises, fiction, poetry and drama. Today, especially with poor readers, a far greater range of reading materials is desirable, and the appropriateness of any set of books for the whole class is very much in question. Much of this variety is readily available: holiday brochures, newspapers, official leaflets and forms, local library loans. All of it should be, as far as possible, interesting and functional, enjoyable and meaningful, since the pupils should be encouraged to see reading as a means to an end, as well as a pleasure in itself. Much traditional material, especially for the low achiever, gives the impression of being neither the one nor the other; as one reluctant reader put it, 'Please sir, when are we gonna stop reading *reading*, and start reading *books*?' (Weber, 1978).

The tasks we set in reading lessons, or DARTS (directed activities related to texts), should be as varied as the materials. Cloze procedures, where pupils are required to fill in the blanks of a text with every fifth or seventh word deleted, are particularly useful, and give rise to much animated discussion, if the text is interesting. The addition of a word processor and printer to your microcomputer can enable you to produce your own cloze texts, chosen for particular children or groups, and typed by other pupils. Cloze can also be used to judge the readability of a text. Photocopy a page of the text, paint out the required deletions, and photocopy again. If a child enters appropriate words in 90 per cent of the spaces, that child can probably manage the book. Children can also be given a short story with the sentences or paragraphs jumbled up, or an incomplete story they are required to complete. They can illustrate stories, make posters and covers for books, and answer open questions on, for example, what the story means to them.

All these activities lend themselves very well to group work, where oral work will arise, but there should always be a place in every English class for USSR – uninterpreted sustained silent reading. With lower-ability groups, these periods may not be long, and may not always involve fiction, though there are many books written for reluctant readers having both an appropriate reading age and interest level. For pupils with more serious reading problems, use cassettes in a recorder with headphones, with the whole or part of a story on it, read at a suitable speed. Sixth formers can be involved in the recording of these cassettes. It provides a good role model for the teacher also to be seen to spend some of this time in reading for pleasure.

Part of the variety of materials should include texts not usually included in school work. Surprisingly, one such generally ignored source is the pupils' own written work. With the author's permission, other pupils should be able to read a story which has received a good mark, but there should also be occasions when everyone proof-reads someone else's work, to suggest correction and improvements. Here again, the word processor is invaluable. There is also a place in the English classroom for comics and popular newspapers like the 'Sun' or the 'Mirror'. The contents of these can be described and analysed, with comparisons made, for example, between one newspaper and another, or between boys' and girls' comics or magazines. Lower-ability pupils may require clearly directed questions to guide their discussions, which in turn requires you to be familiar with the contents of these materials.

Donaldson (1978) has shown that many children have considerable difficulty with metaphors, and indeed with any language which is remote from speech. One way into literature in primary schools is through story-telling; and this could still be exploited at the lower secondary level at least. If a story can be found which is of interest to a majority in the class, this can be read to them, interspersed with 'story-telling' sessions, in which they may be able to participate. Always look for suitable books which incorporate dialect, again as a way of bridging the gap between spoken and written language.

The most highly-wrought, concentrated literature is, of course, poetry. After years 1 and 2, this can be difficult to tackle. All too often, poetry is taught as a purely cognitive task, a hunt for meaning, a counting of metaphors and other figures of speech. Such abstractions are pointless with children who are already experiencing difficulties, as well as undesirable from an aesthetic point of view. Concentrate instead on what the language *does*, through sound and rhythm, the pictures it evokes, the story it tells. Avoid beginning a discussion with completely open questions such as 'What did you think of that?'; instead, direct attention to one part of the poem, a line or a verse, and ask more directed questions: 'What's happening here? What's the poet trying to make us feel? Why was that particular word used here?' Selecting poetry, or any other literature, solely on the grounds that it fits in with a particular project on 'Home' or 'War' or whatever, can obscure the individual qualities, meaning and identity of that work. By all means take the project as a starting-point, but consider the poem on its own terms. The particular pleasure and fun of poetry is often brought out by choral verse, which can't always be fitted into a project! Here, the sound patterns of the poem are brought out and made concrete for pupils to whom poetry has always been an alien, meaningless, 'school' activity. After experiencing a couple of choral poems, groups can discuss ways of presenting different poems chorally, and then try them out on the rest of the class.

One final point on reading skills. It is tempting, with pupils who are obviously not good readers, to concentrate on the lower-order skills of decoding and word recognition. Many children go through school in this way, never able to see the wood for the trees. Higher-order skills are important for them too: finding and using books to get information, and relating this to their own lives. Comprehension questions should be directed not only at the simple strategies of labelling or referring to incidents, but also the more difficult recognition of central meaning and reflection on that meaning in relation to the child's own experience (Tough, 1982).

Writing

This skill comes third in the order of priorities, because for many children, it will be the least used and most alien; it's a 'school' skill and not a 'life' skill, as far as they're concerned. The priorities within the skill should emphasize utility; when they leave school, our pupils should be able to:

> write a letter in straightforward English, well presented and in clear handwriting, with all the common words correctly spelt;

> fill in forms correctly and clearly.

However, simply to concentrate on these end-products throughout the secondary school years would be narrow, boring and therefore self-defeating. Some classroom writing activities should be ends in themselves. Apart from exercises such as comprehension and letter writing, pupils should also be writing for themselves: making a list of questions to be asked on a preliminary work experience visit, making notes for themselves in a drama planning session, working these notes up into a plan of action, and writing creative or factual stories. The academic essay is unlikely to prove stimulating or useful to low attaining pupils, and endless attempts (as they will be !) to teach the paragraphing and punctuation of direct speech in stories are a waste of time in the writer's view.

When setting writing tasks, try to ensure that they arise as often as possible from other tasks, oral or reading, or preferably both. Encourage the writing of pieces for other audiences, and a variety of purposes: real letters to specialist travel firms or government offices, asking for information; for other children or groups in the class or elsewhere in the school. Put two children in front of a word processor and printer for maximum motivation, joint planning, and ease of correction. Writing shouldn't always be set for correction; if it's for enjoyment, leave it at that.

Spelling is always a problem, but often it is made into too much of a problem. The emphasis should be on intelligibility first and foremost, with the spelling of the commonest words coming a close second. Certain words are often confused: where/were, of/off, loose/lose; homophones like to/too/two, their/there, no/know, weather/whether. Tackle each of these words one at a time as they arise; display sentences with the problem word picked out in a different colour; get pupils to compile lists of words they frequently misspell, but again, in the context of their own sentences: these troublesome words must be seen within meaningful sentences. The rush of school life doesn't encourage careful handwriting, but it has an important part to play in good spelling. When children look up or are given a correct spelling, encourage them to use the 'look-cover-write-check' technique, helping them to see the way the word is constructed, to re-write it themselves, carefully and neatly, without reference to the model, and then to check that the two versions match. Play up the visual aspect of the word rather than the application of spelling rules, which in English are complex enough to baffle the brightest mind.

Intelligibility is, again, the first consideration in punctuation. The sentence construction of most low achievers is unlikely to require an indication of the more sophisticated pauses like colons and semi-colons. The allocation of separate paragraphs of speech to each speaker in a dialogue is more important than the correct use of inverted commas, which many children find impossibly difficult as well as ultimately irrelevant, and a pragmatic response to the often ubiquitous apostrophe which sometimes seems to accompany every terminal 's' even among more able writers, is to ban its use altogether as far as selected children are concerned. They'll certainly make fewer punctuation mistakes that way!

Marking is the great bugbear of the English teacher's life. Much of it is done for reasons of accountability, to keep parents and the school hierarchy happy. When the stress is on frequent red marks in books, little benefit arises for the pupils. Marking is probably most useful when done in the presence of the writer. The 'conferencing' technique, where, in a predictable setting and atmosphere, the pupil can talk openly to the teacher about the writing task, is intended to encourage reflection primarily on the content of what is being written, rather than the form. Indeed, this is the problem with frequent and therefore hasty marking: too much concentration on form, at the expense of content and function. Conferencing enables the teacher to become an active participant with the pupil in making and conveying meaning, rather than a distant observer and judge. Such participation can shift the slower pupil's usual focus on the static elements of nouns and adjectives, towards more vivid action sequences, using more varied verbs and adverbs, through specifically targeted questions.

Expressive writing is not unique to English in the curriculum but it is more important here than elsewhere, and difficult to obtain from slower pupils. Don't expect to obtain it at the drop of a hat, at a set time each week. For most of us, real expressive writing can only arise from deeply felt, first-hand experience. Trying to make use of such experiences is not a straightforward matter. Intimate situations make the most urgent demands on a writer, but it would be unwise and even unethical to try to tap into many of these. Here again, the choice of good literary material or a powerful television scene is crucial, probably on an individual basis, and drama too, on the best occasions, can provide a powerful immediacy of experience which, for some, could be the way into written expression of real meaning to them. Don't quibble about spelling or punctuation then!

Conclusion

The introduction of the GCSE examination in 1988 has seen an end to the early splitting of English classes into GCE and CSE groups, as well as the now outdated idea that only the top 40 per cent of pupils are examinable. Most English teachers have probably found the changeover to the new system less novel and trying than teachers of other subjects. The good English teacher has, after all, always emphasized useful, practical skills, learnt through issues and problems which pupils find real and interesting. The English grade criteria are grouped into the same three 'domains' as the main headings of this chapter, and the new emphasis on course-work and continuous assessment effectively represents official approbation of participatory rather than didactic teaching methods. The long-standing concern of English teachers with 'process' rather than 'product', with understanding rather than rote learning of facts, and the widespread use of group work and discussion, are all key elements in the new approach represented by the GCSE.

   Although the GCSE requires separate assessment in the three domains, the good teacher will attempt to combine activities in all four of the language skills of talking, listening, reading and writing. The commonest mistake of inexperienced teachers is planning to get too much done in one lesson. The lower the ability level or motivation of pupils within the class, the more variety you will need in each lesson, but always try to finish early, with time for a short unrelated little activity: read a poem without asking any questions about it, write an anagram on the board, or just ask questions directed at individuals about the task they have completed. A class leaving in disorder will infect the new arrivals, whose quality of work will thereby be badly affected. Your pupils won't appreciate the variety and flexibility they find in your lessons, unless the other qualities of clarity and structure are also present.

References

DONALDSON, M. (1978) *Children's Minds*, London, Fontana.
TOUGH, J. (1982) *A Place for Talk*, London, Ward Lock Educational/Drake Educational.
WEBER, K. (1978) *Yes they Can!*, Milton Keynes, Open University Press.

Resources

One of the best single sources for a wide range of activities and useful classroom texts is the Open University In-Service Education Pack, *Children, Language and Literature* (P530).

The *Microspecial Pack* of twenty-five computer programs, devised by the Scottish Microelectronics Development Programme, is designed to enhance the curriculum for pupils aged 14 to 16 with moderate learning difficulties. The programs include a simple word processor, an adventure game which forms the basis for oral and written activities for two or more children, a cloze exercise (to which the teacher can add further texts), a word game, and several other activities which can stimulate discussion and problem solving in groups, or individual written work. A computer station which includes a BBC 'B' micro, colour monitor, disk drive and printer is required.

Several publishers have brought out series of books especially for reluctant readers. Among the best of them are the following:

Allan Sharp's 'Storytrails' published by Cambridge. These are twenty-two 'branching stories', very popular with teenagers, which require active involvement on the part of the reader. The series includes such alluring titles as 'Invitation to Murder' and 'The Dark Awakening'.

The 'Cascade' series from Collins consists of hardback books chosen for their literary merit. When ordered in library packs, each title is accompanied by free teaching notes.

Longman's 'Knockout' series includes short story and poetry anthologies, as well as novels covering a wide range of themes, with texts graded according to difficulty.

Aidan Chambers has edited two series for Macmillan: 'M Books', which are general titles drawn from contemporary literature, and presented in an attractive, illustrated format; and 'Topliners', which are especially written for reluctant readers.

Chapter 10

Modern Languages and Low Achievers
Mark Fowler

In this chapter we shall consider the value of teaching modern languages to pupils with learning difficulties and those who have been identified as 'low achievers'. We shall report on work conducted (where accounts are available), summarize arguments and suggest some ways forward.[1]

Although modern languages were for some time the prerogative of the more successful learner in school, the arguments for the provision of modern languages to all learners are very strong. In addition to the arguments, there is now increasing evidence that the experience is beneficial for all learners.

Let us consider firstly some of the evidence. We shall consider some examples where modern language learning has been of benefit to learners whom one might have considered unsuited to such learning. In a recent article in *Modern Languages in Scotland*, Christine Brown reported on her experiences as a special needs teacher helping to teach French and German to pupils with special education needs. It was agreed that the benefits were great, particularly for the pupils' own self-esteem (which is rarely boosted elsewhere within secondary education). Learning a modern language 'enhances a poor self image – through success in oral work, for example, or through the motivating power of mastery learning' (Brown, 1985).

It is worth noting here the emphasis placed on success, particularly in oral work, and the motivation provided by the graded test scheme. Success and motivation have enhanced the poor self-image. We learn, too, that the pupils 'can still have the intellectual thrill of communicating through a foreign language, however badly they do it' and 'can still take part in the full curriculum' (*ibid.*, p. 30).

Sadly, it is rare that we find voices within the special needs department supporting the case for modern languages so strongly. However, the theoretical arguments are put equally strongly in the article. Where some teachers might argue that as pupils cannot speak English properly(!) the exercise is pointless, comparisons are made with other subjects.

> Why teach them maths when they can't count much beyond ten? Just because pupils with learning difficulties cannot *master* these subjects does not automatically exclude them from exposure to as much as may be of benefit to them (*ibid.* p. 130).

This very practical article provides helpful suggestions for how the special needs teacher and the foreign language teacher can work together in team and cooperative teaching to their own and the pupils' benefit. Also recorded are the pupils' reactions to the experiments. Whilst positive, they point up some of the problems likely to be encountered by such pupils on a 'long haul' language course. These will be examined further below.

Pupils with severe mental limitations have, too, successfully engaged in learning French. Alex Glass reported on a modular approach to teaching French to secondary pupils with moderate learning difficulties. The special education department of the school in Scotland formed a link with a special education school in south-east France and arranged a visit. This visit then became the focus of a modular course based on environmental studies geared to the foreign country. The benefits were tremendous to both pupils and teachers:

> No enterprise in recent times in the S E department has triggered off so many different beneficial educational activities and done so much not only to increase the general linguistic awareness of the pupils but to enhance their own self-esteem ... No group of pupils ever used the French that they knew to better advantage. They were absolutely uninhibited about speaking what they had learned (Glass, 1984).

Clearly, the trip and the learning experience had been valuable, both in cognitive terms – their 'linguistic awareness' – and their self-esteem. The pupils had used to the full their (perhaps once in a lifetime) visit abroad. They had thus been given opportunities to be by themselves in the small town and 'proudly returned with their purchases and stories of their achievements' (*ibid.*).

Therefore pupils with learning difficulties have profitably engaged in learning modern languages, as a browse through the journals will indicate. Pupils with sensory and physical handicaps, too, have benefited from the experience. In a school where the writer was teaching until recently, a young blind girl shared the curriculum as any other secondary pupil. Working in close cooperation with her German teacher and her classroom assistant she was able to develop all her language skills, including writing, using her braille typewriter.

Her Majesty's Inspectorate recently reported on a survey of twenty-two schools where foreign languages are taught to all pupils (Her Majesty's Inspectorate, 1987). In marked contrast with a report ten years earlier (Her Majesty's Insepctorate, 1978), the findings regarding low-ability pupils are generally positive. In both achievement and attitude less able pupils had benefited from the experience.

> There were many examples of successful teaching and learning among the most and least able and even the latter achieved worthwhile levels of attainment. Most encouraging was the pupils' attitude (all abilities) to the country of the language which they were learning and to travelling abroad ... the attitudes of the least able pupils were generally positive. (Her Majesty's Inspectorate, 1987).

This very informative report conforms with the experience of many foreign language departments.

Having considered briefly some case evidence we shall now examine the arguments for teaching modern languages to these pupils. Essentially two forms of justification are advanced:

(1)   The language is a necessary skill for later life – its vocational and social value.

(2)   Language learning is education – an 'escape from the monoglot's prison' (Hawkins, 1981) – and a contribution to awareness of language.

The first of these arguments is often dismissed when discussing low achievers in particular. It is indeed true that many of these pupils are unlikely to need a modern language for any vocational purpose – with the exception, perhaps, of the other languages of the United Kingdom such as Welsh, Urdu, Bengali, etc. Furthermore, the language they learn at school may not be the one they need later. Similarly, opportunities to use the language for any social purpose are unlikely, particularly given the degree of fluency they are likely to attain. However, if we examine this question more closely, we see that the modern language experience may be of great social value. The language and the language skills they acquire can be of immense value in their life now and as adults on two accounts. Firstly, the international, and increasingly European, quality of life in Britain has meant that the tokens of communication, the symbols, myths and values which we use to relate to our experience of life, have a strongly European quality. Imagine the pupil who tries to make sense of and so be free to use his/her environment ranging from the legendary 'Vorsprung Durch Technik' to 'Le Car', 'Viva España', 'Allô allô', 'Le Croissant' and – in Wales – 'Swyddfa'r Post'. Whilst not having met all the words before the young learner will have encountered the system and no longer remain an outsider. Furthermore, you will probably be aware how keenly many learners, young and adult, display the odd word of a foreign language, however out of place it may be, when in contact with a foreigner. Whilst it serves no openly communicative purpose, it indicates a willingness to establish social contact with the foreigner in his/her own language. It is also a compliment to the foreigner showing that the learner believes that the foreigner's language is worth learning. In sum then, the ability, however limited, to speak or know something about the foreign language and culture is thus an important mark and means of access to modern, western society. Witness those who in secondary modern schools had no experience of a foreign language and who feel that their adult life has to some degree been deprived. In the case of Welsh, not, of course, a foreign language in Wales, the large numbers of adults of all abilities attending evening classes in the language is evidence of the sense of deprivation many feel having not learnt Welsh in school.

Let us consider the second argument, the 'escape from the monoglot's prison'. Hawkins has very effectively argued the case that modern languages free the learner from the closed world of his mother tongue and allow him to see the relativity of language. The learner thus has the opportunity to move outside his own language and play with tokens. It has always been rewarding for me to hear poor achievers in school playing with new sounds and meanings, experimenting with their vocal chords, trying new elements of script and contrasting new and old concepts. 'What must it be like to eat a roll with the chocolate baked inside it and then dunk it in hot chocolate?' In contrast with, for example, geography or an English-based European studies, this is a very personal, individual initiation *through* a language into a language and culture. The value of this experience, provided it is successful and sensitively conducted, cannot be overstated.

Furthermore, the experimentation with language learning itself can broaden the learner's awareness of language. This, it is argued, helps him to develop 'analytic competence', the ability to stand outside language and reflect upon it – an ability believed to be of great importance to, amongst other things, reading (Bruner, 1975, in Hawkins, 1981). It has been noted that where pupils are withdrawn from French for remedial English, progress in reading English slows (see discussion in Hawkins, 1981, 1983). There is evidence, too, that skills developed in learning a foreign language do help cognitive skills. Other arguments have also been forwarded on the basis that learning a modern language offers a new start for the learners allowing them to review and explore concepts they have met before but not fully developed (time, calendar, shape, order, texture etc.) in a new, neutral medium. The evidence obtained from research in Welsh as a second language is particularly helpful here (see Jones, 1968; Schools Council, 1978). Other advantages include educating the ear, encouraging concentration and listening skills, matching sounds to symbols (especially where the match is clear, as in Spanish or Welsh), new structures and meanings (see the fuller discussion in Hawkins, 1981, 1983). Furthermore, given the more active teaching methods that are becoming typical in modern language classes, a broader range of social and personal skills are being effectively developed in a more neutral classroom context (Waite, 1986).

We have seen, then, that learning a modern language can be a purposeful and successful experience for low achievers and pupils with learning difficulties. The key to understanding the role of modern languages for these pupils is to understand what success means for them. To do this we need to look, firstly, at what they will do and, secondly, at how they will do it.

What, then, will the pupils do in their modern language learning? We have learnt much, as modern languages teachers, from the recent expansion of provision of modern languages.[2] Perhaps the most fruitful initiative has been that referred to obliquely in Christine Brown's article – graded tests or graded objectives known often as GOML (Graded Objectives in Modern Languages). Against a background of increasing concern about low achievers and also work in applied linguistics a number of Local Authorities set up local schemes designed with two aims in mind:

(a)   encouraging the use of language for practical communication;
(b)   devising a series of graded steps of achievement.

The success of these schemes is undoubted (Buckby *et al.*, 1981; Dunning, 1983), particulary with low achievers for whom many of these schemes were specifically designed (e.g. OMLAC, 1978). The benefits were essentially increasing the relevance of the language, emphasizing what the learner can *do* for the purposes of communication and recording achievement. The traditional emphasis on accuracy and analysis of language was thus replaced by emphasis on the content or effect of the message. The increase in motivation resulting from such schemes was recorded by HMI: '. . . undoubted benefits of greater enthusiasm displayed by pupils for learning and continuing to learn a foreign language' (Assessment of Performance Unit, 1985).

The schemes provide short-term, clearly defined goals sorted into levels which can be understood and adopted by the low and high achiever alike. The goals emphasize oral communication with reading and writing growing in importance at later levels. Tests are available for which criteria have been established ensuring that all those who perform according to the criteria are successful. Certificates are awarded as tangible proof of achievement.

The success of such schemes highlights the significant features of modern languages provision that are essential for the learners. However, certain disadvantages have arisen which, too, will help us draw up our list of objectives for these pupils.

Most schemes work on the assumption that objectives in teaching and testing are the same for pupils of all abilities and only progress towards them is different. Skills are developed or added, the range of functions and notions is increased, and grammatical and vocabulary demands are expanded. It is tacitly assumed that level 3 is more difficult than 1 or 2 and that skills and knowledge from earlier levels are used again. The corresponding tests become more difficult, requiring, typically, a greater number of, and more complex, oral tasks. Furthermore, the tasks become increasingly unrelated to the learners immediate environment. The vocabulary requirements and the length of discourse (perhaps 4 or 5 role-play statements) reflect the assumption that considerable cognitive development has accompanied the learner's progress. It is not too surprising that earlier motivation is dissipated and progress, originally encouraged by the levels, is hindered by them.

What conclusions, then, can we draw from these?

(1)   The language pupils learn must be practical and relevant to the low achiever. If dealing with things unfamiliar, they must be 'potentially real' to him/her, that is, likely to be encountered by him/her when dealing with speakers of the foreign language. Language relevant to his/ her environment and experience *as a learner* in contact with native speakers will be developed for purposes of communication.

(2)   The objectives must be short-term, attainable and understandable. Ideally, they should arise from the learner's own interests.

(3)   Receptive skills – or 'perceptive' skills as James described them highlighting the active character of reading and listening (James, in CILT, 1972) – should be emphasized. Pupils will be given adequate opportunity to develop productive skills as they choose.

(4)   An ability to understand and, where relevant, produce meanings relevant to young learners will be developed. It is unrealistic to assume that a highly developed communicative competence (Canale and Swain, 1980) will be the aim. Pupils will be encouraged to see language learning as a valuable experience of learning to communicate, with its own objectives (see below). It will not be seen as a failed attempt to create an ability to cope with any native speaker.

(5)   Learners will be encouraged, within the constraints of their ability and interests, to move beyond holophrastic understanding and production. Whilst analogy and generalization remain difficult for these learners, it is valuable for them to encounter the rule-governed features of language

both intuitively and explicitly. It is an important feature of language learning that the learner attempts to adopt a rule-governed strategy which is modified in the light of processing. It also allows the learner to move beyond the problems of short-term and long-term memory. Whilst this aim might be sensitively pursued, it is unlikely to appear in any assessments. Practical *use* of the language will be the primary objective.

(6) Learners will be encouraged to reflect upon languages as tools to find their way around the world, to see similarities between languages, reflect upon the composition of words, etc.

(7) Modern languages do not equal French. It may be more valuable for a low achiever to have gained successfully a little knowledge of two or three foreign languages than to have spent three or four years indifferently at one on a 'long-haul' course (see, for example, Cross, 1979).

(8) Opportunity will be provided for the learner to choose the language he or she wishes to develop and also be involved in negotiating the targets and means of attaining them (Buckby, 1980).

(9) Learners will be encouraged to develop an empathetic appreciation of other or foreign cultures and languages and be aware of their impact on our ways of life in Britain.

(10) Whilst encouraging the development of memory, the courses will not assume a large degree of retention and re-application of material. The development of a modular approach to modern language for these pupils is of great value. Such an arrangement might also permit two or three languages to be attempted at an initial phase. Later modules may be added to extend the same languages in other skills or areas of communication. Pupils thus begin their 'apprenticeship' of learning foreign languages, developing fundamental skills of listening and speaking, and having several opportunities to exercise skills of analogy.

(11) Assessment will match these objectives and will not follow a vigorous cumulative approach or assume rapid cognitive development.

(12) The experience of language learning must be enjoyable, broadening the pupils' appreciation of and demands upon the world rather than narrowing them. We must avoid, too, the danger of 'substantial groups of children whose frustration in French is united with general anti-foreign prejudice and "little Englandism"' (Hornsey, in CILT, 1972).

(13) A component of 'language awareness', it is claimed, will help to fill out the learner's general language education and language learning

experience. A number of schools have operated such schemes which focus on the phenomena of languages, looking at forms of language, language structure, how languages are acquired and used and how they have grown and developed. Arguments are forwarded that both mother tongue development, especially reading, and foreign language learning are advanced (Hawkins, 1984). Materials are available commercially, and work is being monitored by a working-party of the National Congress on Language in Education.

How, then, will these pupils learn foreign languages? Whilst it would be foolish to argue that there is one approach, some comments might be of practical help.

Firstly, we need to note the role that interaction itelf has in the classroom. Buckby looked at this in his article, both in explicit pedagogic terms – what is relevant and interesting to the pupils was assessed by regular questionnaires – and in social terms – with emphasis on mutual respect and real interest in what is said (Buckby, 1980). The classroom environment in which the learning takes place is intensively interactive, and it is this which, in my opinion, sets the tone of the interaction in which the language will be learnt. Where 'real' or social interaction is poor – where there is only action and reaction (or conflict) the environment for learning the language is poor. Excellent pedagogic methods in themselves cannot compensate for this. It may be useful to consider this first when dealing with low achieving pupils (Malamah-Thomas, 1987). In many cases it is these who have been given the worst deal with regard to, and put the greatest strain on, classroom interaction.

It is most important to help create a good learning environment. This requires, at least, a degree of empathy for the target community and language and a sympathetic and relaxed classroom atmosphere. A positive view of the country or community needs to be established, perhaps through careful presentation and discussion based on partner or group project work. It is likely that areas of similarity which are more likely to be of interest to young learners will be explored in English (fashion, pop music, etc) using foreign resources. One might discuss magazines, films with the volume turned down, other library resources (essentially picture-based) and above all, the language assistant, once carefully prepared. Some pupil-initiated language discovery can be made at this stage, as learners working together look for cognates (words which are similar to English words) or talk with the teacher and others about features of the language they find different. Similarly, they might listen to short stretches of spoken language, in groups, and try to identify three of the five words that are very similar to English. They might also experiment at copying these sounds, recording their attempts on a cassette recorder or attempting to say new words which are similar to English. A dry, factual approach must be avoided, and an active approach, encouraging their own discovery, will be developed. Emphasis will be placed on *oral* discovery through English, with regular discussions with the language assistant and other colleagues. Where the other languages of Britain are taught, pupils will be encouraged to 'discover' their impact on the community, copying names of shops or signs, etc.

A scrap-book, as opposed to a project file with its formal demands for writing and presentation, will be of value. Pupils can thus collect pictures from magazines (as many pupils are reluctant or unable to copy at all well), signs, cartoons and the odd explanation or comment. This will provide a tangible record of their initiation into language learning. For language learning it is, in the same way that primary school children learn to hold pencils and draw as a necessary preparation for learning to write. Indeed, it is strongly argued that the attitude of the learner, and particularly empathy for the foreign culture and language, have great control on the language progress of the learner (Burstal *et al.*, 1974; Krashen, 1982; Littlewood, 1984).

It is essential that this preparation of attitude is positive and rewarding, practical and above all interesting. Group work in the class, which we assume will be mixed ability at this stage, may be based on project tables, containing some of the resources required, plus information on where to get further help. Workcards or sheets *may* be helpful, providing learners with prompt questions and suggestions about where to proceed next (for example: 'Look at the cover of this magazine. Can you find three French words you can understand?' or 'Look at the food on the plates. What do you think of it?'/'Draw the things you can see on everybody's plate. Do you eat those things too?'/'Find out what the German assistant likes to eat. Cut out the food and stick it on this plate' [a drawing!]/'Look at this magazine. What is it about? Pop music, sport? What kind of person would read this?'/'Look at the pictures. Can you draw (or cut out) a picture of the person who reads this paper? Can you guess what the name means?' etc).

The role of the teacher at this stage is very important for s/he will also seek to negotiate the tone of class interaction here. Frequent contact with the low achiever will provide the psychological support to increase confidence and allow the teacher to become the oral resource, social and pedagogic, that is so needed by some pupils. The teacher will also confirm progress and react to the learners' discoveries, whilst also suggesting that they look at another aspect if interest is flagging, or indeed change to a different activity. It is important that the element of choice is present in these activities. If there are, for example, five global tasks, it will be helpful if a minimum of only one or two have to be done. This ensures that a degree of work *is* completed, it is pupil-directed and avoids the cumulative failure experience felt by so many low achievers. Other pupils may of course complete more tasks. As we move to the more explicitly linguistic element, it is important that, whatever methods are used, pupils can understand what it is that they are trying to do and understand what significance this has for them. This goes for the overall aims as well as the specific details of each lesson. Herein lies the strength of the GOML schemes, where objectives are described in advance and pupils observe in detail their progress. This raises problems when it comes to the inevitable answer 'But I won't go to France, sir' and it is essential that the teacher encourages honest discussion. Debate will focus on why the language study is of value to the learners, beyond the simple argument that they may (or more likely, may not) need the language abroad in the future. At the same time, we must also recognise the immense value of the school visit which may be the only opportunity of travelling abroad for many of these pupils.

Pupils will be encouraged to develop receptive skills, particularly listening, and whilst speaking will not be obligatory, opportunities will be provided to encourage the confident. A range of very practical listening strategies will be adopted, moving outwards from cognates, and perhaps requiring action rather than writing, such as in Total Physical Response (Sano, 1986). Group and partner work will help ensure that the peer pressure to remain silent before the teacher is not so great. In conversation, the teacher is more likely to accept English replies to questions in the foreign language and the use of anglicisms as an attempt to communicate and not seek to correct form. The 'reduced psychology' of the learner who battles to speak in the foreign language may not be tolerated by the low achiever who already suffers from a low sense of his or her own significance. It is important that a detailed plan of progress is available such as GOML profile cards which can be discussed with and by the students. Allowing time in the 'free' lesson every two weeks to discuss progress with pupils will also ensure that the progress is noticed by them and, where appropriate, recorded on a progress card. Such an arrangement will also provide an occasion for real, individual interaction in addition to the normal class conversation. It also provides the teacher with a ready excuse to give to the pupil the individual teacher attention demanded in class lessons.

A fairly flexible view of progress must be adopted if the desired aims are to be fulfilled. As we have seen, most GOML schemes are based on the notion of mastery of a range of language items. The suitability of such an approach must be questioned with pupils whose retention of the necessary language items may be very poor. It would, perhaps, be useful to allow pupils to move on as teaching is completed rather than repeating work on the same topic. Where graded objectives schemes are used, it needs to be recognized that the likelihood of the low achiever completing all the tasks required, particularly at the later, more demanding levels, is very slim. It may be useful to adopt or amend a scheme allowing these learners to gain credits as they complete work in class, not in any summative test. One might allow credit, for example, for a role-play activity completed over a period of two weeks, recognizing that a five or even three prompt card represents too great a demand to be completed in one attempt. This does, of course, require a less strict view of accuracy and fluency. Given the difficulty experienced by many of the weaker learners and their apparent reluctance or inability to use repair strategies in communication, the pupils' use of the odd word or two to express their meaning will still require considerable inference and backtracking on the part of the teacher.

Many of these pupils have great difficulty in adapting the language at their command to unfamiliar – or even familiar – communication needs (functional competence). Similarly, they have great difficulty planning their communication as dialogue and adapting as it progresses (strategic competence). It may be possible, when assessing, to allow pupils to use the dialogues they have already met and simply adapt them for their purposes. Similarly, greater flexibility can be shown with resource books, etc., in reading or listening tests.

Much of the material included in some syllabuses, despite claims that it is 'communicative', is in my opinion of negligible value and interest to our learners, especially low achievers. For example, what value will arranging to have oil checked for a car or paying by banker's card abroad have for 14-year-olds? In adult life these tasks will be of little importance even to the few who do travel abroad. It is important, too, that the tendency to teach so-called 'survival language' to these pupils enshrined in some graded objectives schemes is tempered. It is likely to be of little significance or use to them even on the once in a lifetime day trip and relies heavily on a feature of the language learning situation which low achievers find particularly hard to sustain, namely a leap of imagination. The learner is required to sustain this leap throughout the course. Now s/he is in a foreign country in a particular setting which may change from minute to minute (at an ice-cream stall, at a French post office, at a patisserie, in customs, in a French home) with a bewildering array of different people (penfriend, shop assistant, customs official, penfriend's father) performing a wide variety of tasks and functions (getting an ice-cream or stamps, inquiring about prices, negotiating, giving information, checking information etc).

At the initial stage, this imaginative leap is a refreshing, even exhilarating experience for the low achiever trapped within a humdrum experience of predictability. However, these leaps cannot be sustained or switched on by command. Therefore, whilst the use of realia or copies of them (bottles of wine, stamps, papier mâché croissants, etc.) are very effectively used by teachers and pupils in simulation, they soon provide diminishing returns, particularly in a 'long-haul' course. Furthermore, such teaching emphasizes the transactional at the expense of personal interaction and creativity. It is of small personal significance and for this reason it does not provide the 'deep meanings' (Stevick, 1976) considered more likely to be learnt quickly.

It is important, then, to exploit the *real* environment in which they find themselves, within school (not just the classroom) and outside, developing, too, language which is significant for them as individuals. The language used needs to be of significance to them in the real environment, not just the pretend one. It is, after all, a large enough leap from the real world to agree to use the foreign language anyway. Therefore the language used will relate to concrete items, with emphasis on developing vocabulary rather than structures, moving outward from cognates. The local environment can be used to great advantages, as indeed a number of projects have recently begun to do (for example, Bristol Urban Studies Centre). Pupils might, for example, give and follow directions in the foreign language to find their way around the local town. They might prepare a cassette on their own town (in English or 'cued' foreign language) and prepare to process a similar cassette from the foreign country. The material itself needs to be of some personal significance to them, particularly at later stages, for example, finding out about what Germans think of us, whether they smoke or not, what they do in the evening. (Hermann, 1986). Tasks may be based on this which demand comprehension rather than production of language, where rehearsal for recording one or two simple questions for a link group in France provides a focus for the learning which may have been initiated and agreed by the pupils themselves. Exploration of effect will be encouraged, as pupils respond to varieties of music, tastes, pictures, things funny or frightening, paintings, clothes, etc. Most of this work will require selection from alternatives or guided frames as commonly used in foreign language teaching. Surveys can be conducted as group or partner activities where essentially the same function is used (e.g. seeking opinion) but the topic is of significance to the pupil here and now: for example, a survey of attitudes ('Que penses-tu de..?') about smoking, fox-hunting, Madonna, glue-sniffing, etc.

The likelihood of the last suggestion being performed as a free activity by very low achievers is very small. This brings us to the final point in this brief consideration. For many low achievers, language study in school is not, realistically speaking, likely to result in a broad ability to communicate independently in the foreign or community language(s). For most if not all of these learners, the experience of foreign language learning at school will have been an introduction to language learning and a filling-out of their general language education. As such, it will have benefited their general education as members of a multi-lingual world in the multi-lingual countries of Britain and had positively beneficial effects both cognitively and on their general mother tongue skills (Hawkins, 1981). To use Hawkins' terms, the experience will have been an 'apprenticeship' which has its own objectives and criteria for achievement. For example these learners will not be expected to generate language spontaneously in most situations, but are more likely to make adaptations of language resources to express their own meanings, as indicated above. Where talks and activities require specific language items, these will be provided as resource material. This will enable the learner to complete the task by using resources at his/her disposal rather than fail because s/he cannot do it all. This will also encourage a more realistic view of language learning in school in which the learner learns how to use language resources rather than rely on poor retention and newly developed skills. A new framework for assessment will thus be used allowing positive statements to be made regarding performance *in relation to support provided*. It is important that teachers and students recognize this, not as failure to develop communication skills, but as *a* means of communicating. Such objectives may valuably be discussed with the pupils and may provide a means for the dangers of a mastery approach to be avoided, so allowing pupils to move on successfully. Success is thus understood as success in relation to criteria relevant to them.

The teacher will need to consider carefully which foreign language or languages will be offered to the students in which order. It has long been recognized that whilst detailed comparison of the accessibility of languages is difficult, some comparisons are useful. It is clear, for example, that the phonology of spoken French poses greater problems for English learners than that of German. The relationship between the written and spoken forms of Spanish is much closer and more systematic than that of French. Whilst it is difficult to draw conclusions from the research conducted by the Assessment of Performance Unit, it is worth noting some of their findings:

> The highest proportion of both girls and boys finding the language both easy and enjoyable was among pupils learning German ... Speaking – higher proportions of boys learning German held positive rather than negative views; the contrary applied for French or Spanish (p. 391); The pattern in German, of higher scores in listening than in reading, contrasts with results in French and Spanish (p. 394). (Assessment of Performance Unit, 1985).

It may be that the choice of language presented first will influence the attitude of the learner to other languages.

Furthermore, the teacher will need to consider the feasibility of offering a language that is already spoken by a number of students in the school and community. The linguistic advantages offered to the students by the opportunity to start a language or develop one that is already known may greatly enhance their linguistic education.

In conclusion, we need to look briefly at the organization of modern languages teaching in relation to pupils with learning difficulties and low achievers. I hope that the arguments and suggestions above have shown that modern language learning is relevant to such pupils and outlined ways for departments to prepare overall plans to include them. However, the debate that has raged over mixed-ability teaching after year one has not ended. There still remains little evidence on which to draw conclusions,[3] except that the number of departments able to teach mixed ability beyond year one seems to have increased considerably.

However, in 1978 Her Majesty's Inspectorate concluded, on the basis of seven years' research and in common with many others (e.g. Wringe 1976; AMA 1979):

> there seem to be no grounds for believing that mixed ability grouping can offer any advantages to the modern language class even in the hands of an able teacher; in the hands of the less skilled or experienced it can have positively harmful effects (Her Majesty's Inspectorate, 1978, p. 118).

Nonetheless there are now many departments who have taught mixed-ability groups successfully. Furthermore, the research conducted by the APU in 1984 found no association between performance of learners and any particular class arrangement (Assessment of Performance Unit, 1986).

Varnava has argued the case for mixed-ability teaching very effectively. Considerable disadvantages may arise when setting is used. Very soon a 'sink' class is produced whose own self-esteem is very low, often negating the very positive achievements of the first (mixed-ability) year. Under-achievement then becomes instituted and a downward spiral of poor motivation, cooperation and learning is accompanied by classroom conflict and dropout. Furthermore, the grouping of ability is self-reinforcing and allows classroom alliances of disruption and poor motivation to be further extended and strengthened. Before long, the 'sink' group becomes defined more by the characters of its constituents and their disruptive alliances than by their poor achievement. When this group is then further weakened by the frequent withdrawal and addition of pupils for 'remedial' work or changes to other sets the class becomes a nightmare for both pupils and teacher (Varnava, 1975; Wragg, 1976).

Conversely, mixed-ability classes beyond year one, where sensitively operated, can encourage self-esteem and cooperation allowing pupils of different abilities to work on related themes at their own pace and depth. The responsibility of the teacher is both to organize efficiently the resources and methods of group work and to *allow* the pupils to work for themselves. This approach requires a conviction that pupils working together do not in themselves create disruption or lead to the learning of error. Such methods and attitude a department must work and plan for together. The implications for differentiated tasks and resources are huge as very few are available commercially at present. If departments are to institute mixed-ability teaching, the aims and methods need to be clearly perceived and agreed by all and appropriate resources provided.

In conclusion, we may say that plans to extend foreign language learning to all abilities are already in effect in many schools. There are also national plans (DES, 1987, 1988) to extend the provision of foreign language learning to age 16.[4] However, the expertise and conviction needed to ensure that the pupils' experience is stimulating and valuable will certainly need support. Few materials are available commercially to cope with very weak learners and the problem is even greater with less commonly taught languages such as Spanish and Italian. Departments will need to plan and work together, to cooperate with the special education departments, and in cooperation with other schools to provide the resources and build up the expertise.

Notes

[1] Whilst this chapter deals principally with the teaching of foreign languages, many of the arguments also apply to the teaching of Welsh in English-medium schools in Wales.

[2] Before the establishment of comprehensive schools, only a small proportion of pupils had the opportunity to learn a foreign language. The situation changed dramatically in a short space of time. In 1962 25 per cent of children in England and Wales started a foreign language; by 1977, 90 per cent, and in 1987 the figure is nearer 95 per cent.

[3] The APU survey of 1984 found that most schools have mixed-ability grouping for the year 11–12 and then some form of ability grouping for the 12–13 age group and beyond.

[4] 'In Wales this will be in addition to the study of Welsh, which will be a core subject for bilingual schools and, subject to the Secretary of State's power to make exemptions, a foundation subject in non Welsh-speaking schools' (Letter from Welsh Office, 26 January 1988).

References

AMA (1979) *Teaching Modern Languages in Secondary Schools*, London, Hodder and Stoughton.

Assessment of Performance Unit (1985, 1986) *Foreign Language Performance in Schools*, London, Her Majesty's Stationery Office.

BROWN, CHRISTINE (1985) 'The better for the experience: foreign language learning for pupils with learning difficulties', in *Modern Languages in Scotland*, No. 27, January.

BRUNER, J.S. (1975) 'Language as an instrument of thought', In DAVIES, A. (Ed.) *Problems of Language Learning*, London, Heinemann.

BUCKBY, MICHAEL (1980) 'Teaching pupils of lower ability', in *Disadvantage in Education*, Vol. 3, No. 1, Spring.

BUCKBY, M., BULL, P., FLETCHER, R., GREEN, P., PAGE, B. and ROGER, D.(1981) *Graded objectives and tests in modern languages teaching; an evaluation*, London, Schools Council.

BURSTALL, C. (1974) *Primary French in the Balance*, Windsor, National Foundation for Educational Research.

CANALE, M. and SWAIN, M. (1980) 'Theoretical bases of communicative approaches to second language teaching and testing', in *Applied Linguistics*, Vol. 1, No. 1.

CENTRE FOR INFORMATION ON LANGUAGE TEACHING AND RESEARCH (CILT) (1972) *Teaching Modern Languages Across the Ability Range*, London, CILT.

CROSS, DAVID (1979) 'Motivating the majority – monoglot to polyglot in three years', in *Audio-Visual Language Journal*, Vol. 17, No. 2.

DEPARTMENT OF EDUCATION AND SCIENCE (DES) (1987) *The National Curriculum*, London, Department of Education and Science/Welsh Office.

DES (1988) *Modern Languages in the School Curriculum*, London, Department of Education and Science/Welsh Office.

DUNNING, R. (1981) *French for Communication*, Leicester, University of Leicester Press.

GLASS, ALEX (1984) 'French and pupils with mild mental handicap', in *Modern Languages in Scotland*, No. 26.

HAWKINS, ERIC (1972) 'Teaching modern languages across the ability range', in Centre for Information on Language Teaching and Research, *Teaching Modern Languages Across the Ability Range*, London, CILT.

HAWKINS, ERIC (1981) *Modern Languages in the Curriculum*, Cambridge, Cambridge University Press.

HAWKINS, ERIC (1983) 'Language study for the slow learner', in RICHARDSON, G., *Teaching Modern Languages*, London, Croom Helm.

HAWKINS, ERIC (1984) *Awareness of Language*, Cambridge, Cambridge University Press.

HER MAJESTY'S INSPECTORATE (HMI) (1978) *Mixed Ability Work in Comprehensive Schools*, London, HMSO.

HMI (1987) *An inquiry into practice in 22 comprehensive schools where a foreign language forms part for all or almost all pupils up to age 16*, London, HMSO.

HERMANN, K. (1986) 'What's communicative about asking "Wo ist die nächste Haltestelle bitte?"', in *British Journal of Language Teaching*, Vol. 24, No. 1.

HORNSEY, A.W. (1972) 'A foreign language for all?', in Centre for Information on Language Teaching and Research, *Teaching Modern Languages Across the Ability Range*, London, CILT.

ILYIN, D. (1983) 'What can be done to help the low ability student?' in *System*, Vol. 11, No. 2.

JAMES, C.V. (1972) 'A note on language skills', in Centre for Information on Language Teaching and Research, *Teaching Modern Languages Across the Ability Range*, London, CILT.

JONES, W.R. (1968) 'Research in bilingual education', in *Educational Research in Wales*, London, HMSO.

KRASHEN, S. (1982) *Principles and Practice in Second Language Acquisition*, Oxford, Pergamon.

LITTLEWOOD, W. (1981) *Communicative Language Teaching*, Cambridge, Cambridge University Press.

LITTLEWOOD, W. (1984) *Foreign and Second Language Learning*, Cambridge, Cambridge University Press.

MALAMAH-THOMAS, A. (1987) *Classroom Interaction*, Oxford, Oxford University Press.

MILLE, S.H. (1978) 'Teaching modern languages in mixed ability groups', in WRAGG, E.C., *Teaching Mixed Ability Groups*, Newton Abbot, David and Charles.

OMLAC (1978) *New Objectives in Modern Language Teaching (2)*, London, Hodder and Stoughton.

OMLAC (1981) *New Objectives in Modern Language Teaching (2)*, London, Hodder and Stoughton.

RICHARDSON, G. (1983) *Teaching Modern Languages*, London, Croom Helm.

SANO, M. (1986) 'How to incorporate total physical response into the English programme', in *English Language Teaching Journal*, Vol. 40, No. 4.

SCHOOLS COUNCIL (1969) *Development of Modern Language Teaching in Secondary Schools*, London, HMSO.

SCHOOLS COUNCIL (1978) *Bilingual Education in Wales 5-11*, London, Evans/Methuen.

STEVICK, E.W. (1976) *Memory, Meaning and Method*, Rowley, Mass., Newbury House.

VARNAVA, G. (1972) 'Modern Languages: a basic part of the curriculum', in Centre for Information on Language Teaching and Research, *Teaching Modern Languages Across the Ability Range*, London, CILT.

VARNAVA, G. (1975) *Mixed Ability Teaching in Modern Languages*, London, Blackie.

WAITE, I. (1986) 'Language teaching and personal development: an answer to the problem of relevance', in *British Journal for Language Teaching*, Vol. 24, No. 3.

WRAGG, E.C. (1976) *Teaching Mixed Ability Groups*, Newton Abbot, David and Charles.

WRINGE, C. (1976) *Developments in Modern Language Teaching*, Wells, Open Books.

Possible Resources (to be used selectively)

French

Courses and Schemes

Local Graded Objectives Schemes: contact LEA or CILT

A Paname	– Arnold-Wheaton
Eclair	– ILEA/Mary Glasgow
Salut!	– Cambridge University Press
Action!	– Nelson
En Bref	– Blackie
Chouette	– Arnold-Wheaton
Tour de France	– Heinemann

Hexagone	– Oxford
Français: Graded Objectives	– National Language Unit of Wales
Français: Niveau Débutant	– National Language Unit of Wales

Other Resources

J'aime Ecouter 1, 2, 3, 4	– Mary Glasgow
Service Compris	– Mary Glasgow
Destination France	– Longman
Get by in French	– BBC
In France	– Nelson
A French Fun Book	– Longman
Dès le début	– Video + booklet – BBC + Longman

Readers

Bibliobus	– Mary Glasgow
Collection Papillon	– Nelson
Napoléon Series	– Arnold-Wheaton
Machin Series	– Arnold-Wheaton

Software

Quelle tête/jeu des ménages	– Cambridge
French connections	– Cambridge
6 French Games	– AVP Gwent

German

Courses and Schemes

Local Graded Objectives Schemes: contact LEA or CILT

Einfach Toll	– Stanley Thornes and Hulton
Partner	– ITV + Longman
Einfach Klasse	– Oxford University Press
ZickZack	– Arnold-Wheaton
Get by in German	– BBC
Deutsch: Graded Objectives	– National Language Unit of Wales
Deutsch: Anfängerstufe	– National Language Unit of Wales

Other Resources

Alles Klar	– Longman
Destination Germany	– Longman
A German Fun Book	– Longman
In Germany	– Nelson

Readers

Lesekiste   – Mary Glasgow

Software

Kopfjäger/Umziehen   – Cambridge
6 German Games   – AVP Gwent

Spanish

Courses and Schemes

Local Graded Objectives Schemes: contact LEA or CILT

Get by in Spanish   – BBC
Destination Spain   – Nelson
Español: Graded Objectives   – National Language Unit of Wales
Español: Nivel Principiante   – National Language Unit of Wales

Other resources

Juegos de Palabras   – Mary Glasgow
In Spain + Workbook   – Nelson
Dicho y Hecho   – BBC
A Spanish Fun Book   – Longman

Welsh

Courses and Schemes (secondary level, second language)

Cwrs Cymraeg Ysgolion Uwchradd   – National Language Unit of Wales,
                                      Pontypridd, Mid. Glam.
Clebran   – Clwyd LEA

Language Awareness

Language Awareness (series)   – Cambridge
World Language Project   – Hodder and Stoughton (forthcoming)
Language & Languages   – Oxford

Chapter 11

Meeting the Needs of Low Attainers in Music
William Salaman

Every pile has its bottom. Schools, maybe more than other institutions, appear almost to revel in sorting out their workers into categories of excellence. Whatever the general standard of attainment, there will always be some who are labelled 'bottom of the pile'. These unfortunates are the low attainers and all too often their classification and fate depend upon their ability or lack of ability in literacy and numeracy. When we examine the teaching of subjects distantly connected with literacy and numeracy we observe the disproportionate influence that these loosely connected skills wield over teaching methods and effectiveness, serving as they do, a broad basis for most of the banding, streaming and setting that go in secondary schools. The aesthetic and sporting areas, which are among the least suited to such categorization of students, can produce high attainment among 'low attainers' which should serve as an embarrassment to those who cling to notions of low attaining children as types. As we mature we become increasingly aware of our strengths and weaknesses. I am happy to describe myself as a reasonably high attainer in music but a very low attainer in high-jump. Did my PE teacher regard me as a high attainer or low attainer, I wonder? The question is crucial because discussion of the topic of this chapter must centre either upon those who are labelled broadly (and unfairly) 'low attainers' or upon those who appear to perform poorly in music lessons in particular. In a better world, I would choose to discuss the needs of the latter group — those who find difficulty in singing in tune, whose grasp of instrumental playing is hampered by clumsy coordination or whose response to music is faint. This would be to assume that such individuals could be gathered together into a musical 'remedial' class, an unheard-of luxury. Basing the discussion upon reality rather than fantasy, I shall look at the musical needs of the former group, those who find themselves in the C stream for reasons ranging from their competence in the three Rs to their attitudes and behaviour, but certainly not to their musical aptitudue or skill.

Despite a recent surge of interest in the teaching and care of children with special needs following Warnock (1978) and the 1981 Act, there has been a comparative dearth of literature about pupils one step above those statemented as having special needs. Similarly, the teaching of music to low-attaining children has received very little attention lately. Stimulating books by Dobbs (1966) and Ward (1976) provided a strong focus for the teaching of music to less able children in the 1960s and 1970s but the interest has all but evaporated, leaving one to wonder whether the problem has been solved or is insoluble. It seems that the problem is in the process of being solved through developments in the teaching of music generally and through a greater concentration among music teachers upon the essential nature of the subject. These will be explored later. For now, we should attempt to analyse what the problem was and, in many schools, remains.

Some Causes of Low Attainment

Low attainers are perceived as failures. As has been suggested above, they fail principally in core curriculum areas, but the label sticks and, all too often, the sole area of success that a school can claim is that of convincing such children and the world that they are failures through and through. Psychologists and sociologists may find causes of failure in family relationships, social class, housing conditions and the like, but this is to impose one problem upon another. The nature of failure in one particular examination or test must arise out of the assessment itself. We are encouraged to believe that any properly designed formal test should produce results which follow a fairly standard curve of incline from top to bottom. If 90 per cent of pupils obtain 90 per cent of the marks, the test is too easy. If 90 per cent of pupils obtain 10 per cent of the marks, the test is too difficult. However, if half the pupils 'do well' while the other half 'do badly', the design of the test has been judged correctly. Put another way, we are forced to conclude that a decent test should produce plenty of failures. That decency can be so distasteful should be a cause for serious concern. Though tests may provide incentives for pupils and form a reliable basis for school reports, they can also create failures where success and failure should not be issues. For children of lower general ability, the stigma is more pronounced and, very often, adversely influences the levels of attainment reached in subjects where tests are not applied, morale having dropped to a point beyond rescue. Further, the concern with formal assessments which permeates the 'academic' depart-ments within a school can spill over into departments which should not be involved with such procedures under normal circumstances but which have been drawn into the practice so as to be sheltered under an umbrella of respectability within the school. Music is typically one such subject. Until recently, much of secondary school music teaching has been dominated by the study of facts *about* music. Readers may remember (possibly with little pleasure) music lessons devoted to the study of the life of a composer or the mathematical relationships between note lengths. These features are easily tested. Similarly, the story of a programmatic piece of music, the mechanics of orchestral instruments and the minutiae of musical forms have provided ample material for homework and end-of-term examinations and, indeed, ample material for the creation of low attainers and failures. A way around the production of so much failure might be the simple abolition of formal testing in music. This would force teachers of music to examine the intrinsic value of the work being done. With the umbrella of respectability folded away, the *musical* benefits of such factual study are difficult to list (as indeed they were in the first place). The main solution to the problem is to re-examine curriculum content. It is only fair to say that many teachers of music have been doing this recently, spurred on by the GCSE examination and its radical criteria. The outcome of such reappraisal has been a renaissance of musical activity in classrooms and a welcome blurring of the distinction between low and high attainers. One may go further than this. Practical and musical activities which have, in the past, been found to benefit slower learners are now being made available to all pupils. The tail is beginning to wag the dog and out of this development important new principles of music education are becoming established. These are making the concept of a 'low attainer' less tenable than it used to be and are causing the aesthetic foundations of music education to assume a position which they should have held long ago.

The Curricular Implications of New Thinking in Music Education

Some subjects in school are more pupil-orientated than others. The traditional music lessons, described in the paragraph above, are subject-orientated, music being treated as a gravel-pit of facts and skills which can be transferred pebble by pebble, into reluctant buckets. The course must be devised and administered by the teacher because the teacher is the only person qualified to impart the information to the pupils. We might see a number of parallels between this kind of pedagogy and that used in the traditional teaching of mathematics. However, if we wander down the corridor to the art room, we will find pupils offering *their* creativity and experience to the art teacher. The teacher guides, suggests, advises, but does not dictate. The work of the pupils may not startle through its excellence, but equally, it is not a success or failure in accordance with rigid marking schemes, nor is it placed in rank order. Any shortcomings in the work should be discovered and analysed by the pupils themselves so that their critical faculties are being developed alongside the executive ones. This description is not unduly rosy. For many years, visual art has been treated in schools as an expressive, creative subject offering children a chance to immerse themselves in the present rather than forcing them to serve as assistants at the alter of the past or as slaves to the prospects for the future. The value placed upon the utterances of children as children, eloquently advocated by Herbert Read (1943), David Holbrook (1967) and others has been given serious thought by music educators. To transfer the philosophy from visual art and creative writing to music is far from simple and many music teachers have found the task disappointingly taxing, but as work along these lines develops in music classrooms around the country, increasingly reliable approaches are being offered. At the same time, it is becoming clear that the low attainers, those who have been labelled failures for so many years, can prosper in the practical and creative spheres of music-making, thus reducing substantially the impact of the phrase 'low achiever'.

Keith Swanwick (1979) has provided music educators with a cogent yet readily understood analysis of musical behaviour, an analysis which is providing a footing for much of the activity pursued in British music classrooms and which serves also as a framework for the GCSE National Critera for Music (DES, 1985b). He sees involvement in music as being a function of one or more of three distinct yet inter-related facets. These are Composing, Audition and Performing. There is no need to examine this analysis in great detail, but some explanation would be useful for an understanding of its educational application. **Composing** is seen as a deliberate construction of a 'sound object' intended for an audience. It does not necessitate the writing down of the sound object nor need it entail the use of existing conventions in music. Lest we imagine that the resultant sound object is simply the product of an undisciplined free-for-all, it should be realised that successful work in this field should show awareness of some of the aesthetic principles which govern *all* creative work: a sense of shape and balance, contrast, unity, an appropriate relationship between basic material and duration, etc. Experience has shown that composition in class is generally best conducted through group-work where pupils experiment, exchange ideas and make joint decisions. **Audition** is a special kind of listening. The listener is not just a 'hearer' as is the case with background music. Being entertained by music is not the main thrust of audition either. It refers to the listener as *audience*. Music can engage one's attention as compellingly as drama or dance. It is this active involvement through listening which is gaining increasing attention among music teachers.

Performing suggests the making of music with voices and/or instruments. The problem here, especially in the case of instrumental performance, is one of technique and musical literacy. It is difficult to perform if one has no skills with which to perform. To teach concurrently thirty children to play instruments is an awesome but not insuperable task. Notwithstanding all the problems of space, noise, equipment and management that an active course of this sort requires, music education is definitely moving in this direction, aided strongly by the GCSE National Criteria (DES, 1985a) which insist that pupils be engaged in such activities anyway. We shall examine each of the facets described briefly above from the viewpoint of a 'low attainer'.

Composing

If a pupil has difficulty with the reading and writing of words, it is likely that similar difficulties will be encountered in the reading and writing of music. This being so, conventional composition, which demands many sophisticated skills, is almost tailor-made for the ensurance of failure. The advantage of the freer approaches which are being pursued in classrooms today lies in their general avoidance of technicalities, at least in the earlier stages. There is no exact parallel to be drawn between this approach in music and the approaches found in creative writing and visual art, but some comparisons may be useful. It is some years since the emphasis in creative writing shifted away from matters of grammar and spelling towards the telling expression of individual thought. Predictions that the result of such a shift would be an illiterate population have proved to be unfounded, but even so, a retrenchment to a position of compromise has been evident. The principle remains, nevertheless, that individuals have something of value to write about and that the substance of their thoughts can outweigh the importance of the means used in recording them. In visual art, freedom of expression has superseded technical training for decades but, as with creative writing, technical matters are introduced early to assist the expressive intentions. Until recent years, music in class has dwelt on technical matters to the total exclusion of compositional activity since music appeared in the curriculum during the nineteenth century, so the shift towards the pursuance of composition can be seen legitimately to be one of the most radical developments in the history of music education. Whereas pupil writers and artists have at least a modicum of technical skill with which to embark upon their creative work, pupil composers usually have none at all. The great majority have to start from scratch. Nearly all are 'low attainers'. This is not to suggest that progress will be the same for all pupils. Some are bound to develop swiftly while others lag behind, but all can achieve at their own level and, when working in a group, can share the achievement of the group as a whole. Music is a non-verbal means of communication which acquires meaning through general consent. Where pupils agree upon the effectiveness of their decisions, their work attracts a validity which has to be respected. Much work in this field offers little more to an audience than evidence of experiment with compositional procedures. A piece which explores contrasts between sound and silence, for instance, may attract derision from those who expect balanced melodies and functional harmony. To experienced music teachers, the processes and the results can reveal depths of compositional thinking which are of immediacy and educational value. When conducting work of this sort, a teacher transfers a proportion of musical responsibility to the pupils, some of whom will be bound to reject the opportunities offered. Others will welcome the chance to demonstrate what they can achieve, once freed from the shackles of abstract concepts, tasks based on memorized learning and formal testing. Among these pupils there are bound to be some low attainers whose only failure lies in their inability to fulfil the school's prediction of low attainment!

Audition

The special kind of listening that the word audition implies has been explained, so the word listening will be used hereafter since it is more familiar, but the meaning of audition is retained. Because music has no generally accepted verbal or pictorial meaning, many people are bewildered as to how to approach it. For some, there is an emotional response which borders on the physical, providing an enhanced and enriched awareness of their own reality and of the significance of the moment in which the response is felt. For others, the response is more intellectual, the music 'argument' providing the chief focus of attention. For a music teacher, the first task is to generate a response which is essentially musical. It is distressingly easy to lose sight of the aesthetic purpose of listening to music. Information about the music and its composer can be supplied (and tested) with much less effort. To devise a course in listening which will engage the attention of pupils of all abilities is an immensely demanding task. Rather than supply 'entertainment', possibly in the form of pop records or light classics, we should look to the lessons learned through composing. The growth of compositional skill should lead to a more profound awareness of the compositional procedures used by others, whether they be classmates or professional composers. The uses of repetition, ostinato, pedal notes, sequence etc. together with the exploration of higher-order concepts such as balance, contrast and density are common to the beginner and professional alike. The established composition is both a model for and a confirmation of pupils' personal experiences. (It is curious to note that art teachers rarely draw their pupils' attention to existing works in this way. Maybe it should be a cause for concern that 'Art' and 'History of Art' are separated subjects at all levels of education.) The skills of reading music are introduced into listening activities more easily than into those of composing or performing since no executive skill is expected. One can follow the notation of a piece of music as it is being played rather as one can follow the words of a poem as it is being read. We do not have to spell the words, write them down or even read them out. We simply follow. With music, the score provides a 'picture', vague at first but becoming more precise as understanding deepens, which both focuses attention and sharpens awareness. As with composing, listening can provide all pupils with challenges which lead to achievement as opposed to hurdles which threaten failure.

Performing

I have mentioned that composing is a comparative newcomer to the musical curriculum. Listening in one form or another has been part of the musical diet in schools since the invention of the gramophone. Of the three activities under discussion, performing was the first to be pursued in schools. Singing was introduced into the curriculum to improve the quality of hymn and psalm singing in nineteenth-century churches and chapels. From this beginning there have developed numerous schemes of singing and instrumental playing ranging from the playing of toy percussion to working with highly sophisticated synthesizers. With such a choice available, it is impossible to pinpoint activities especially well suited to the so-called low attainers. However, mere involvement in such activity itself suits everyone other than the determinedly antagonistic. To make music alongside others can be enormously rewarding provided the material is aptly geared to the capabilities of the participants. In mixed ensemble work, whether pursued as a class or group activity, roles can be found which allow for varying degrees of aptitude, once again highlighting positive achievement and eliminating the inevitability of failure.

Likely Developments

Music in schools is changing at a brisk pace, each new innovation often supplanting the last. However, the basic principles of musical involvement remain well ensconced and it appears that the benefits gained from establishing music as an active, creative and, above all, *musical* pursuit will not be surrendered lightly. I have suggested that our low attainers should benefit from the new thinking as richly as anyone else. Indeed, within the walls of the music classroom, 'low attainment' becomes an increasingly meaningless expression. There should be ample opportunity for all members of the class to fulfil their potential musically and little necessity to compare one person's contribution against another's. Some form of pupil profiling would appear to offer the most reliable and fair way of assessing work, especially since group activity blurs distinctions between the contributions of individuals. These are healthy trends which are helping to emphasize the expressive core of music education. Parallels which may be found within the development of other arts subjects in schools, notably visual art, creative writing and drama, suggest that new strength will be added to the teaching of music in schools and that within a few years it will become a wholly practical subject. Signs of such developments can be discerned already and their success has been documented. We can hope that the value of practical music education will be suitably recognized and rewarded and that all children will become the beneficiaries.

References

DES (1978) *Special Educational Needs (The Warnock Report)*, London, HMSO.
DES (1985a) *GCSE The National Criteria*, London, HMSO.
DES (1985b) *GCSE The National Criteria for Music*, London, HMSO.
DOBBS, J.P.B. (1966) *The Slow Learner and Music*, Oxford, Oxford University Press.
HOLBROOK, D. (1967) *Children's Writing*, Cambridge, Cambridge University Press.
READ, H. (1943) *Education through Art*, London, Faber.
SWANWICK, K. (1979) *A Basic for Music Education*, Windsor, NFER.
WARD, D. (1976) *Hearts and Hands and Voices*, Oxford, Oxford University Press.

Books for Further Reading

DES (1985) *Music 5–16*, HMSO.
PAYNTER, J. (1982) *Music in the Secondary School Curriculum*, Cambridge University Press.
SALAMAN, W. (1983) *Living School Music*, Cambridge University Press.
SWANWICK, K. and TAYLOR, D. (1982) *Discovering Music*, London, Batsford Educational.

Chapter 12

Low Achievers in Physical Education
Dilys Price

Who are the low achievers in Physical Education?

In every school there are young people who hate physical education. There are many reasons for this and in the past some physical education teachers have considered these problems and their causes to be outside their area of concern. Today the consequences of this attitude are beginning to be recognized as being dangerous for the health and well-being of the community and the economy. Ill health, lack of fitness, emotional problems, mental illness, boredom, stress, poor self-esteem, lack of confidence and lack of energy can often go back to dislike of physical education in childhood as one of the contributing factors. This dislike may be due to physical inability, poor teaching, lack of movement and sports activities or even bad experiences at some time in physical education. Sometimes, children, while enjoying some physical activities in play, do not enjoy areas of traditional physical education. As physical educationalists we have begun to recognize our responsibilities to try to tackle these problems and to alter these far-reaching negative attitudes to physical education and physical activities.

Some children are undoubtedly physically less able than others. They are often but not always in the group we label 'slow learners' and the failures they know in the classroom and the resulting sense of poor self-esteem and lack of confidence is often compounded by their failures in physical education.

Many are deprived youngsters, who are disadvantaged by their environment: poverty, broken homes, poor diet, poor facilities for play, and emotional traumas. They fall behind and fail in physical activities. Often these children have been handicapped in many ways, some suffering trauma at birth, deprivation afterwards and physical and emotional abuse later on.

They are spiralled into failure so that their intentions and struggles to succeed in physical education are overcome by other forces working against them.

Sadly, another group sometimes at risk are young people with physical handicaps who are integrated into mainstream education. Some children in wheelchairs or with cerebral palsy or spina bifida, for instance, are left out of physical education. They are also being deprived of an important aspect of their emotional and social development.

Other handicapped young people may join in physical education lessons, but experience a continual lack of success with its consequent sense of failing and isolation.

For all these youngsters detailed individual assessments and adapted physical education programmes are essential to help them remain motivated and be successful in physical education. And physical education teachers must now learn these skills and find time for them in their busy professional lives.

Clumsy or motor impaired children have always been with us but have only recently been recognized as needing help. More awareness of their particular needs in physical education classes as well as extra remedial sessions are necessary to help them to improve their skills and to employ compensatory physical strategies. In the past problems of 'physical illiteracy' have been allowed to develop and spread into emotional and social problems. Such children have grown to hate physical education, often wanting desperately to succeed at first, but later resigning themselves to failure.

There are also young people who, although reasonably physically able, are not skilled in the traditional physical education curriculum. These could do well in other areas of physical education if they were fortunate enough to be in a school with a wide, diverse and flexible physical education curriculum.

Nowadays there are many young people of different cultures and backgrounds in school and they too have difficulty in adapting to some physical education lessons, feeling ill at ease and insecure in activities and behaviours that are alien to them. It is necessary to be aware of their problems and to adapt the curriculum and to prepare alternative teaching strategies to bring them into successful and profitable physical education.

Lastly, for many children, an over-emphasis on competition, technique and skill has proved to be inappropriate. These aspects are valuable, but for many children they need to be balanced with the aspects of play, expressive and exploratory activity and self competition.

Some youngsters, perhaps heavier than most, unskilled or lacking confidence, unable to overcome the fear of jumping onto a box in the gymnasium or join in a basket-ball game in the sports hall, may enjoy walking and gradually gain confidence and enthusiasm for hill walking and scrambling. They may feel there is more purpose in these activities, and eating sandwiches for example by a waterfall may reinforce a sense of happiness, self-worth and success! — especially if there has been some effort involved in reaching it!

Whatever form it takes, a sense of individual failure and losing should not be an objective in our lesson structure — instead, getting the youngster motivated to do his or her individual best, to work with the concept of excellence as the aim, (with all the spin-offs of self-satisfaction and the self-confidence which effort and commitment bring) should be what we want to bring into a young person's world. These can be the achievement of all youngsters of all abilities (or inabilities). Excellence can be achieved at every level, and every child can gain the self-confidence which striving and reaching towards excellence can bring.

Physical education curricula and methodology need to be adapted to bring about self-confidence, fitness and health, social development, move-ment skills and the motivation to remain physically active for life.

Warnock (DES, 1978) saw that 20 per cent of young people are, at some point, in need of special educational help. We need to look hard at what we teach and the way that we teach physical education. Are we aware that approximately 20 per cent of the children we teach may need remedial help in movement at some point? Because this is likely. Are we adapting, assessing and adapting again to achieve the best results in physical literacy, motivation, health and skills for our young people?

The Clumsy Child

Invariably, those who are involved with the teaching of physical education will come across the clumsy youngsters, or, more precisely, children who are affected to a greater or lesser extent by a lack of motor coordination. It is these young people who are chosen last in team games or whose allocation to a team is met with groans.

The problems of clumsy children are by no means minor, particularly to the pupils concerned. They may become withdrawn at a very early stage in their school careers; lack confidence in practical areas; refuse to attend school on physical education days or generally cover feelings of inadequacy by clowning through school. While schools tend to withdraw for extra sessions children who have learning difficulties in mathematics or English, this is seldom the case in physical education and allowances must be made for the children who have motor coordination problems which may last throughout their school careers.

Clumsiness is relative, and it is the degree of clumsiness that makes the situation a problem. There are people who are clumsy to the point of desperation in some areas, but manage other tasks and exercises quite competently. And there are some people who are utterly clumsy at almost everything, from tying a bootlace to kicking a ball or stepping off a bus.

The causes of clumsiness are various and not always identifiable. There are often problems in motor organization or perception or both. The causes include minor cerebral palsy, impaired formation of the neural interconnections during brain growth, and subclinical epileptic activity (McKinlay and Gordon, 1980).

More boys than girls suffer from clumsiness and Brenner *et al.* (1967) found that 6 per cent of the seven-year-olds in their study had some perceptual motor disabilities, that is, one or two children in every normal primary class.

Although specific remedial action must be considered it needs to be emphasized at all stages that a holistic approach is essential. One cannot deal solely with one part of behaviour, when clumsiness relates to the person as a whole. It is with the whole being one is concerned, with his or her mental, emotional and physical needs.

Through adaptations of physical education teaching content and method teachers can help the clumsy youngsters in a variety of ways. Pupils can be helped to build a positive self-image, to develop a feeling of security in the class environment where failure can be tolerated and where success in movement at some level is established; where the students are motivated to effortful activity and concentration by stressing self competition and success rather than class competition and the inevitable failure and decrease of effort and motivation which group competition brings to clumsy young people.

One problem is to determine what clumsiness is. Morris and Whiting (1971) suggest that a young person is motor-impaired or clumsy if she or he is 'unable to perform the particular patterns of skilled behaviour demanded by the environment'. The emphasis is on diagnosis by behaviour rather than by cause (which may be multi-faceted or not possible to identify or treat) and treatment, in the form of adaptions, education and compensatory techniques, can produce enhancing and beneficial effects on movement behaviour.

Early identification in the school setting is extremely important and the Stott, Moyes and Henderson Test of Motor Impairment (1972) has now been adapted for use by teachers (Henderson, 1984). If Brenner's estimate of 6 per cent of seven-year-olds suffering from perceptual motor disabilities is near the mark, it means that hundreds, if not thousands, of children in junior and senior schools have been struggling for years to overcome their clumsiness. The stress and emotional turmoil involved in such frustrating struggles must be alleviated. Movement programmes have a critical role to play. For many young people who lack parental and teacher understanding and support, the conquest of clumsiness may be impossible.

The needs are clear:

1.   Teachers and other caring agencies first need to be aware that clumsiness can afflict intellectually gifted youngsters as well as the mentally and physically handicapped.

2.   Knowledge of the student's ability and intelligence is necessary to make a sound assessment of motor coordination.

3.   Social/family factors impinge on both ability and coordination.

4.   All young people should be assessed in relation to their age peers and social context.

5.   All teachers need to have available an acceptable check-list and empirical norms against which to assess students.

The strategy is therefore:

1.   that all teachers, alerted to the problems of clumsiness, must attempt to identify, first by general observation in the classroom, playground and gymnasium, and secondly by their own prepared check-lists in more precise testing periods, young people who are at risk in terms of physical imcompetence.

2.   that teachers need to attempt to remedy the problem by adapted, compensatory and appropriate supplementary physical activities.

3.   that (through the head teachers) they do consult with the educational psychologist, consultant paediatric neurologist or physiotherapist about pupils whose problems are not alleviated by remedial and compensatory strategies so that they can then work as part of a multi-disciplinary team to overcome the young person's difficulties.

Remedial Work/Approaches

Difficulties in one or more of these areas of the check-list which indicate marked clumsiness, will, of course, engage the teacher's concern. Remedial methods will vary with the kind and extent of clumsiness, but there are general principles underlying the approaches to dealing with these children.

1.   First is the recognition by the teacher of the emotional result for the child of failing with one's peers.

2. As clumsiness is most obvious in its physical manifestations, there are clearly movement connotations. It is necessary to pin-point some specific failures — eg. balancing, catching a ball, writing — and provide therapeutic exercises at the appropriate level. Any exercise which the youngster is quite unable to perform adequately would only give rise to more frustration. Gradualness and planned gradation are the keys.

3. Movement activities are central. The pupil learns best and most naturally through motivating and playful or recreative activities, and a movement programme at the level the student is able to enjoy must be the starting point. Gymnastics and dance focus on the body, for instance balancing, moving, stepping, jumping and turning. There is no doubt that movement improves movement and coordinated body skills learnt in the gymnasium and sports hall and dance studio will transfer in increased skills in everyday life. Add to this Freud's statement that 'the ego is first of all a body ego' (Salkin, 1973); that successful body experiences give a growing child a sense of his or her own worth in a more immediate way than success in any other area, and one begins to see the essential importance of frequent and reinforced movement education — focused on educational gymnastics and educational dance and outdoor pursuits, with the emphasis on enjoyment and individual readiness. Formal and informal approaches, direct and indirect teaching all have their place. Observation of the youngsters' success in movement skills and activities and the level of self-confidence will guide the teacher to the appropriate content and approach.

4. Movement skills should be broken down into progressive tasks so that the pupil can progress by appropriate steps (e.g. allow thinking time; simplify or change the rules of the game). Body awareness is basic to improving the capabilities of one's body and parts of that body. Isolating parts of the body can simplify tasks (e.g. a youngster sitting on the floor and concentrating on hand and arm movements does not have to think about weight-bearing, walking or bumping into others).

5. When considering the clumsy pupil in a class of thirty, it is sometimes hard to remember that we are aiming to develop all pupils to their full potential. The more clumsy the young person, the more careful must be the planning of the physical education lesson: even the least able can succeed if given appropriate activities. The ability of the teacher to create an atmosphere of tolerance for the pupil is invaluable and will certainly be more likely to promote a positive response from the clumsy child or young person.

6. Gross body movement exercises will make possible improvement in finer activities. McKinlay and Gordon (1980) think it is likely that shoulder exercises will improve finer control, such as writing. It is by remedial, compensatory and frequent movement programmes and activities that the physical manifestations of clumsiness are most likely to be overcome.

7. Motivation and courage to work at movement activities with energy will only come to the pupil from the teacher. It is essential that the teacher, while providing appropriate movement skills and progressions, holds up to the young person a mirror of his or her self-worth in every way possible, thus motivating the pupil to increased effort and making all activities worth while.

I would draw teachers' attention to a useful check list of activities (Arnheim and Sinclair, 1979), to which they may wish to refer when preparing their own remedial movement programme:

1. Tension and release.
2. Locomotion and balance.
3. Rhythm and space.
4. Rebound and airborne activities.
5. Projectile management.
6. Management of daily motor activities.
7. Selection of play skills.
8. Motor fitness.
9. Aggression management.
10. Water environment.

It is likely that any remedial movement will result not only in better posture and balance, body image and self-confidence, locomotion skills and enjoyment of movement, but also in improved organisation and attention span, emotional control, socialization and self-concept (McKinlay and Grimley, 1977).

Adaptations for the Low Achievers in Physical Education Areas: Methodology

There is no one right way to teach, there is no one right curriculum.

There are however certain criteria for a good teacher. The good teacher is like an explorer, endlessly seeking new methods and rediscovering old ones; assessing and reassessing present methods and constantly evaluating them in the light of students' progress to see if they are achieving the goals set, and the needs of the students.

The good teacher is committed to bringing to all pupils the joy of effort and the pride of achievement. To achieve this nothing is more important than the teacher's ability to observe, record, assess and evaluate. The Warnock Committee (DES, 1978) puts this as one of its main recommendations in the initial training of all teachers. There is no doubt about it, that to achieve the best results students need to be assessed in detail, formally and informally at frequent intervals. Linked to this is the importance of setting out clear aims and objectives. Without clear global aims and specific objectives, assessment of the programme and the progress and development of the child within it is impossible.

I am certain that aims should include:

1. Increased movement skills and realistic sense of physical abilities.

2. Improved body-image and increased self-confidence.

3. An understanding of the concept of excellence and the knowledge that at every level this can be achieved, whatever the pupil's ability (or disability).

Other aims should be to make pupils aware and skilled in the use of their bodies, able to use and not abuse them: able to relax and be skilled in relating to stress, to have strong and elastic muscles, resilient ankles, knees and hips; a spine able to stretch, twist, bend and arch efficiently; heart and lungs that are efficient and well exercised. In other words, throughout school and later in adult life to help young people to have and to keep an efficient machine, which they use appropriately and have knowledgeable control over, and which is a source of self-confidence, recreation and health.

A good teacher must be able to vary teaching methods to achieve these aims. Movement activity, exploration and experience are important, as is the progression of structured and direct tasks. It is important that all movement tasks undertaken bring a sense of success, satisfaction and achievement.

Self competition is always important, but for some young people any other type of individual competition fails to motivate. Youngsters however can get pleasure in cooperating together and this cooperative spirit is essential to happiness. I believe that it is dangerous to the individual and others if competition is the sole motivation for effort in sport activities. Kinaesthetic enjoyment, self competition, a striving for excellence, creative achievement and the enjoyment of cooperative and social physical activities are the more valuable in real life terms. Surely the world is at the stage where an awareness that we link in harmony with each other has become a prerequisite for survival. The understanding of the inter-dependence and inter-relatedness of each for the other, the knowledge that 'no man is an island', is essential for our survival and health and happiness.

Dance

This is an area which can be of immense value to low-achieving pupils, because there is such a range of physical, creative, intellectual, social and emotional possibilities within it. The expression and communication inherent in it can be at many levels, and is often enjoyed by young people who find other forms of communication difficult. The appreciation of communication through 'body language' can help personal development and self-confidence immensely.

Dance lessons can have a physical stress because dance is a physical art. But students can also work together with differing physical abilities and can gain satisfaction from dancing however physically handicapped or motor illiterate they may be. By making the focus imaginative, musical or even social, dance can provide many valuable experiences in shared activities of different abilities. Dance can stress the dramatic, creative or intellectual. It can range from folk dance (where all follow a set pattern) to dance drama or mime (where each individual may have his or her own movement.) Dancing can be lyrical or lively, free or set, stylized or natural and there is opportunity for every student to experience success and self confidence as s/he communicates individual or group movements to others. Dance can link to the past, present of future, to art, music, poetry, literature, can be individual or group, set or free, lyrical or lively, assertive or quiet, linked to reality or fantasy, to emotions, intellect, kinaesthetic feeling or action.

I would say that there are two simple keys to successful dance teaching. Firstly, always, in each lesson, allow half the class to watch the other half. It always has the effect of increasing effort and concentration. Dance is to do with communication and 'sharing and showing' must be part of the dance context. Secondly, praise. This is essential because in dance there is not the in-built feedback of hitting the goal or getting over a bench, and the teacher must provide feedback by positive comment and praise. (Incidentally, working in twos provides feedback by a peer also, as each works with one another, so I always include partner work in each lesson).

Notes on the Teaching of Dance

Laban's analysis of movement (1948) provides an excellent frame for dance preparation and coaching. Preston Dunlop (1980) gives a detailed exposition of possibilities, tasks, progressions and methods of teaching around these themes and her book should be used as a source book.

Every creative movement lesson should ideally include the following:

1. **Physiological Area**

(a) Movement tasks to mobilise trunk (curling, arching, twisting, extending, bending).

(b) Movement tasks to strengthen arms (taking weight on hands, pushing or travelling on hands and feet, extending, lifting, opening, pulling, pressing, gesturing).

(c) Movement tasks to strengthen and mobilise legs (running, jumping, gesturing.

(d) Tasks to extend cardiac-respiratory system (i.e., exerting the student).

2. **Creative Area**

(a) Some choice (e.g., starting position).

(b) Some free exploratory work in a task (e.g., the pupil can find different parts to balance on, or cut different patterns in the surrounding space, or make up a stepping sequence).

(c) A small sequence, or dance, should be composed by pupils each lesson.

(d) Some imaginative idea used at some place in the lesson (e.g., 'imagine you are slithering along the floor dragging a heavy weight', 'roll like a pebble on the sea's edge'. Or use a short poem, or mythical, historical or real-life situation — which may, or may not, be linked with classroom work). *N.B.* Ideas played out in movement always become very meaningful and movement can be a marvellous start for creative writing and understanding of situations, historical, cultural and environmental.

(e) Try to play one piece of music in each session, even if it is only to warm up at the beginning or to relax to at the end of the lesson. (Be careful to vary the music and use many different kinds, not just 'top twenty pop' although familiar music may be a good starting point).

(f) Dance lessons will become more creative as the students become more confident in their bodies through experience of skills and of vigorous gross movement activities, and these will develop body image. It is essential that the teacher helps youngsters feel good about themselves and their bodies — that the pupils gain a positive concept of themselves.

3. **Movement Analysis Area**

(a) Body awareness — actions, body parts.

(b) Space awareness – floor and air patterns, directions, levels, extension, body shapes.

(c) Effort (dynamics and rhythm) awareness — different rhythms and change of speed and force, working actions, rhythmical phrases.

(d) Relationship awareness – partners, trios; with, against, leading, following, canon, question and answer.
(Try and have *contrasts* of Body/Space/Effort/Relationship in each lesson).

4. Form of Lesson

(a) Start the lesson with energetic, gross motor tasks, until the students are a little tired. Then lead them onto activities demanding more concentration and choice.

(b) Share and show work done.

Gymnastics

This is one of the best areas for achieving success in movement skills for many students. Formal and informal approaches to skills learning should both be used and an understanding that gymnastics is not a narrow area, but a wide one embracing many activities of the body and movement and does not only or mainly emphasize 'skill' and 'apparatus', is essential if the success-orientated work is to be achieved.

Keith Russell, Associate Professor, University of Saskatchewan, said at the 1985 British Amateur Gymnastics Association Conference on 'Gymnastics in Physical Education':

> we must move away from these [narrow] approaches if gymnastics is
> to become a significant educational force and is to mature into a
> lifetime/fitness activity.

He went on to say that one good approach is through Movement Education (Body/Space/Effort-Dynamics/Relationship) and the other is through a programme synthesizing many aspects of gymnastics into its most fundamental six 'Dominant Movement patterns'. This is, as with Laban's (1948) taxonomy, to isolate the most basic aspects or themes of movement and to systematically expand on these themes. I believe the Laban Educational approach is still one providing most opportunity for gymnastic success in the low-achieving pupil because of the breadth of the gymnastic possibilities within it. It is not the only one and the B.A.G.A. Coca Cola Awards (Recreational Gymnastics) 6–1 provide another excellent, badge-orientated way of achieving. There are others, and the Russell analysis shown in Figure 12.1 could provide appropriate help for some teachers for success-orientated teaching.

Gymnastics – Specific Theme	Laban – Analysis of Movement			
	Body	Space	Effort	Relationship
1. landings	Vary the:	Vary the:	Vary the:	Perform
2. static	1. starting position	1. levels	1. time/ duration	1. self
3. swings		2. pathways		2. with partner
4. locomotions	2. finishing position	3. directions	2. force/effort	3. on mats
5. rotations		4. ranges		4. onto apparatus
6. spring				5. over apparatus
7. combinations				6. from apparatus
				7. on apparatus
				8. in the air

EXAMPLE

4. rotation around transverse axis (roll)	1. from squat 2. to kneeling	1. low 2. straight 3. forward 4. confined	1. quick 2. soft	1. self 2. on mats

Figure 12.1: *Gymnastic Activities and Laban Analysis*

The working party of British Advisers and Lecturers of Physical Education are at present working on a booklet (including a video) entitled 'Gymnastics in the Secondary School Curriculum', (1988) and this should be very valuable. They advocate thematic teaching. They point out that the best teaching will sometimes use whole-group practice and an identical skill or blend of skills, while at other times choice is widened to provide greater scope for individual interpretation. They stress that the gymnastics be taught in a non-competitive way. (Those who are motivated by competition have every opportunity in club situations to work competitively.) They also stress that gymnastics in the curriculum should be conceived as being part of a larger whole, enriching and being enriched, that all forms of gymnastics are constantly changing and draw their material from a broad, completely rooted, constantly evolving gymnastic heritage, and that innovation has always been part of the gymnastic heritage.

This paper makes some important points which I think the teacher of the low achiever will find helpful:

1. Approaches to teaching and learning will depend on the educational needs of the pupil at any given time as perceived by the teacher, moving from formal to informal.

2. The thematic approach makes for a 'broad-based' curriculum which is desirable in schools and particularly with children of different gymnastic abilities.

3. Gymnastics in schools can start work with a low skill threshold and is non-competitive.

4. Gymnastics in schools focuses on developing pupils' knowledge and understanding and realizing their individuality so that they become increasingly self-determining. They stress that these aims require a wider range of teaching and learning procedures.

5. It is necessary to evaluate pupils' movement development relative to individual differences.

Lastly, it is worth mentioning the importance of stressing a 'physical/motor enhancement' in which the teacher systematically enhances physical or motor attributes through the use of gymnastics. This approach is needed within all the physical education areas in today's climate of concern at the unfitness of many young people. Attention needs to be given to the improvement of students' physical and motor attributes within gymnastics and the whole of the physical education curriculum. This should underpin gymnastics, but also games, dance, swimming, athletics and outdoor pursuits. Obviously some areas will more easily relate to the improvement of certain physical or motor attributes rather than others and this is why a wide and balanced physical education programme is desirable.

Games

Too often youngsters fail in games activities because games teaching is often geared towards narrow skill and technique learning, or winning at all costs.

The National Coaching Foundation, in *Play the Game* (1986) states that over the past years there have appeared alarming trends in children's sports, namely, over-rigorous competition and training programmes and the stress of winning at all costs. They make the point that there is a place for more play, fun, free expression, experimentation and discovery even in games. As with gymnastics, the over-stress on technique and skills has failed and there is room for emphasizing the principles of games, small games and new games.

> Rather than measure the value of sport in terms of whether a child can win or not, score or not, defeat or be defeated, emphasis should be on the development of a sense of personal worth and achievement... Everyone can achieve excellence — it is a matter of attitude and intention rather than where you are, in the order of things (National Coaching Foundation, 1986).

Games should be fun and by adapting rules games can be played and understood quickly. This is particularly important for the low achiever, too many of whom gain a sense of failure in games lessons and therefore miss out on the values which games have to offer. It is extremely difficult for young people to experience all games and to achieve success in them, therefore there is a need to provide a games curriculum which leads to games education and to successful participation. There is a shift towards the idea of games for understanding which will include games principles, games making and small games, thus helping youngsters to enjoy the possibilities that games have to offer and to become skilled in games strategies and games situations.

Coventry LEA (Rohnke, 1984) suggest that there should be three components in games teaching:

1. **Games centred games.** This will involve teaching for understanding, looking at principles of games and their tactics and will involve:

    (1) *competence* in games playing related to the principles of play and tactics;

    (2) *personal fulfilment* and satisfying activities;

    (3) *opportunities* to solve problems in games situation.

2. **Games making.** This will give pupils opportunities to devise games helping them with games concepts and the practise of games skills at suitable levels.

3. **Ball skills (including small games)**. This will allow youngsters to experience a whole range of activities, helping them with competence and understanding.

The following categories can help teachers to prepare games schemes involving game principles, and successful activities and suitable strategies to further these:

> Invasion games
> Net/wall games
> Fielding/run scoring games

Targets
Game forms
Enabling games
Principles of play
Games making/creating games
Representing games

The focus suggested now (Almond *et al.*, 1986) is to shift from practising techniques within a major game, to understanding games forms which represent certain principles of play, to explore these in small and new games and for children through this approach to become more satisfactorily involved and skilful physically, intellectually, socially and emotionally.

In very real terms our aims in games must include effort, perseverance, success, cooperation, athletic enjoyment and skill.

Outdoor Pursuits and Linked Activities

Learning in an outdoor environment should be part of the school curriculum. There is immense value for some children in these outdoor activities, particularly for many low achievers. They find an eventual achievement of enjoyment in these activities greater than any other. The Newson Report (DES, 1963) said that outdoor pursuits had a special value for the average and less than average child and 'built up self confidence and social skills of the inadequate and unsocialised'.

In my personal experience I have seen children blossom in self-confidence and improve by the minute in physical skills during outdoor pursuit exercises. I cannot stress too much how important I think it is that low achievers walk, cave, canoe, sail, and take part in other such holistic adventurous activities. The stress on needing and helping each other, the exposure to the natural environment and the strong physical activity add up to the 'meaningful' experience in which learning takes place (Maslow, 1972).

The Cheshire Probation Outdoor Pursuits Committee Conference (1978) reinforced this view of outdoor activities, saying that they:

bring about improvement in the way individuals see themselves
...discovering their potential and the extent of their own physical
and mental abilities.

Rohnke (1984) describes the situation and achievement of the low achiever attempting these activities very well:

As they dare to try, they begin to experience physical success and
recognise that the seemingly difficult is often quite possible. The
struggles are often the beginnings of maturity which we believe

entails, in part, having a real experience with a wide range of natural human reactions — fear, joy, fatigue, compassion, laughter, pain or love.

The evidence is that for many, but particularly for youngsters with the problems of low achievers, adventure and outdoor activities can bring about very definite growth in self-confidence with all the spiralling benefits that this brings.

Often the progression to an outdoor pursuits course needs to be gradual. An adventure need not take place a long way from home and need not require expensive equipment or a high level of skill. For instance a 'night trail' can be planned close to the school and be the first progression of a longer term course in outdoor activities (Rohnke, 1984).

Swimming

This is an area which is important and valuable. Where children find it hard to swim it is worth giving extra time and increased help because of its value for physical health, self-confidence, leisure and social activity, safety and emotional development.

Water therapy is used by professionals working with the body, with speech problems, maladjustment and other mental, emotional and physical disabilities. For the low achiever, water activity is of prime importance and should always be part of their physical education curriculum.

Athletics

This area too has a place in the physical education programme. But for the low achiever, there needs to be a balance of activity and skill teaching and an emphasis on the enjoyment of self competition and the importance of individual activity, done in the pursuit of personal improvement and effort.

The teacher must see that s/he prepares an atmosphere in which the winners do not suffer from a sense of superiority and the losers from a diminished sense of confidence. If this is not possible, I suggest an alternative activity.

The Five Star AAA awards can be useful to motivate youngsters with a tangible badge. However, in my opinion it is not a good idea to turn the summer term over completely to athletics. The test is to see if all the young pupils are able to continue to grow in self-confidence and effort. If not, widen the curriculum again.

Health-Related Fitness

This is an area which is an increasingly important, on-going and innovative aspect of our present physical education programme. Courses, articles and books are addressing themselves to the problem of this lack of fitness of the present generation which we know is due to lack of activity, poor diet and smoking. Hopefully, this interest and knowledge will continue until the situation has improved.

There are two aspects to this. The first is to encourage a more active lifestyle and this must be reflected in a physical education programme which has as a primary aim the enjoyment of physical activity. This can only be good news for those of us concerned with pupils with special needs, for it is they to whom we must address our skills in getting motivation, self-confidence and physical skill and activity going.

The second component can be called 'looking after yourself' and will involve:

Diet and nutrition
Relaxation and rest
Posture
Abuses
Depression, stress and anxiety
Well-being
Healthy habits
(Rohnke, 1984)

Within the practical physical programme one will undoubtedly see an importance given to such activities as weight lifting, cycling, aerobic dance, breathing exercises (including the Alexander Technique and bioenergetics), and self-enhancement techniques. Aspects such as flexibility, coordination, stamina, tone and balance will gain in importance. (I believe that in the near future we may even have classes which will include massage skills. I have seen young people with a mental handicap successfully coping with these techniques and gaining real benefit in terms of reduction of tension and stress).

Gradual increased effort will follow simple activities as the youngsters enjoy and feel the positive results of movement action and movement success.

Some Notes on Teaching Aerobic Dance

Aerobic dance must stay within the young people's success range and enjoyment. At the end of every session the youngster should feel an enhanced self-image through movement success and positive feedback. Start from what the individual can do, but each time get the class to do a little more. This 'overload', small as it is, is very valuable, but exhaustion and extreme regimentation are not! And a sense of failure is definitely *not* valuable.

If the session demands too little effort and the teaching is tired, uninspired and *unaware*, the aims will not be achieved. I believe we must expect our youngsters to become very able, fit, happy and confident in movements while accepting that this will take time. Idealism must go hand in hand with practice. Our self-discipline, liveliness and joy is an essential part of our work in teaching.

Aims

1. Aerobic fitness.
2. Mobility.
3. Rhythmical, musical, social and dance activity.

Basic Points

1. Components: aerobic fitness, flexibility and mobility, strength, speed, coordination.
2. Concentrate on breathing out, 'like a train'.
3. Aerobic dance is energetic, *continuous* and fast. (Jane Fonda's 'work out' concentrates on slow stretches). Valuable to use both activities.
4. Build activities up gradually, relax afterwards.

Adaptations for Low Achievers

1. The basic ideas can be taken in *moderation*. Don't be afraid to make adaptations to suit needs.
2. At first students will need frequent stops.
3. They may like to do an exercise slowly without music first and then add music for the repeat.
4. Don't stay too long on one tape or exercise, build in variety.
5. Be moderate in your demands at first.
6. Music can include folk, gospel and even classical as well as 'pop'.

Suggested session outline for aerobic dance session

1. (a) *Breathing* (like a train).
   (b) *Jog, kick, bounce,* hop, step, etc.
2. (c) *Twists and stretches:* up, sideways, down, etc.
3. (d) On all fours, *trunk arches and curls.*
   (e) *Leg stretches* and *bends,* etc., on all fours.

4. (f) *Sit-travel.*
    (g) *Arms circle.*
5. (h) *Stand; jumps,* bounces, etc.
6. (i) Slow breathing, stretching, walking, gesturing.
    (j) Conclude in circle together walking right (4), left (4), in (4), out (4). (This provides a quiet ending to the aerobics).
7. The class may like to put together a simple circle sequence, based on:
    (a) stretches up
    (b) reaches sideways
    (c) reaches forward
    (d) kicks
    (e) jumps on spot
    (f) turning on spot
    (g) clapping
    (h) walking in a circle, left
    (i) walking in a circle, right.
8. Lie, relax.
N.B. (i) Sometimes yoga activities can follow an aerobic session. Try and include stretching, bending, arching, twisting and inverting in each lesson.
    (ii) Relaxation and self-enhancement makes an excellent conclusion to an active session.
    Play suitable music.

Suggested Outline for Relaxation Session

Briefly, an example of a relaxation section at the end of an active class (although whole lessons could be profitably given over to this) could be as follows:

1. Imagine each part of the body relaxed and heavy. Start from the feet, naming each part.

2. Breathe deeply and slowly for ten breaths. Visualize each number in turn drawn on a blackboard.

3. Wander through a secret place of your choosing. Enjoy the objects, sounds and colours.

4. Remember a time when you felt confident and happy. Go through it and remind yourself of all the qualities you like about yourself.

5. See the energy around you. Visualize its patterns and colours as you wish.

See it
      (a) protecting
      (b) soothing
      (c) attracting.

6.   Go on a magic journey in your mind.

7.   Come back feeling refreshed and relaxed.
(Quiet music can be used to help the session).

This is a new area, but one which I believe will gain an increased importance in our management of stress, energy and confidence. It is already being used widely by athletes and elite sports people and management organizations as well as practitioners concerned with ill health and disease. I am sure it will become a major area in the education of youngsters, and will enable many more than at present is the case to reach their potential in childhood and adult life. It has been neglected too long by us educationalists. We must now redress the balance.

Conclusion: Value of Movement Activities to other Areas of the Curriculum

Any teacher concerned with the low achiever in school needs to be aware of the great help that a successful movement activity programme has on other areas of the curriculum. Without doubt, any confidence gained in physical education results in increased concentration, self-confidence, social and communication skills in other areas.

Piaget (1955) writes of three stages of development and states that the sensory, motor and concrete operational stages must precede development in the conceptual stage. Frostig and Maslow (1970) and Kephart (1960) and other American educationalists use movement activities to help perceptual motor development.

If we can help youngsters gain joy in a wide range of physical education activities, we know they will gain so much: self-confidence, health (mental and physical), a prognosis for health in later life, increased abilities in other area of both education and 'real life' situations. In the end it is *our real interest* in these low-achieving young people, as well as our teaching skills, which is necessary to help them. Without a belief in their dignity and their unique individual worth, our value to them will be at best superficial, at worst, damning.

References

General, including Outdoor Pursuits

ARNHEIM, D.D. and SINCLAIR, W.A. (1979) *The Clumsy Child — Motor Therapy*, USA, Mosby.

BRENNER, N.W., GILLMAN, S. and ZANGWILL, O.L. (1967) 'Visuo-motor disability in school children', *British Medical Journal*.

BRUCE, V.R. (1969) *Awakening the Slower Mind*, Oxford, Pergamon Press.

CHESHIRE PROBATION OUTDOOR PURSUITS COMMITTEE (1978) Conference Report.

COSTONIS, M.N. (Ed) (1978) *Therapy in Motion*, USA, University of Illinois Press.

DES (1963) *The Newson Report*, London, HMSO.

DES (1978) *Special Educational Needs (The Warnock Report)*, London, HMSO.

FROST, I.G. and MASLOW, A.H. (1970) *Movement Education Theory*, USA, Follett.

HENDERSON (1984) *see* STOTT, MOYES and HENDERSON.

KEPHART, N.C. (1960) *The Slow Learner in the Classroom*, USA, Merrill.

MASLOW, A.H. (1972) *The Further Reaches of Human Nature*, Harmondsworth, Penguin.

MCKINLAY, I. and GRIMLEY, A. (1977) *The Clumsy Child*, Association of Paediatric Chartered Physiotherapists.

MCKINLAY, I. and GORDON, N. (Ed) (1980) *Helping Clumsy Children*, Churchill Livingstone.

MORRIS, P.R. and WHITING, H.T.A. (1971) *Motor Impairment and Compensatory Education*, London, Bell.

PEARCE IN PARKER, T.M. and MELDRUM, K.I. (1973) *Outdoor Education*, Adline Press.

PIAGET, J. (1955) *The Child's Construction of Reality*, London, Routledge and Kegan Paul.

ROHNKE, (1984) *Physical Education for Life*, Coventry LEA.

SALKIN, T. (1973) *Body Ego Technique*, USA, Thomas.

STOTT, D.H., MOYES, F.A. and HENDERSON, S.E. (1972) *Test of Motor Impairment*, Windsor, NFER

REVISED VERSION (1984) *Henderson Revision of Test of Motor Impairment*, Windsor, NFER.

Dance

BRUCE, V. and TOOKE, T. (1966) *Lord of the Dance*, Oxford, Pergamon Press.

LABAN, R. (1948) *Modern Educational Dance*, London, MacDonald and Evans.

LOFTHOUSE, P. and CARROLL, J. (1969) *Creative Dance for Boys*, London, MacDonald and Evans.

LONG, A. (1976) *Praise Him in the Dance*, London, Hodder and Stoughton.

MINTON, S. (1986) *Choreography. A Basic Approach using Improvisation*, London, Eddington Hook.

NORTH, M. (1973) *Movement Education*, Hounslow, Temple Smith.

PRESTON DUNLOP, V. (1980) *A Handbook for Dance in Education*, 2nd ed., London, MacDonald and Evans.

RUSSELL, JOAN (1969) *Creative Dance in the Secondary School*, London, MacDonald and Evans.

SLADE, P. (1977) *Natural Dance*, London, Hodder and Stoughton.
SMITH, J. (1976) *Dance Composition*, London, Lepus.
WATTS, E. (1977) *Towards Dance and Art*, London, Lepus.

Gymnastics and Games

ALLEN, T.E. (1969) *Sense and Sensitivity in Gymnastics*, London, Heinemann.
ALMOND, A., BUNKER, D., and THORPE, R. (1986) *Rethinking Games Teaching*, Department of Physical Education and Sports Science, University of Loughborough, Leicester.
BRITISH ADVISORS AND LECTURERS (1988, in press) *P.E. for Children with Special Educational Needs in Mainstream Education.*
BAALPE (1984) *Safety Practice in P.E.*
BAALPE Bulletin of Physical Education (1986) *Gymnastics in Schools*, Vol. 21, No. 1, Spring.
BAALPE (1988) *Gymnastics in the Secondary School Curriculum* (accompanying video), (to be published).
BULLETIN OF PHYSICAL EDUCATION (1983) *Games Teaching Revisited*, Vol. 19, No. 1, Spring.
CROSBY, S.N. and JONES, M.A. (1978) *Gymnastics*, Clwyd Education Authority.
FACEY, P. (1984) *Physical Education for Life: A Framework for Developing the Physical Education Curriculum*, Coventry Education Authority.
LISTER, D.A. (1988) *Gymanistics in the Secondary School Curriculum* (with video), BAALPE.
MARTENS, R. (1978) *Joy and Sadness in Children's Sport*, USA, Human Kinetics.
MAULDON, E. and LAYSON, J. (1965) *Teaching Gymnastics*, London, MacDonald and Evans.
MORISON, R.A. (1969) *A Movement Approach to Educational Gymnastics*, London, Dent.
NATIONAL COACHING FOUNDATION (1986) *Play the Game. For Children in Sport. Play Board.*, National Coaching Foundation.
RUSSELL, KEITH (1985) *Gymnastics in Physical Education*, unpublished paper (British Amateur Gymnastics Association Conference Paper).

Relaxation and Self-Enhancement Techniques

MADDERS, J. (1987) *Relax and be Happy*, London, Unwin.
OSTRANDER, S. and OSTRANDER, L. (1986) *Superlearning*, London, Souvenir Press.
SHONE, R. (1987) *Creative Visualisation*, Wellingborough, Thorsons.
SIMONTON, O.C., SIMONTON, S.M. and CREIGHTON, J.L. (1986) *Getting Well Again*, London, Bantam.
TODRIS, M. and INKELES, G. (1979) *The Art of Sensual Massage*, London, Unwin.

Swimming

ASS. SWIMMING THERAPY (1981) *Swimming for the Disabled*, E.P. Publication.
ELKINGTON, H. (1978) *Swimming. A Handbook for Teachers*, Cambridge.

Health-Related Fitness

ANDERSON, T.R.L. (1970) *The Ulysses Factor*, London, Hodder and Stoughton.

BROSNAN, B. (1982) *Yoga for Handicapped People*, London, Souvenir Press.

CHAITOW, L. (1983) *Your Complete Stress-Proofing Programme*, Wellingborough, Thorson.

COOPER, K.H. (1980) *Aerobics*, London, Bantam.

COOPER, K.H. (1986) *Running without Fear*, London, Bantam.

CORBIN, C.B. and LINDSEY, R. (1983) *Fitness for Life*, USA, Scott, Foresman and Co.

CORBIN, C. and LINDSEY, R. (1984) *The Ultimate Fitness Book*, London, Leisure Press.

CORBIN, C. and LINDSEY, R. (1985) *Concepts of Physical Fitness with Laboratories*, London, Wm C. Brown.

CULLUM, E. and MOWBRAY, L. (1986) *Y.M.C.A. Guide to Exercise to Music*, London, Pelham.

DES (1983) *Learning out of Doors*, London, HMSO.

ETHERIDGE, D. (1986) 'Outdoor Education at a Comprehensive School' in *Bulletin of Physical Needs*, Vol. 22, No. 1, Spring.

FACEY, P. (1984) *Physical Education for Life, A Framework for Developing the Physical Education Curriculum*, Coventry Local Education Authority.

FINGE, A. (1984) *Yoga Moves*, USA, Wallaby.

GALLWAY, T. and KRIEGEL, B. (1981) *Inner Skiing*, London, Bantam.

GROVES, L. (1979) (Ed) *Physical Education for Children with Special Needs*, Cambridge University Press.

HAUSOR, G. (1971) *Look Younger Live Longer*, London, Faber.

HAZELDINE, R. (1985) *Fitness for Sport*, London, Crowood Press.

KELLETT, D. *Health Related Fitness. Its Place in the School Curriculum* (Resource pack and video.)

LOWEN, A. (1976) *Bioenergetics*, Harmondsworth, Penguin.

MAISEL, E. (1974) *The Alexander Technique*, London, Thames and Hudson.

PARKER, T.M. and MELDRUM, K.I. (1973) *Outdoor Education*, London, Dent.

ROYAL CANADIAN AIRFORCE (1965) *Physical Fitness*, Harmondsworth, Penguin.

SMITH, R.W. (1977) *Man-chi'ng Cheng T'ai Chi*, USA, Charles Tuttle Co.

WILSON, A. and BEK, L. (1983) *What Colour Are You?* (Yoga), London, Truston Press.

WILMOTH, S.K. (1986) *Leading Aerobic Dance-Exercise*, London, Eddington Hook Ltd.

SECTION III:
CROSS-CURRICULAR ISSUES

Introduction

Section III of this book tackles a number of major issues which affect teaching and learning in all areas of the curriculum. As such it is aimed at both pre-qualified and post-qualified teachers who are keen to improve the educational experience of many low-attaining pupils. It opens with a chapter by David Fontana on personality which stresses the part played by self-esteem in the learning process, and the vital importance of all children being given the chance to succeed. This leads in to the chapter by Graham Upton which explores the nature of learning difficulties and a range of possible causes. Having looked at hereditary influences, socio-economic background and the part played by the school, Upton then goes on to suggest guidelines for teaching and organization which are geared to providing success for all pupils.

Carol Aubrey's contribution on responses to disruptive behaviour looks at the background to the present position and then leads on to an examination of the well-organized and well-managed classroom. She focuses on effective teaching and gives many pointers as to how this can be achieved. Pupil management and classroom management skills are analysed and strategies explained. As an overview of the main variables to be found in successful classroom management, this chapter will, I am sure, be referred to time and time again by teachers. It is accompanied by a useful list of books, manuals and resources.

John Harris' chapter on the role of language in creating special education needs provides a revealing insight into the way which teachers and pupils, whilst appearing to speak the same language, frequently do not understand each other. Given that pupils, as the chief 'recipients' of school language, are more disadvantaged than teachers by any breakdown in communication, Harris demonstrates that it is incumbent on every teacher to be aware of the nature of language and the implications of its various styles and usage.

Proficiency in using language is seen to depend on both appropriate experience and good teaching.

Sara Delamont's chapter examines the relationship between gender and low achievement and underlines the consequences of sex differentiation and sex discrimination. She points out that the higher the attainment level of secondary pupils the less sex differentiation there is in the curriculum and that observation research indicates the corollary to be true. Girls with learning difficulties are therefore more likely to be 'excluded' from certain areas of the curriculum than boys. Examination of such areas shows them to be linked to higher paid employment prospects than the subject areas which the girls are encouraged to show interest in. Delamont gives many examples of the differentiation and discrimination observed in schools but also includes discussion on strategies for change, reminding us, however, that shifting attitudes will depend on committed teachers.

The final chapter in this section by Tina and David Frost examines the impact on teaching of the new initiatives of TVEI and CPVE. For those who are still unsure of the aims and objectives of such courses and still less clear of their implications for the teaching of low-attaining pupils, this contribution will be most welcome. The Frosts draw together many strands which have run through the writings of other contributors to this volume: the need for a practical approach which is perceived by the pupils to be relevant and interesting, the need for all lessons to be planned with achievement of success inbuilt, the need for flexibility and constant assessment leading to modification where necessary and the need for enthusiastic teachers who have respect for their pupils as individuals. Guided by such principles, the effective teaching of all pupils will be possible for all teachers and will contribute towards a whole-school approach to meeting special educational needs.

Chapter 13

Personality
David Fontana

It is sometimes said by psychotherapists that the single most important cause of psychological problems in the individual is the inability to value oneself. This inability (let's call it low self-esteem) is seen not only in those anxious and neurotic people whose lack of confidence turns life into a fearful experience for much of the time, but also in those aggressive, tough individuals who bolster their personal inadequacies by attempting to dominate and intimidate others. Put another way, and translated into the school context, both the isolate and the delinquent child suffer at the psychological level from the same basic lack of any real sense of personal worth. Research evidence (see Fontana, 1986, for a summary) shows both types of child to be chronically lacking in self-esteem, and in the positive realistic and optimistic response to life which stems from this self-esteem.

In one short chapter there is not the space to examine in any detail the precise psychological mechanisms responsible for low self-esteem. But we can say that typically low self-esteem children come from backgrounds in which others fail to offer them the warm and accepting relationships upon which children depend for their self-image. Children are not born knowing who they are. They acquire this knowledge as a direct result of the way in which the significant adults in their lives behave towards them. If they come from homes in which these adults love and prize them, then they early begin to see themselves in the same terms. If on the other hand they are brought up in an atmosphere of rejection and hostility (or even indifference) they early on begin to see themselves negatively and aquire the guilt and self-directed aggression which goes with this negativity.

Working with a group of ten-year-old boys who he has subsequently followed through into adult life, Coopersmith (e.g. 1968) discovered that high self-esteem boys are usually blessed with parents who show an interest and respect for them as people. Parents who share ideas with them, listen to their opinions, allow family decisions where possible to be taken democratically, who are fair and consistent in their behaviour towards them, who know their likes and dislikes and who their friends are, and who are accepting and affectionate towards them physically. Parents who, in short, show their children that they are significant individuals, that they *matter*. Low self-esteem boys on the other hand usually seem to have parents who are the exact opposite, who show limited interest in them, who are arbitrary and unfair, who rarely take their views into account, who know little about them, and who are generally physically cold and rejecting.

Research of this kind indicates strongly children's need to be thought well of by others if they are to think well of themselves. Show children that you value them, that you respect their abilities, that you care about their lives and circumstances, and they will learn to value, respect and care about themselves. Show them on the other hand that they really don't count for very much, and they will come almost inevitably to take the same view of themselves. And when we talk about valuing and respecting and caring about children, I must stress that we mean valuing them as valid people in their own right, instead of constantly measuring them against our yard-stick and finding them wanting. It means accepting their abilities and emotions as natural expressions of each child's unique personality, and allowing them in turn to accept and get to know these things for themselves. Through this self-acceptance and self-knowledge they can identify and work with the need for personal change, allowing this change to be a function of their own understanding of life, rather than a confused (or rebellious) response to the demands and authority of others.

Coopersmith's studies have been carried out with boys, but precisely the same mechanisms are at work with girls, except that girls have the added disadvantage of society's tendency to condition them into a culturally subservient role. Research such as that by Lewis (1972) shows that girls have a harder task than boys to develop self-esteem. Not because they are less loved and valued within their families, but because parents are less likely to listen to their opinions, and less likely to allow them the emotional self-expression and emotional assertion so necessary to satisfactory personal development. Though I am coming to the role of the school shortly, let me add here that this discrimination against girls is continued (often unwittingly) at school level, with boys allowed early on to feel a greater significance in their social and academic roles.

One last point though before we turn to the school. If self-esteem is the single most important aspect of personality development, and if it is cruicially dependent upon the behaviour of others towards us during the formative years of childhood, does this mean that the individual's genetic endowment, his or her inheritance, has no part to play? Not at all. Psychologically, the individual is throughout life a creation of inheritance and environment, nature and nurture, and the interaction between the two. What this means in terms of personality is that the individual is born with what psychologists call *temperament*, the raw material of personality. Differences in temperament are apparent in babies from the early weeks of life onwards (see e.g. Thomas, Chess and Birch, 1970), and these differences are remarkably persistent throughout life. One baby is temperamentally adaptable and cheerful, another is cranky and difficult, another is rather passive and withdrawn. It is the nature of this temperament, and the way in which it reacts with the environment, that determines the sort of people we are. In the case of one child, therefore, the kind of environment that breeds low self-esteem will prompt a rebellious and aggressive reaction. The child feels bad about himself or herself, but takes out these bad feelings on others. No less filled with self-rejection than the next child, he or she nevertheless may adopt a tough response towards the world, blaming it in a confused and destructive way for his or her own problems. Another child, different temperamentally, will turn aggression inwards, blaming and punishing himself or herself with feelings of guilt and worthlessness.

Because heredity and environment react at every point, socio-economic factors will also play a part here. Given similar temperaments, a child from a lower socio-economic group may be more likely to respond with toughness and aggression than a child from a more privileged grouping. The first child comes from a sub-culture in which toughness and aggression and a rejection of authority may be prized, so that by adopting these responses he or she gains some of the prestige denied in his/her early up-bringing. The second child comes from a sub-culture in which aggression brings less reward and in which authority is generally respected. As a consequence the child is more likely to develop conformist behaviour and to accept blame for any apparent personal shortcomings. The psychological damage experienced by the children is the same in both cases, but the symptoms manifested by them differ sharply.

The Role of the School

Within the school, children face influences very similar to those within the home, but with one important addition. Within the school they are brought more obviously and sharply against a realization of personal inadequacy. Teachers draw attention to their abilities and performance. They are compared and compare themselves with other children. Like it or not, from the moment they enter infant school until the moment they leave the high school, children are faced with the language of success and failure. Not just as expressed in marks and grades, but as expressed in teacher comment and in general teacher attitude. Some children are left in no doubt that the school values and prizes them, others are left equally certain that the school looks negatively at their abilities and/or their general behaviour.

The inevitable result is that while some children receive a continuing boost to their self-esteem, others receive a continuing assault upon it. Do not let me suggest that this is deliberate school policy. Much of it goes on unconsciously, with teachers genuinely unaware of the effect that their behaviour is having upon their children. Do not let me suggest, either, that teachers and schools should abandon their sense of standards and simply devote themselves to indiscriminate praise of all and sundry. But do let me suggest that no teacher can fulfil his/her proper function in relation to children without a clear understanding of child personality and of the influence that teacher actions have upon it.

Children enter school bringing with them all their life experiences to date, plus the way in which innate temperament has reacted to these experiences. The job of the teacher is to work with the child as he or she now is, assisting the child in the interactive processes of learning the knowledge and skills the school has to offer and of developing a positive and healthy personality. To do this, the teacher must take children not at face value but at the deeper levels where reactions to life experiences are being formulated. This is what psychologists and teachers mean when they talk about the psychological *needs* of the child. One child's aggressive and difficult exterior, another child's withdrawn manner, another child's studied indifference, may all be signs that the child's need to feel a significant, acceptable, and ultimately successful human being are not being met.

My earlier discussion of those factors within the home that lead to the development of high self-esteem in a child gives a clear indication of how the teacher, in turn, can play a part in this development. Just as the parent can show, by word and deed, that a child is important, that he or she matters, so can the teacher. Just as a parent can show an interest in the child, a respect for his or her opinions, a readiness to share decision-making wherever possible, so can the teacher. Obviously this doesn't mean that the teacher, any more than the parent, should abdicate a role as final authority and arbiter of standards, but it does mean that the teacher can indicate clearly that all children are valued members of the class, all children have a worthy contribution to make, all children have a right to their individuality.

Much of this indication will come from the teacher's general relationship with the class and with its members. A relationship based upon friendliness, interest, respect, and genuine recognition of worth lies at the heart of what I am saying. But there are more tangible factors that are vital too. The main one, and it should be engraved as a golden rule upon the heart of each one of us engaged in the practice of teaching fellow human-beings, is that each individual *must be given success at some level, high or low*. Children already suffering from low self-esteem, from the constant experience of failure as people and as pupils, need the vital experience of success, no matter how basic the level initially, if they are to build that self-confidence and self-belief without which progress cannot be made. Once the teacher has offered this basic success, whether it be with written work, with oral work, with classroom tasks, with relationships, then the child can be helped to edge standards upwards. By first finding something the child can do, something the child can get right, the teacher lays the foundations for a more extensive realization of the child's potential.

Since most low self-esteem children and young people suffer low esteem in the eyes of their classmates (or can only attract high esteem through toughness and disruptive behaviour), the wise teacher will see to it that the success offered to such children is public success. Without overdoing things or making the strategy too apparent, the teacher will see to it that the rest of the class are aware of the success a low self-esteem pupil is now enjoying. A word of praise here, an approving comment there, may be all that is needed. Particularly where the class admire and respect their teacher, then the clear signs that he or she values the individual, indeed values all members of the class, will have a marked impact on class attitudes.

At the same time that he or she is building up the self-esteem of the vulnerable child, the wise teacher will also see to it that the self-esteem of everyone else is also protected. A high self-esteem child is less wounded by criticism or public failure than a low self-esteem child, but no child is immune from hurt. Unexpected failure, as when children receive poor marks in areas where they normally shine, is particularly daunting, as is the public humiliation of having to admit in front of the class to bad results. Thus the teacher is always ready with an appropriate, supportive comment. The marks weren't good, but perhaps that was because the child misunderstood the question; or because the groundwork hadn't been fully explained in class; or because the work had to be rushed for some reason. Whatever form of words the teacher chooses, it is essential to indicate to children that they mustn't be downhearted. There's always a reason when we don't come up to our own expectations. Poor marks are not a way of downgrading a child, simply of finding out what work still needs to be done.

This attitude towards marks and grades should permeate the teacher's whole approach. The purpose of any kind of testing should not be to test the child's attainment (or worse still 'ability') but to guide teacher and class in seeing where they go next. Low marks are of interest only in that they show a child needs more help, more guidance. To the golden rule that all children should be allowed to experience success we can add another one, that any activity in the class which discourages children from believing in their capacity to tackle a particular learning task or which discourages them from trying again, is bad education. And so is any activity which holds children up to ridicule in their own eyes or in the eyes of classmates.

Of course, in applying this rule we must bear always in mind that children differ from each other in what they construe as discouragement. To high self-esteem children, and particularly to children who also have extraverted, outgoing temperaments, a challenge, properly presented, is welcome. They enjoy the stimulus it provides. To low self-esteem children, such as a challenge, carrying with it the ever-present fear of failure, is a daunting prospect, and one against which they will defend either by hopelessness ('I can't do it') or by rejection ('It's a waste of time'). Only when the teacher knows the class well can the task be presented to children in the appropriate way: with a challenge to one child, with support and encouragement to another.

Conclusion

Personality, essentially, is the way in which we feel about and present ourselves to the world. It is the way in which we experience our own lives. To children and young people who are taught to experience themselves as failures, as of little significance, the world is a negative and dispiriting place. In the face of it, they develop strategies to try and protect their lack of personal worth, their overriding sense of failure. In one individual these strategies may take the form of hostility towards others; in another, an unwillingness to compete, to set oneself realistically high standards; in another, indifference or scorn or cynicism towards everything; in another, an exaggerated conceit which is quite the opposite of self-esteem (high self-esteem people accept and value themselves as they are, without any need to pretend to perfection). In all cases, one thing is clear. Individuals are unable to develop a realistic way of looking at themselves or at the real world. Locked into a personal sense of failure, they filter all experience through the bars of their prison, unable to function as objective observers of themselves and others, or to accept the common humanity which is the lot of all of us.

In its development, personality is crucially affected by the experiences which the home on the one hand and the school on the other have to offer. I once read a description of the teacher as a person who comes bearing gifts to children. Whether this is too fanciful a description or not I leave others to judge. But one gift that all teachers must bring is the belief and the encouragement that will allow children to believe in and accept their own selves. Without this gift, then the teacher would be better advised not to come at all.

References

COOPERSMITH, S. (1968) 'Studies in Self-esteem', in *Scientific American*, February.
FONTANA, D. (1986) *Teaching and Personality*, Oxford, Basil Blackwell.
LEWIS, M. (1972) 'State as in infant-environment interaction: an analysis of mother — infant behaviour as a function of sex', in *Merrill-Palmer Quarterly in Behavioural Development*, 18.
THOMAS, A., CHESS, S. and BIRCH, H. (1970) 'The origin of personality', *Scientific American*, August.

Chapter 14

Overcoming Learning Difficulties
Graham Upton

In ordinary schools the concept of a learning difficulty is often seen as being synonymous with remedial class placement or the pre-1981 Education Act category of Educational Subnormality. In such schools the concept of a learning difficulty is thus restricted to those children who have severe and obvious problems. In practice, the category is also usually specifically restricted to learning difficulties in the basic skills of reading, although in some schools it also takes in failure in mathematics, spelling and hand-writing.

In the light of the deliberations of the Warnock Report and the directives of the 1981 Education Act it is clear that the use of the term learning difficulty is too narrow. Indeed, such an understanding of the concept can be seen to hide the fact that large numbers of children experience learning difficulties. A sixth former, for example, who is absent from school for two weeks is likely to experience some learning difficulty on return to school; as is the child whose catarrh causes occasional hearing loss and the child for whom the death of a close relative causes a temporary disturbance in his or her emotional well-being and subsequent ability to concentrate in class.

A common practice in the past has been to identify children as having a learning difficulty only when there is a severe discrepancy between their chronological or mental age and their performance. An often-used criterion for deciding whether a child has a learning problem has been a two-year discrepancy between assessed performance in reading (usually on a standard reading test) and simple chronological or mental age (based on performance on a test of intellectual ability). At the same time in many Local Authorities and schools the identification of children with learning problems has been directly related to the availability of special class places or special teaching. Thus, if a high school has staffing to provide only one remedial class, then only the twenty (or fifteen or twenty-five) children with the lowest attainments will officially be classed as having learning problems. Other children, irrespective of their level of attainments, will of necessity be placed in ordinary classes, frequently without support. Whatever the policy it is clear that both approaches result in the identification of only those children whose problems are the most severe. Yet children whose problems are less severe are equally in need of special attention — a child whose reading level is one year behind his or her chronological age could experience considerable difficulty in coping with reading material in an examination stream.

This concern with only the most severe problems has also tended to obscure the fact that children can experience learning problems in any area of school work. The concept of learning difficulties has, as was noted above, focused on failure in the basic skills. The importance of this cannot be underestimated as children who fail to master the three Rs are clearly disadvantaged in all other aspects of their education and obviously need help to overcome such pervasive difficulties. However, a more adequate definition of the term must recognize that failure in other areas of school work deserves attention also. (See Chapters 11 and 12 for a fuller discussion). Equally, there is a need to recognize that learning difficulties can be transitory. In the past almost all special help has been directed towards problems which are relatively long-term in nature — special class placement, for example, can cover a child's entire school career. Yet for many children the problem may not require special class placement or even regular remedial help. Learning difficulties may occur in any school subject and may only require minimal intervention from the ordinary class or subject teacher. A more adequate definition of the term must acknowledge that there are children in every class who experience learning difficulties; children who fail to profit from instruction in the same way as the rest of the class.

Why do Children Experience Learning Difficulties?

Why children experience learning difficulties is a question which puzzles many teachers. Rightly so, perhaps, because this is a question for which there are no simple answers. Two case studies illustrate the difficulty of determining causes. Both of these children exhibit clear learning difficulties but in each case it is only possible to hypothesize about the causes of their problems.

John

John is in the second form of an ordinary comprehensive school. He is in an ordinary class but is a very poor reader. When he was tested (on the Neale

Analysis of Reading Ability) at the end of Form 1 when he was 12½, his accuracy of oral reading was 8 years and 6 months, his speed of reading was 8 years and 3 months and his comprehension was 9 years and 5 months. His spelling was equally poor and a piece of his free writing reveals the extent and severity of his spelling problems.

> 'one Saturday moring it was raing very hard I did not thing that the corrse wood be palpell but I still went to the corrso we perite went but we had to play becouse it was a finel it was a vere hard mach becouse we were slipeng all over the corrse. I was lucke to win that mach becouse I hade the edvenich of being abell to macke him run when he slit on the wen sand.'

To some extent this piece of work highlights the puzzling nature of the problem John presents. If the spelling errors are ignored in this passage, the expression, and the quality of thought that is reflected in it, are good, as can be seen in the following corrected version of the writing.

> On Saturday morning it was raining very hard. I did not think that the courts would be playable but I still went to the courts. It was pretty wet but we had to play because it was a final. It was a very hard match because we were slipping all over the courts. I was lucky to win that match because I had the advantage of being able to make him run and when he ran he slipped on the wet sand.

In oral work in class, especially in individual conversation, John clearly functions at a much higher level than his reading or spelling suggests. This discrepancy was reflected in an intelligence test given to him at the same time as his reading test. On this test (the Weschler Intelligence Scale for Children) John obtained a Verbal score of 103, a Performance score of 118 and a Full-scale score of 111, which scores place him at the upper end of the average category. Similarly, his mathematical attainments were of a much higher standard than his reading and spelling. Because he had been withdrawn for some remedial teaching he had not followed the usual mathematics syllabus and his performance in maths cannot be compared to that of his contemporaries. However, on a test of basic computational skills (the Schonell Graded Mathematics — Arithmetic Test) he was found to be functioning at levels close to that expected of his chronological age.

In other ways, John also displayed a high level of general ability and competence. His school report describes him as a strong, athletic boy and an excellent tennis player who has reached the equivalent of county standard for his age. His family background also could by no means be seen as one which might have led to such a severe learning difficulty. The family live in a somewhat run-down inner city area but the physical conditions of the home are good. The house is, in fact, a detached one with a large garden in an area of mainly terraced houses. His father is self-employed and has a small but apparently successful delivery business. The house is in good repair and is well furnished. John always comes to school in uniform and is invariably clean and tidy. Nor is he lacking in support and encouragement from his parents. While his father was 'never too bright at schoolwork' his mother trained as a nurse and both seem committed to the importance of education. His two elder sisters are in the same school, both in upper band classes and both expected to proceed to 'A' level work.

John is clearly an anxious child and his reading problems seem to be a continuing source of concern to him. However, he relates well with his peers, and seems to have a good circle of friends. In class his teacher says that he is by no means an angel but he is generally well-behaved and is certainly not a behaviour problem in any way. His attendance is excellent. In his entire primary school career he missed only twelve days and in Form 1 had missed no days at all.

That John has a learning problem cannot be disputed. Why he has such a problem is more difficult to determine. He appears to be an otherwise bright child, is well-motivated and comes from a supportive family. The only explanation in this instance seems to be what has been described as a specific learning difficulty — some sort of neurologically-based weakness which prevents the child from learning a specific skill but which does not interfere with other areas of functioning. As John's main problem is primarily in reading he can be described as possibly dyslexic. Such a term is essentially only a hypothesis and its existence has been a matter of some controversy (see below for a discussion of this) but in cases like this it seems the only relevant explanation.

Julie

Julie, on the other hand, presents a very different problem. While in John's case it is difficult to see anything that may be causing his problems, in Julie's case the difficulty is to distinguish between a whole host of influences, any one of which could have caused her difficulties.

Julie is in Form 3, in a remedial class. Her learning difficulty is more general than John's. At the age of 13 years and 6 months her reading was assessed (using the Neale Analysis of Reading Ability again) and her reading age in terms of accuracy of oral reading was 7 years and 10 months; speed of reading, 9 years; and comprehension 6 years and 9 months. Her performance in mathematics was marginally better but still well below that of her chronological age. In other subjects her work is similarly weak. While she was in junior school she had, in fact, been recommended for special school placement twice, but on both occasions this had been resisted by her parents. Assessments of her level of intellectual functioning have suggested a generally depressed level of performance. Immediately before her transfer to secondary school she was tested on the Weschler Intelligence Scale for Children and recorded a Verbal score of 84, a Performance score of 75 and a Full-scale score of 77. These scores place her well below the average range.

The reasons for her problems seem to lie in a complex array of individual difficulties and adverse family and social influences. First of all, Julie has a number of physical ailments and health problems. She is asthmatic, has a minor heart defect and was diagnosed in early childhood as possibly having suffered some degree of brain damage at birth — 'difficult birth' is recorded in her medical records as are 'convulsions' in the pre-school period. She does not take part in any physical activities at school and is 'excused' from all games and PE. Indeed her family presents an extraordinary range of chronic health problems. Her mother was also asthmatic, grossly overweight and had a heart ailment which resulted in her death while Julie was in Form 2. Her elder sister is also a chronic asthmatic and her younger brother is severely mentally handicapped. Her father is under medical treatment for a back injury suffered at work.

The physical and emotional conditions of life of the family are also very poor. The home is a small and somewhat dilapidated terraced house in a very run-down inner city area. It is in a very bad state of repair, and reported by Social Services to be extremely dirty and poorly furnished. Julie's father is a spray-painter but is rarely in work. Since her mother's death, the housework and cooking seem to have been delegated almost entirely to Julie, although it is suspected that this was happening previously also. Immediately after the mother's death the children were taken into care for a short period but the father is currently judged to cope reasonably well with the family. It is, however, not a family which provides a great deal of motivation for education. Julie, for example, has missed a lot of time from school. In the second form (when her mother died) she was absent for seventy-four days but prior to this had missed an average of forty-four days a year. All of these absences were apparently condoned as excuses were always provided by the parents. When she is at school Julie is also something of a behaviour problem. She has been described by her teachers at various times as 'a most unstable girl' who 'frequently breaks into temper tantrums', 'suffers from dizzy spells' and 'often complains of feeling unwell'. She belongs to a small group of very aggressive and anti-social girls who seem to be frequently involved in fights, both in and out of school.

In sum, we have in Julie a child against whom everything seems to have conspired to create her academic failure. Her health problems, family background, adjustment problems, lack of special schooling and her generally limited ability could all be seen as the causes of her academic failure. Whether any of these is more important than the others is not clear but such a differentiation of influences is to some extent academic in that, in reality, all must have contributed to her difficulties. This is clearly a case of a pupil with serious learning difficulties and a depressing combination of severe adverse environmental and individual problems. It is not, however, atypical of the difficulties experienced by many children.

In practice it is difficult to be specific about the causes of any child's learning difficulty. At the same time various factors have been found to be associated with the existence of learning difficulties and these do give some insight into the problems some children present. Some of these are characteristics of the individual, some originate in the child's family or social environment while others originate in the school.

Intelligence

Perhaps the most common explanation of children's learning difficulties is the notion that they reflect limited intellectual ability. Thus, in school staff-rooms children are often referred to as 'thick' or as 'dumbos' or with some other similarly pejorative term while more formally we talk of 'slow learners' and 'the less able'.

There is evidence on a variety of levels which support such thinking. At the extreme end of the intellectual spectrum, for example, children whom we label as mentally or intellectually handicapped have severe and usually very obvious learning difficulties. Similarly, at the other end of the scale there are 'gifted' children who seem to find learning more easy than most other children. IQ scores, in spite of all the criticism of them that abounds, do also have a high positive correlation with school attainments. However, other than in cases of severe mental handicap it is difficult to ascribe causality to a child's limited intellectual functioning.

The reasons for this revolve around the definition of intelligence. To talk of intelligence as a cause of a child's learning progress or failure assumes the existence of intelligence as an underlying feature of an individual's make-up. Such a feature is viewed as setting limits for development; it is presumably genetically based and primarily determines, rather than is affected by, learning. While some authors still espouse such views the majority conceptualize intelligence as developing out of the interaction between this genetic endowment and environmental experiences (see Rutter and Madge, 1976, Chapter 6). In this sense, intelligence itself consists of learned behaviours and this is reflected in the sort of items contained in intelligence tests. Any child's performance on such a test will reflect his or her already acquired academic success in reading and mathematics which frequently constitute a large part of such tests.

From this perspective, to use the concept of intelligence or an IQ score as a guide to a child's expected level of performance is clearly unacceptable. The measure of intelligence is a measure of attainment and this cannot be validly used to predict performance in other (especially similar) areas to those sampled in the test. While we might expect a child to perform as well in a reading test as he or she does in an intelligence test a depressed level of functioning on one test should not be used to set limits on our expectations for performance in other areas. In cases where a child's IQ score exceeds his or her attainments in other areas this may help us to have positive expectations for that child, but such reasoning can be dangerous when performance in both areas is low. One example may serve to illustrate the problem.

Robert

Robert is now in the bottom stream of the third form in a comprehensive school. When he entered high school he came from a special class in Junior School and was placed in a special class in the High School. His attainments were certainly low with reading and mathematics ages around the 8 to 9 year level. He arrived with the label of a slow learner and an assessed IQ of 76. To the teachers Robert was clearly a child from whom one could not expect a great deal — indeed, in view of his low ability his attainments could be considered to be quite reasonable. During the year, however, his teachers became increasingly convinced that Robert was a much more able child than his IQ score suggested. No details had been provided about the IQ testing but enquiries eventually revealed that a group verbal test had been used and that this had been administered some four years previously when Robert was virtually a non-reader. That he had scored so poorly on a test which requires the child to read the items silently was not surprising. Re-testing on a test which was conducted orally and which also involved a high proportion of non-verbal items (the Weschler Intelligence Scale) produced scores in the average to above-average range.

Clearly this use of an inappropriate test was reprehensible and hopefully represents a rare occurrence. But the fact that this did happen is not the point of the example. Rather it was the effect that this labelling had on the teachers who taught Robert that was important. Expectations for Robert were very different when he was seen as a slow learner with an IQ of 76 to when he was seen as a boy of at least average ability. Similar difficulties have recently been highlighted in the assessment of children from ethnic minority groups whose abilities do not appear to be adequately assessed by tests designed for a group with differing cultural experiences.

These comments should not be taken to suggest that children do not differ in intellectual ability. Clearly, they do, and equally obviously these differences must affect performance in school. At a common sense level, limited intellectual ability can be seen as a cause of a child's learning difficulties, but when we try to be more precise than common sense will allow we run into difficulty. If we could assess innate differences in ability then we could be more accurate. But innate differences in ability presumably depend on the efficiency of neurological functioning and at present we do not have the technology to assess that. What we do have are tests designed to measure relatively small aspects of intellectual development. The use of these measures to predict levels of functioning in other areas, however, is clearly something which is open to dispute and wherein great caution must be exercised.

Home Background

Home background is similarly frequently seen as an important determinant of school success and failure. The identification of the important features of home background is fraught with difficulty but even a feature as obvious as father's occupation has been found to be linked with academic progress from an early age. Evidence from the National Child Development Study (Davie *et al.*, 1972) provides striking evidence of this. This study, which is a longitudinal one and which has involved a sample of some 17,000 children (all the children born in Britain in one week in 1958) has, among many other things, looked at children's performance in school and related it to the Registrar General's classification of occupations. In this system families are placed in social class groups according to the father's occupation — no account is taken of the mother's occupation and the lack of a male 'head of household' results in no social class classification. The categories as used in the National Child Development Study are as follows:

Class

I	Higher Professional
II	Other Professional and Technical
III(i)	Non-Manual — other Non-Manual occupations
III(ii)	Manual — Skilled Manual
IV	Semi-skilled Manual
V	Unskilled Manual

When children's performance at school at the age of seven was related to this categorization the results revealed a striking association. In Figure 14.1 it can

	Class I	Class II	Class III (non-manual)	Class III (manual)	Class IV	Class V	Total percentage of population
LOW ORAL ABILITY	4%	10%	10%	24%	29%	39%	22%
BELOW AVERAGE AWARENESS OF THE WORLD AROUND	5%	12%	14%	30%	37%	53%	37%
POOR PROBLEM ARITHMETIC SCORE (0–3)	12%	20%	20%	30%	33%	40%	30%
POOR 'SOUTHGATE' READING TEST SCORE	8%	15%	14%	30%	38%	50%	30%

(Source: Davie *et al.*, 1972)

Figure 14.1: Social Class and Academic Achievement

be seen that children from the lower social class groups have many more problems than children from higher groupings. As Davie *et al.* point out in relation to reading at 7 years of age:

> the chances of an unskilled manual worker's child being a poor reader are six times greater than those of a professional worker's child...the chances of a social class V child being a non-reader are fifteen times greater than those of a social class I child (p. 102).

And, in more general terms,

> the difference between social class I and II and those from social class V is equivalent to nearly 17 months of reading age at age seven (p. 176).

Four years later at age 11 when these children were tested again the gap had widened to 27 months.

Such findings typify the outcome of many other studies and as Rutter and Madge (1976) note 'it has been commonly claimed that parental poverty and low social status lead children to fail at school' (p.80). The weight of evidence suggests strong inter-generational influences on attainment but this does not mean that we can assume a direct causal connection between particular aspects of family background and school performance. Clearly we can't because while 50 per cent of Davie's social class five children were poor readers at age seven, the other 50 per cent were not. Thus, home background, *per se*, cannot be seen as a cause of learning problems.

How then can this inter-generational continuity be accounted for? Many possible explanations exist. At one level, life, for children from deprived home backgrounds, is simply more demanding and problematic. Children who come to school from home circumstances such as those of Julie referred to above can hardly be blamed for having a limited interest in academic learning. Similarly the attitudes of some families towards education in general and to schools in particular are hostile; an attitude which has been exacerbated in recent times for many young people by high levels of unemployment and increasing disillusionment with the value of education as a passport to vocational success.

At the same time, it is important to recognize that for many children schools constitute an alien environment where they are required to cope with activities which have no apparent relevance to the immediate demands of their life. From this perspective, it is interesting to speculate to what extent the differences in reading attainment identified by Davie *et al.* can be accounted for by the use of reading schemes where children go to concerts and on Sundays for picnics in the countryside with their Mummy and Daddy. Equally, teachers' expectations should not be underestimated as powerful determinants of children's performance in school. (For a fuller discussion, see Chapter 2). Arguably, the child with learning problems who comes from a depressed home background will be seen as having less chance of overcoming their problems than the child from a more affluent family. For some children school can be a place where you prove that you are able, for others it is a place where you must prove you are not unable; and this is an important difference.

Emotional and Behaviour Problems

The relationships between emotional and behavioural development and academic success has frequently been the subject of research (see, e.g., Ramasut and Upton, 1983). The results of this are amazingly consistent, and demonstrate an undisputable relationship between poor educational attainments and emotional and behavioural problems. Different studies have revealed some variation in the association. Typical of the pattern of many authors, however, Upton (1978) using data from the National Child Development Study found the association shown in Figure 14.2 in relation to reading ability amongst 11-year-olds.

These scores show a clear trend whereby the poor readers tend to show a higher degree of maladjustment than the good readers, the majority of whom can be seen to be well adjusted.

Why such a relationship exists is not clear in spite of many attempts to explain it (see, e.g., Davie *et al.*, 1972). Some have focused on the possibility of emotional and behaviour problems causing school failure as a result of the child's poor concentration and poor relationship with teachers and high anxiety. Others have reversed the causal chain and explain the emotional and behavioural problems as the result of failure and consequent feelings of inadequacy, parental anxiety and over compensation. Yet others have viewed the emotional and behavioural problems and the learning difficulties as disparate manifestations of the same underlying problems (e.g. brain damage; unstable home circumstances; parental rejection).

While the above explanations have obvious value, they all imply one-directional causality. To some authors (see, e.g., Upton, 1983) it seems more appropriate to conceive of the relationship between the two as being more complex. A more satisfactory model on which to base such explanations is seen as a circular and interactive one in which the various elements referred to above might interact with one another in a dynamic fashion. Thus, like the proverbial vicious circle, the emotional and behaviour problems, the learning difficulty, the parental behaviour, the teacher behaviour and the child all interact with and react to one another to generate the pattern between the emotional and behaviour problems and learning difficulties.

Once again, however, the association is one of correlation rather than cause. While the pattern is strong it is clear from Figure 14.2 that the association is not invariable. Thus, many children who exhibit learning difficulties do not display emotional or behavioural problems, and vice versa. Unfortunately, there is currently no way of knowing why the link sometimes exists and why at other times there is no such connection. The strength of the link, nonetheless, merits our attention and awareness of it is clearly valuable in any attempt to understand any specific classroom problem.

Reading Ability[2]	Behaviour Rating[1]			
	Low Score	Moderate Score	High Score	Very High Score
Bottom 30%	46.3	28.9	17.5	7.3
Middle 40%	69.9	20.2	7.5	2.3
Top 30%	81.5	14.1	3.7	0.7

1. Based on teachers' ratings using the Bristol Social Adjustment Guide.
   A low score indicates good adjustment, a very high score poor adjustment.
2. Reading ages classified according to score from low to high.

Figure 14.2: Behaviour Rating Score and Reading Ability

Specific Learning Difficulties

As noted in John's case study some people have postulated the existence of specific learning difficulties. One of the earliest definitions (1968) of these, but one which is still current, is that of the United States National Advisory Committee on Handicapped Children. It states that:

> Children with specific learning disabilities exhibit a disorder in one or more of the basic psychological processes invoved in understanding or using spoken or written languages. These may be manifested in disorders of listening, thinking, talking, reading, writing, spelling or arithmetic. They include conditions which have been referred to as perceptual handicaps, brain injury, minimal brain dysfunction, dyslexia, developmental aphasia, etc. They do not include learning problems which are due primarily to visual, hearing, or motor handicaps, to mental retardation, emotional disturbance, or to environmental disadvantage.

In other words what is envisaged here are puzzling cases such as that of John where children have a learning difficulty in one of the basic skill areas in spite of apparently good ability in other areas of functioning. Problems of this kind in reading (dyslexia) have attracted most professional and public interest but attention has also been given to similar difficulties in arithmetic (dyscalculia), writing (dysgraphia) and language (dysphasia).

For many years the concept of a specific learning disability has been the subject of considerable controversy (see Young and Tyre, 1983). While many have ardently advocated its existence others have denied it. For example, until recently the DES refused to recognize dyslexia as a problem for which special educational treatment could be provided. In 1972 a specially appointed DES Committee reported 'there is... very little empirical basis for the view that dyslexia "exists" as a specific condition' (DES, 1972). They argued that the problem could not be distinguished from other instances of reading difficulty. More recently, largely as the result of parental pressure, attitudes in Britain, at least, have changed and the 1981 Education Act included reference to specific learning difficulties.

While the official recognition of the concept has allowed the provision of special help for children thus identified, the problem itself has been no more clearly defined than it was previously. In most cases, it remains a definition by inclusion; one which can explain the existence of a problem when no other explanation appears sufficient. While this may sound vague and unsatisfactory, the concept can in some cases prove to be a helpful explanation for a problem; one which presents the most puzzling of problems in a positive light. In John's case it certainly helped teachers to adopt more constructive and sympathetic teaching methods. It is a concept which can be helpful in understanding an otherwise inexplicable problem, albeit that such an explanation is relevant in only a small number of cases.

The School

In recent years considerable attention has been given to the extent to which schools themselves may be regarded as causal agents in the generation of learning problems. The factors which have been reviewed so far in this chapter have all involved aspects of individual, familial or social pathology. Traditionally, explanations of learning problems have implicated such factors as affecting the child's ability to benefit from the educational process and resulting in failure to learn. In such conceptualizations of learning problems the school has been treated as a black box, the inner workings of which were seen to be at most a neutral, and in most cases a positive, influence on the child's educational progress. Since the early 1970s, however, there has been a growing awareness of the existence of marked school differences in the attainment of pupils.

Elsewhere in this book (see Chapter 6) research literature in this area has been thoroughly reviewed by David Reynolds and it is inappropriate to cover that ground again here. However, it would be equally inappropriate to attempt to identify causes of learning problems without reference to the school. While it may be painful for teachers to recognize that they may excuse as well as prevent and ameliorate learning problems, it does not reflect well on the integrity of the profession to do other than recognize the potential of the schools as a negative as well as a positive influence.

Within schools, the role of the teacher in creating academic success (and failure) is crucial. Clearly most teachers would wish to see their contribution to children's learning in a positive light but there are situations where the teacher can be seen as a cause of learning difficulties. In mathematics, for example, children are taught for the first seven years of schooling by teachers who frequently have limited mathematical abilities themselves and in reading the now classic study by Morris (1972) drew attention to the lack of preparation of most primary school teachers to teach those children who leave infant class with only a limited command of basic reading skills. It would not be surprising if children in the charge of such teachers fail to make maximum progress. Similarly, stereotypical attitudes among teachers towards mathematics and science could be seen to underlie the wide differences which exist between the attainments of boys and girls in these subjects at secondary level.

Does it matter if we don't understand Causation?

It is apparent from this brief summary of factors which have been seen as having a causal link with learning problems that much remains unknown. More research may help to clarify the situation and in the future it is possible that a more specific delineation of cases may be achieved. In most cases, however, it is not important or necessary to know why a problem exists in order to help a child to overcome it. What is important is what is done about the problem; what the teacher attempts to do to overcome it.

All too often knowledge of a cause can lead to inaction rather than action. Faced with a knowledge of the problems experienced by Julie, many teachers may be inclined to adjudge the situation beyond help. Yet, need any of Julie's home or health problems necessarily affect her learning or her relationship with her teacher? The experience of special education is frequently that this need not matter. Such children when placed in a special class frequently respond positively and make good progress in spite of their problems. Given appropriate work and a positive relationship such children often overcome serious and previously intransigent learning difficulties. Children with severe learning difficulties which arise from sensory, physical or mental handicaps need specialized help in order to overcome their problems but this does not appear to be the case with the majority of children who experience milder forms of difficulty. In the author's experience such children require little more than good teaching and a positive climate in which to work.

Guidelines for Teaching

A. Establish a Positive Relationship

When confronted by children who present learning dificulties, perhaps the single most important factor is the teacher's attitude to the children and their problems. To have spent time preparing work to which children fail to respond can be a frustrating and annoying experience. The reaction of many teachers is to see the child in a negative light and to lay the blame for the problem solely on the child. It is all too easy to assume that there is something wrong with the child, that otherwise the child would surely respond to the teaching that was provided. Thus, as was noted in the previous section, we tend to emphasize problems of individual and family pathology to explain such problems. In staff-room jargon problems seem to be all too often explained away in terms of the children being described as 'thickos', 'hellers', 'nutters', 'estate children' or as 'yet another one of those Robertsons'.

On the other hand, if we can view the difficulty as being more of a problem for the teacher, then we can free ourselves to interact more positively with these children. While this is undoubtedly easier to say than to do, the importance of good relationships cannot be overestimated. A good illustration of the significance of relationships when working with children who present learning difficulties has been provided by Lawrence (1973). Lawrence was concerned primarily with children with reading problems but his ideas have clear evidence to all areas of school learning. Lawrence started with the assumption that in remedial reading it is the relationship between the teacher and the child that is of prime importance and that things like the reading scheme used and the choice of teaching method are of secondary importance. Lawrence, furthermore, sees the main barriers to a poor reader's progress as being emotional and attaches particular importance to the negative self-image the poor reader frequently develops. To Lawrence any attempt to help a child with reading problems should focus on helping the child to develop a more positive view of himself or herself which he feels can only be achieved through a positive relationship.

To demonstrate the validity of his views Lawrence conducted a two-stage project. In the first part of this he took four village primary schools and selected twelve poor readers from each school matched for sex, age, IQ and reading attainment. A different type of intervention was then provided for each group of children. In the first school the children received individual personal counselling for one session per week over a period of two terms; in the second school the children received similar individual counselling but also received remedial reading instruction; the children in the third school received remedial teaching only; while those children in the fourth school received no additional assistance to that provided by their ordinary class teachers. The counselling which the children in the first two groups received was characterized, according to Lawrence, by the following features:

Methods used with Counselling Group

1. The counsellor introduced himself or herself as a person interested in children and who liked to ensure that they were happy.

2. The establishment of an uncritical, friendly atmosphere, involving total acceptance of the child was attempted.

3. The counsellor tried to provide a sounding board for the child's feelings — direct interpretation was avoided.

4.   The interview was child-centred throughout.

5.   As a rule direct questioning was avoided.

6.   Discussion at first was only possible through the medium of pictures and drawings. The child was shown other pictures as a stimulus to feelings.

7.   Early in the period the child was asked for three main wishes and each discussed more fully.

8.   Throughout the interview the counsellor tried to be alert for opportunities of praising the child's personality (not skills), and in so doing, building up self-image.

9.   The following areas of the child's life were covered over the counselling period: relationships with parents; relationships with siblings; relationships with peers; relationships with other relatives; hobbies and interests; aspirations, immediate and long-term; worries, fears, anxieties; attitude towards school; and attitude towards self.

The results of this part of the project were startling, to say the least. When Lawrence looked at the progress the children had made in reading during the two terms occupied by the project, the group which had improved most was the group which had received only the counselling. This group had made more progress than the group which had received remedial help as well as the counselling; they in turn had improved more than the group which had received remedial reading only and the group which had been subject to no specialist intervention. The results obtained seem to suggest that remedial teaching is, in fact, of little value. However, it must be pointed out that no attempt was made by Lawrence to determine the quality of the remedial teaching and that methodologically the comparisons made cannot be justifiably taken to imply the absolute value of the counselling approach.

   The second phase of the project produced even more surprising results in some ways. While the first part of the project had produced remarkable results it is open to criticism in that the counselling had been provided by a specialist, a facility which is not readily available in most schools. However, in Lawrence's view what the counsellor had done in stage one was no more than to value these children and to provide them with help characterized by skills which are not the exclusive domain of the specialist counsellor. Rather, he saw them as natural features of any positive human relationship. To illustrate this contention, Lawrence decided to repeat the experiment using non-professional people as counsellors. He, first of all, took two schools in which he tried out his ideas in a tentative pilot study and then extended this to include four other schools. He took twelve children who were experiencing reading problems in each school and split them into two groups of six matched for age, sex, IQ and reading attainments. The children in the one group then received 'counselling sessions' once a week for two terms while the other group acted as controls and received their usual classroom instruction.

On this occasion the counselling was provided by mothers of other children at the school. They were selected by the head teacher of the schools (on the basis that they were sympathetic, intelligent and interested) and provided with three training sessions before the counselling started and a further three as the project progressed. The results were not as clear-cut as in the initial project but in three of the four groups the counselled group did make significantly greater progress in reading.

While attempts to replicate Lawrence's findings have not always been successful (see, e.g., Coles, 1977) his focus on the importance of relationships certainly accord with the present author's experience of remedial teaching wherein the children who make the most progress are the ones with whom a positive relationship is established. Clearly, there is a classic chicken and egg situation here and it is not possible to say whether the good relationship precedes the improvement or vice versa. To ignore the importance of the positive interaction and to focus solely on the traditional role of teaching would seem to be more than a little foolish. The negative reactions which many children who fail display does, of course, mean that developing such positive relationships is not always easy. However, it is an orientation with which it is clearly important to persevere.

B. Have Positive Expectations

While it is important not to overestimate what children are capable of achieving it is equally important not to underestimate their potential. However, with children who present learning difficulties their previous failure can all too easily come to set the teacher's level of expectations for future progress. That a child has failed in the past often results in the expectation that he or she will continue to fail. Such an assumption can, of course, be a perfectly valid assessment of a child, but in other cases this can be an unfairly negative expectation. Unfair not only in the sense that it may not be a correct evaluation of a child's ability but unfair also in that it may affect our interaction with that child in ways that overtly and covertly influence the child's progress. It does appear that our expectations for children can come to serve as self-fulfilling prophecies for those children.

Thus, if we expect children to fail it is likely that they will do so, while if one expects them to succeed then success is more likely.

A striking illustration of the importance of teachers' expectations has been provided by two American researchers called Rosenthal and Jacobson (1968). (This is also discussed in Chapter 2). In order to assess the extent to which teachers' expectations can affect children's performance they devised a very cunning experiment. They went into a school where their stated aim was to try out a new test which they said they were developing, the purpose of which was to help pick out children who might be expected to make good progress in the near future. Children who may not be doing well at the moment but who could be 'academic bloomers' in the future. Having spent some time in the school ostensibly 'piloting' this new test, they left. But, before they left they told the teachers the names of some children who, according to the results of their testing, might be children who were about to blossom in the way described above. No great fuss was made about this, names were simply presented for information.

At various intervals over the next two years they came back to the school and found that many of these children had made progress as predicted.

What a useful test, you might say. The twist in this story, however, is that the test was not a new test, indeed it was a standard test of general intellectual ability. Furthermore, the names given to the teachers had been selected at random. In other words there was no reason to expect those who made progress to do so, other than their teachers' expectations that this would occur. In addition, it did not appear that the teachers had consciously gone out of their way to promote more work or a more stimulating environment for these children. When asked to recall the names which had been given to them, the teachers could remember only some of the names. In other words, it seems that the progress made by these children reflects an unconscious change in their teachers' attitudes towards them. The fact that the teachers expected more of these children presumably permeated their relationship with the children who in turn came to expect more of themselves and thus produce more.

While one experiment cannot be taken as conclusive and met with limited success (see Pilling and Pringle, 1978), it does highlight the importance of our assessment of a child's abilities. It is not always possible or realistic to be optimistic about some children's chances of success but it does seem that a positive expectation can go a long way to initiating improvement. If children feel incompetent and if in his or her manner the teacher confirms this view then it seems highly likely that the child will continue to hold it and behave accordingly. If, on the other hand, teachers say or imply in their behaviour that they feel the child is capable of better, then it is possible the child may also come to feel that, or at least to question his or her own negative self-evaluations.

C. Provide Work at their Level

If children are experiencing difficulties in any aspect of school learning it is vital that any work which is provided for them is at an appropriate level of difficulty. Work which is too difficult will clearly not produce a positive response among children who have experienced failure. Repeated exposure to work they cannot do can only lead to a lower level of motivation and interest. Unless you are faced with a homogeneous group of children, this means that work must be individualized. To the ordinary classroom teacher this may sound unrealistic. Admittedly it is not easy, but if a genuine attempt is going to be made to help the child in difficulty it is essential. The chapters in Section II give guidance and help in a variety of subject areas. However, it is worth reiterating that the most obvious way in which work must be individualized is in terms of the relationship between the work provided and the child's present level of mastery of the subject involved. In subjects like mathematics the importance of this is obvious for mathematics is, in large measure, a hierarchical subject, wherein the failure to master lower-order skills directly interferes with the learning of higher-order skills. Similar hierarchical learning is also apparent in practical subjects and languages although this case may be arguable. In subjects where the existence of a hierarchical arrangement of knowledge is less obvious, or arguably non-existent, it is not always easy to determine just how the child's present difficulties relate to his or her general command of the subject. However, it would, for example, be inappropriate in any subject to expect a child to undertake work involving critical judgement or inferential evaluation when that child has not achieved a basic understanding of the subject matter.

A common problem in providing work at an appropriate level is the readability of teaching materials. For children who experience any degree of reading difficulty work must be presented at a level commensurate with their reading ability. If a child cannot easily read the material which is presented, be it a poem or mathematics problem, then clearly any work based on that material is unlikely to be completed with a great degree of success. Textbooks, worksheets, blackboard notes and any other written material should be chosen or prepared with this in mind. Otherwise, a reading problem can very quickly become a more general learning difficulty.

Preparing work at an appropriate reading level is not a difficult task and is certainly not one which necessarily requires specialist skills. Reading experts may debate the finer points of establishing specific reading levels but

for most teachers such fine tailoring is unrealistic and is probably unnecessary. Rather, what is required is a 'rough match' between a child's ability to
read and the reading content of any material that is used. Newspapers, for
example, seem to pitch their product at an appropriate level of difficulty for
their target audience without a great deal of specialist help. Indeed, the way
in which different newspapers cover the same story represents a perfect
example of what is being suggested here. Similarly, within any one
newspaper different sections are clearly written at different levels —
compare, for example, the sports page with the international affairs or
business sections.

There are, in fact, no hard and fast rules which govern the readability of
written material but there are some general principles which can be used, viz:

1. Avoid long words (particularly words of three or more syllables or
   more than 7/8 letters).
2. Try to use words that are common and regular in their pronunciation.
3. Use short sentences as much as possible.
4. Avoid complex grammatical structures.
5. Be aware of, and use, the children's language where possible.
6. Keep the number of technical terms to the minimum required.
7. Make sure that any technical terms particular to the subject are
   understood by all the pupils.

Not all long words are necessarily hard to read, nor are all long sentences.
However, as generalizations these pointers can be used to good effect. To
some extent providing work at an appropriate reading level is no more than a
matter of teacher sensitivity. Once you are aware of the need to simplify
material, to do so is not difficult.

D. Provide them with Success

The old adage, 'nothing succeeds like success', is particularly pertinent when
dealing with children who experience learning difficulties. Their previous
educational difficulties frequently result in them becoming disaffected and
showing limited interest in schoolwork. As a result they can come to be seen
by teachers as difficult and unrewarding to teach, which attitudes, in turn,
can lead to even lower levels of motivation, and ultimately to an ever-
tightening downward spiral whereby nothing the teacher does seems to
inspire the slightest flicker of interest or enthusiasm. In order to break this
cycle it is the present author's contention that such children require
experience of success and additional effort to motivate them and to reinforce
them for what work they do carry out.

It is never easy to break into a vicious circle such as is involved here but to do so seems essential to the success of any attempt to help a child overcome a learning difficulty. The most obvious way of doing this is by providing the child with success experiences and such experiences will flow naturally from work which is at the right level of difficulty for the child and which progresses through appropriately sequenced steps (see, e.g., Ainscow and Tweddle, 1979). At the same time it is possible to structure games and other classroom activities to improve a child's self image and many useful ideas for this can be found in Canfield and Wells (1976).

In some cases the level of interest may be so low that an individually prepared reinforcement programme is necessary. Detailed guidelines for how this might be done are provided in publications such as that of Wheldall (1987) but for the majority of children more informal procedures can be effective. It is surprising what effect a word of praise or interested enquiry can have on a child whose previous interactions with a teacher have been more concerned with correcting errors in work or harangues about the need for greater effort.

However, ensuring that children with learning problems experience success in school involves issues of school policy as much as it concerns the individual teacher. Subtle messages about status and worth can be conveyed to children by many aspects of administrative policy. The status of the teachers assigned to work with lower streams, for example, can provide a very clear message to the children about how they are perceived by the school. The common practice of assigning young and inexperienced staff to work with special groups while the more experienced staff get on with examination work is a very clear message to children that their work is not highly regarded and the attitudes of some teachers to low-attaining groups is sometimes less professional than one might hope it would be. The statement, 'I've got some Sixth Form marking to do 3R. What I would like you to do this period is to get on with some work of your own... QUIETLY!! Understood?...', reflects an approach that is heard in many schools on many occasions. Such an attitude would seem unlikely to encourage children to 'try' next time the teacher feels inclined to teach them. The importance of the work of all children should be reflected in all school practice and the success achieved by children accorded equal status.

Institutional Considerations

It has long been recognized in special and remedial education that children who experience learning difficulties need some degree of individualized attention. Thus, special schools and classes have traditionally functioned with lower pupil-teacher ratios than ordinary schools. If an ordinary school realistically hopes to cater for children with learning difficulties, due recognition must be given to this need. For some children this may mean placement in a small class group but for the majority of them it will more realistically mean procedures being designed to ensure that each child's needs are recognized and catered for in ordinary classes without the luxury of any additional resources.

Such an emphasis on the individual clearly goes beyond the sole responsibility of the teacher, although the individual teacher may be the focus of the school's interaction with the child. The extent to which a school is effective in meeting the special child's need for individual attention is a matter for policy as much as it is a matter of the actions of any teacher. In the author's experience central to a school's effectiveness in this regard appear to be:

A. The Concern and Interest of Senior Management

Unless the headteacher and other members of the school's senior management feel that attempts should be made to help children with learning problems it is unlikely that any individual teacher's efforts will be as effective as they might be. Indeed, without the interest of senior management it would seem likely that many teachers could remain ignorant of the needs of such children or feel powerless to help even if they are aware of the problem. At the same time, a little help is always better than none and it is certainly not the present author's intention to underestimate what can be done by an interested and caring teacher. However, the more that can be done to develop a similar awareness among all staff, the more likely it would seem to be that the needs of the greatest number of children will be met.

B. An Agreed Whole-school Policy

While concern and interest are important prerequisites for the success of any attempts to meet the needs of individual children it would seem important that the intent to meet individual needs should be recognized explicity in a whole-school policy. Clear policies need to be established about the identification of learning problems in all departments of the school — what sort of problems does the school consider worth attention, what signs should teachers look for, whom should they inform if they are concerned about a child? It is equally important that it should be made clear what intervention is available and when, for how long and by whom it should be provided. What is the class teacher's responsibility in this? How does each department organize support? What can be expected of any specialist teachers in the school? How and when might outside help (e.g. from an educational psychologist) be sought?

C. A Formal Communication System

If an awareness of the needs of individual children is seen as desirable then some formal procedures must be established as part of a whole-school policy to ensure that relevant information about children is communicated to all staff. It is not good enough for information about a child's learning problem to be passed on by word of mouth or for key material to be entered on to a child's record card on the assumption that it will be seen by teachers. Rather, communication procedures must be established whereby information about children can be regularly and quickly drawn to teachers' attention. A sudden change in home circumstances could be very important for a teacher to understand a child's behaviour in class while a considerable improvement in reading ability noted by the remedial teacher could be very important to other teachers' efforts to provide work at an appropriate level of reading difficulty.

D. Additional/Alternative Teaching where Necessary

In cases where children are experiencing marked difficulties in schoolwork individualization of work may not be possible without alternative or supplementary teaching. As has been the practice in the past it may be necessary to teach some children with severe learning difficulties in special classes where smaller pupil/teacher ratios will allow the teacher to develop highly structured programmes designed to meet specific needs. However, the criteria for providing such separate provision must be clearly established to avoid the creation of a ghetto environment and the danger of these children being segregated from their peers socially as well as academically. Alternatively, some of these children could be withdrawn for short periods to receive specialized help in the place of some other part of the curriculum. The provision of help on a withdrawal basis can be an appropriate way of assisting children overcome more transient difficulties such as those which arise from temporary absence from school or to help overcome the unpredictable difficulties which a child with a minor visual or auditory problem may experience. In some cases this may involve no more than a further explanation of points which the child has not understood or has misinterpreted. In other cases withdrawal may be necessary for more extended periods of time. In all cases, however, care needs to be taken to ensure that contact is maintained with subject teachers to avoid the child falling behind in the main class teaching from which he or she is withdrawn.

Recently it has also been recognized that many problems can be dealt with in the ordinary classroom if additional support is provided. In many schools such support teaching has come to be seen as a more appropriate role for the specialist teacher than the conventional 'confinement' of that teacher to the special class or special education department. Support of this kind has been found helpful in assessment, curriculum development and actual classroom-based intervention (see, e.g., Hinson, 1987) and is more in keeping with the functional integration of a whole-school approach to meeting special educational needs.

Conclusion

The concept of learning difficulties which has been advanced in this chapter should be recognised by most teachers. In line with the deliberation of the Warnock Report it is meant to refer to up to 20 per cent of the ordinary school population, some of whom will be in special classes but the majority of whom will be spread throughout the school. The burden of this chapter has been to argue that such children's problems cannot be explained away by reference to lack of ability, poor home circumstances or other similar influences. Rather, they must be seen as the responsibility of the school in general and individual teachers in particular. Given appropriate encouragement it has been the present author's experience that providing appropriate help is well within the capabilities of most teachers. The majority of these children require little more than sympathetic understanding and work at an appropriate level of difficulty. Failure to cater for this group of children is tantamount to a dereliction of duty and it remains a challenge to all schools and all teachers to avoid this occurring.

References

AINSCOW, M. and TWEDDLE, D. (1979) *Preventing Classroom Failure*, London, Wylie.

CANFIELD, J., and WELLS, S.H. (1976) *100 Ways to Improve Self-Concept in the Classroom*, Englewood Cliffs, Prentice-Hall.

COLES, C. (1977) 'Counselling and Reading Retardation', in *Therapeutic Education*, 5, 1, pp. 10–19.

DAVIE, R., BUTLER, M. and GOLDSTEIN, H. (1972) *From Birth to Seven*, London, Longman.

DES (1972) *Children with Specific Reading Difficulties (The Tizard Report)*, London, HMSO.

HINSON, M. (Ed), (1987) *Teachers and Special Educational Needs*, Harlow, Longman.

LAWRENCE, D. (1973) *Improved Reading through Counselling*, London, Ward Lock.

MORRIS, J.M. (1972) *Standards and Progress in Reading*, Windsor, NFER.

PILLING, D. and PRINGLE, K.M. (1978) *Controversial Issues in Child Development*, USA, Elk.

RAMASUT, A. and UPTON, G. (1983) 'The Attainments of Maladjusted Children', in *Remedial Education*, 18, 1, pp. 41–44.

ROSENTHAL, R. and JACOBSON, L. (1968) *Pygmalion in the Classroom*, New York, Holt, Rinehart and Winston.

RUTTER, M. and MADGE, N. (1976) *Cycles of Disadvantage*, London, Heinemann.

UPTON, G. (1978) *A longitudinal study of children's behaviour and adjustment from age 7 to 11*, unpublished Ph.D. thesis, University of Wales.

UPTON, G. (1983) *Educating Children with Behaviour Problems*, Cardiff, Faculty of Education, University College.

WHELDALL, K. (1987) *The Behaviourist in the Classroom*, London, Allen and Unwin.

YOUNG, P. and TYRE, C. (1983) *Dyslexia or Illiteracy*, Milton Keynes, Open University Press.

Chapter 15

Responses to Disruptive Behaviour: Classroom Organization and Management Strategies

Carol Aubrey

Background and Introduction

Disruptive behaviour has been treated differently by different teachers at different times in educational history. After the 1870 Education Act with the introduction of universal, compulsory schooling, it was likely to be regarded as morally wrong and corrected by corporal punishment. Interestingly, it was not until 15 August 1987 that physical punishment was banned from state schools. By the end of the 1920s, medical and psychodynamic explanations of emotional and behavioural disorders became acceptable and, as Bowman (1981) noted, child guidance and special school staff were trained in psychiatric theory. Children were thought to misbehave because there was 'something wrong with them', that is, there were endogenous causes, or else maladjustment was seen as resulting from inappropriate interpersonal relationships. This model, heavily influenced by Freudian theory, accounted for both the excessively disruptive and aggressive 'acting out' child and the excessively withdrawn child, who might show extreme and inappropriate anxiety in response to his or her own personal and social circumstances. Lunzer (1960) described these two main types as withdrawing or aggressive children. Rutter (1965) and Stott, Marsden and Neill (1975) used similar categories: conduct disorder and emotional disorder, or, in Stott's terminology, over-reacting and under-reacting behaviour. The majority of children were believed to fall into these two categories though it was possible the categories might overlap. In his Isle of Wight study, Rutter described one-fifth of children as suffering from 'mixed conduct and neurotic disorders.'

The 1944 Education Act gave the first legal recognition to such children and the Ministry of Education (1946) described these pupils as:

pupils who show evidence of emotional instability or psychological disturbance and require special educational treatment in order to effect their personal, social or educational re-adjustment.

As Woolfe (1981) noted, the definition is legalistic and weak, and terms like 'emotional instability' and 'psychological disturbance' are hypothetical constructs which lack operational definition in behavioural terms. The fact that a precise definition was not forthcoming meant there was scope for individual professional diagnosis and interpretation. Later the Underwood Report (Ministry of Education, 1955) stated:

a child may be regarded as maladjusted who is developing in ways that have a bad effect on himself or his fellows and cannot without help be remedied by his parents, teachers or the other adults in ordinary contact with him.

The definition avoids specificity but provides a framework for decision-makers. Significantly, the 1981 Education Act goes so far as to abolish all old categories including maladjustment, so presumably a 'maladjusted' pupil has special educational needs legally, only if s/he has a learning difficulty which calls for special educational provision to be made.

However, between the years 1950 and 1974 Laslett (1977) noted the rapid expansion of numbers of residential and day special schools for maladjusted children; and Squibb (1981) commented on the increase of special units over the late seventies, from 199 units between 1973 and 1977, to 239 units by 1979. Of course this reveals nothing about the children involved nor any notion of natural pathology and indicates more about prevailing belief systems, local decision-making and availability of places.

During this period new definitions of maladjustment were emerging, based on social learning theory. These sought to explain inappropriate behaviour with reference to learning, from observing and reinforcement, from observing powerful models in the child's environment based on operant behaviourism of Skinner (1953). Concepts of pathology were thus rejected in favour of analyses of those aspects of the environment which it was hypothesized were maintaining the unwanted behaviour. Recently the term 'disruptive' has become more common and often replaces 'disturbed' or 'maladjusted.'

In the early and mid-seventies disruptive pupils became a public issue and this period saw the growth of local authority provision for such pupils in special units in and out of schools. Particular concern was expressed about violence and aggression in schools and about truancy. In 1977 HM Inspectorate carried out a survey of such units and concluded that disruptive was not a helpful term to describe the wide range of pupils found there. The most common features displayed were their major difficulties in relationships with adults, particularly teachers. *They were neither the most, nor least, able though the majority showed considerable educational under-achievement.* The majority were boys between the ages of 14 and 16 years and many were from 'unsatisfactory' home backgrounds.

This was the period of radical change in local authorities as secondary schools changed to comprehensive education. In some cases this did not lead to greater equality of opportunity, particularly where the grammar school ethos and values, and even curriculum, were retained and the skills of the secondary modern school dismissed. In the wider socio-economic context inner city poverty and youth unemployment grew and at the same time — in the early seventies – an acute teacher shortage occurred in the same inner city areas. This was the period, too, of growth of segregated units for disruptive pupils.

Evans (1981) put forward a range of sensible reasons for disruptive behaviour, whether mild or severe, including:

school size;

excessively authoritarian regimes;

inability of pupils to keep up with work;

pupils having no legitimate means to exercise identity and status or influence events in school, which could be increased if staff made pupils feel second-rate, either through attitudes or through over-valuing academic work.

She suggested it could be seen as a reaction of pupils who might lack the competence or articulacy to express their frustration in other ways. She acknowledged that many factors in pupils' lives were outside the control of school and whilst some disruptive behaviour might be due to stresses in the home or outside environment, some pupils might find school a safer place to vent anger than either of these. She suggested that as educationalists we should know what we meant by disruptive behaviour and went on to describe two discernable types of disruptive behaviour:

First there is the low-key and insidious form of disruption which... has to do with non-cooperation, mild disobedience, lateness for lessons, failure to bring equipment, failure to produce homework, open boredom, unwillingness to concentrate, clowning, chattering, and so on...

This she regarded as difficult to combat since no single action would be regarded as serious enough to be made a large issue and sometimes no single child could be held responsible. Secondly, she went on:

> ...there is the disruptive behaviour of a small number of pupils,
> mainly older but sometimes younger, who would appear to have
> become totally alienated from school... their behaviour can be
> excessive... and includes pupils who are very aggressive, and who
> can, on occasion, seriously damage property or make violent attacks
> on other pupils or staff.

However, as Tattum (1986) acknowledged, to the teacher indiscipline is a fact of school life with which teachers to a greater or lesser degree will have to cope. To focus on the pupil alone is to ignore the interactive nature of human relationships and the very special social context that exists in schools and classrooms. The quality of relationships and the nature of the social context created as vital elements in the process of control and discipline stressed by Tattum, echoes the sentiments of Evans (1981). She noted especially the needs of disruptive pupils for:

(1)   constructive and consistent relationships with adults and peers;

(2)   control of behaviour, particularly responses to criticism, checks and rules; and

(3)   and educational perspective through the encouragement of systematic patterns of work and success.

Clearly, she stressed, disruptive pupils do not form a homogeneous group: 'It is not a simple exercise to assess the weight of various factors which cause disruption and the definitions given apply variously to different pupils at different times.'

Over the last ten to fifteen years, however, classroom research has made available strategies both for creating classrooms as effective learning environments and for preventing, or coping with, most behaviour problems, with disruptive or socially withdrawn pupils. Even for individual pupils with more severe problems, practical and effective strategies exist.

The Well-organized and Well-managed Classroom

Teacher Managing Behaviours

In order to discuss effectively what constitutes good classroom management it is essential first that a major assumption behind such strategies is made explicit: successful classroom managers are effective teachers or instructors. The emphasis here is on analyses of processes in the classroom and on student-teacher interactions which influence learning and teaching outcomes.

This represents a move away from earlier evaluation studies of input/output factors and away from characteristics of pupils or teachers. *The focus of attention is on how effective teaching is organized and the strategies teachers use in effective classrooms.* Good management implies good and effective teaching; the good teacher is both an authority figure and a successful instructor. Research suggests that competent classroom managers are distinguished less by their response to troublesome behaviour than by their skill in *preventing* such problems occurring. On the one hand, this involves appropriate curriculum planning and pacing which ensures children are successfully engaged in suitable academic tasks; on the other hand, it entails ensuring that students learn thoroughly a set of workable rules and routines for classroom behaviour. Successful and well-planned classroom managers increase attention, engagement and academic learning time which leads to high levels of successful educational performance. Consequently less 'down time' is left for inappropriate behaviour, when children do not have enough to do or do not know what is expected of them. Classroom management is inseparable from classroom instruction: a well-organized classroom is a well-managed classroom (Berliner, 1984).

Kounin (1970) first demonstrated that the well-managed classroom functioned as a result of the constant and systematic teacher attention given to creating, maintaining and sometimes re-establishing conditions that enhance effective learning. Such classrooms, which can often appear to be maintained without teacher attention, in fact function as the result of careful planning, organization and timing. Later Brophy and Putnam (1979) and Good and Brophy (1980) replicated this work with younger children, specifying that preparation and planning begin even before the school year commences. Room areas are organized according to the function or activity and equipped with items which are stored for easy access and replacement. Movement of pupils is facilitated by clearly learned routines for 'traffic control' which avoids crowding and bottle-necks. Transitions between activities are clearly indicated by signals and cue carefully-taught children what to do, in which area, with which equipment. Activities begin at a brisk pace with clear lesson beginning and ending and students are clear about teacher expectations and task requirements. *Successful lesson flow involves avoiding:*

> *thrusts* — sudden 'burstings in' on children's work, with insensitivity to timing or group readiness;
>
> *'prop and actone' over-emphasis* — which means deflecting the pupils' attention from the main flow of lesson activity, to attend to peripheral or insignificant matters;

dangles — starting on one activity and leaving it hanging in mid-air by attending to another activity and then resuming the first activity;

flip flops — going back to an activity which has just been terminated;

over-dwelling — engaging in a stream of talk beyond that which is necessary;

fragmentation — the unnecessary asking of individual children to undertake something which could be dealt with by a group instruction or group activity.

Other researchers (Emmer *et al.*, 1980, and Anderson *et al.*, 1980), following and observing teachers of 9-year-olds in the first few weeks of term, found smooth-running routines of successful classroom managers resulted from intensive preparation and organization by introducing rules and procedures for room management, materials storage, daily routines of breaks, and storage of belongings, by formal teaching, just as in academic content. Children learned teacher expectations, received demonstrations of procedures, were given time for questions and given practice where necessary. This was followed up with additional instruction and practice when monitored procedures were not learned appropriately, with cues and reminders when procedures were to be carried out. Consequences of appropriate and inappropriate behaviour were thus made clear.

Not only is a good start an essential beginning of the year but preparation and timing are prerequisites to every lesson beginning as is skill in fitting the lesson to the time available. Wragg (1981) was involved in producing training materials to help student teachers develop control and management skills during practice and established from this that the successful teacher-manager usually arrives at the classroom before the pupils and admits them in an orderly fashion, thus establishing his or her presence before the lesson begins. Lessons are begun briskly and in a well-defined way and attention is invited through suitable questioning, appropriate materials and varied teaching techniques. Priority is given to the establishing of constructive relationships by learning names and getting to know the children. Lesson sequence, materials and organization for pupil group work are pre-planned and possible disruption anticipated by giving careful instructions about task requirements early.

By comparison of good with poor classroom managers, Kounin (1970) established that less effective managers did not differ so much from effective managers in their *response* to disruption, as in their strategies for minimizing the opportunities for children to become disruptive. Successful techniques included (a) 'withitness', (b) 'overlapping', (c) 'signal continuity' and lesson momentum, (d) group alerting and accountability in lessons and (e) variety and challenge in independent seat work.

(a) 'Withitness'

Success managers monitor regularly and scan pupils continuously, thus identifying problem behaviour swiftly, conveying what Wragg (1981) would term 'vigilance' by intervening before problems escalate. This is achieved by being positioned in a spot where all pupils can be clearly seen, the classroom being continuously monitored and the teacher circulating the classroom as appropriate.

(b) 'Overlapping'

Successful managers handle more than one matter at a time: they may monitor a class, while conferring with an individual pupil, deal with a misdemeanour without interrupting class lesson flow, or teach a group and handle an individual enquiry or interruption.

(c) 'Signal continuity' and lesson momentum

If classroom managers are well-prepared and present the lesson briskly, pupils have a continuous 'signal' to attend to the task and inattention prompted swiftly by a brief comment, a question, eye contact or even proximity of the teacher. Such lessons proceed smoothly without interruption either from poor lesson organization or disruption from pupils who lack a clear signal or task to attend to.

(d) Group alerting and accountability

Kounin (1970) found effective managers used presentation and questioning techniques to keep the group alert and accountable. This involved looking around the class before selecting a pupil to make an oral response, choosing sometimes randomly, swiftly going round the whole class for a response, using volunteers, interspersing group with individual responses, using challenge to solve tricky questions and keeping material novel and interesting. This kept students involved through challenge and accountable by the possibility of needing to respond.

In general, work by Brophy and Evertson (1976) and Anderson *et al.* (1979) confirmed Kounin's positive indicators for successful management and pupil learning — 'withitness', 'overlapping', 'signal continuity' and lesson momentum — though results of studies concerning group alerting and accountability techniques were more equivocal. Such strategies may be useful as occasional devices but if they are implemented too frequently it may be an indication that more essential classroom management techniques should be used with greater effectiveness.

However, frequency in teacher-directed questions in guided student practice is important, again not only in primary-aged children for basic skill acquisition, but also with older children. The importance of high frequency of questions has been established, for instance, in teaching mathematics to pupils of 12–14 years, where Evertson *et al.* (1980) showed the most effective teachers asked an average of 24 questions during a 50-minute mathematics period, whilst the least effective teachers asked only 8.6 questions.

Anderson *et al.* (1979) found a correlation between student achievement and time spent in question-answer format and between student achievement and the number of academic interactions per minute. A major teacher function is the response to pupils' answers and correcting errors during guided practice, during checking for understanding and during review. Rosenshine (1983) suggested four types of pupil response:

correct, quick and firm, which occurs in late, initial learning and review, where research indicates a new question is asked to maintain momentum;

correct, but hesitant, again occurring in initial stages of learning in review of new material, where it is suggested the teacher provides short statements of feedback;

incorrect, but careless, occurring in review drill or in reading, where the teacher should simply give the correct answer;

incorrect, but lacking knowledge of facts or processes, occurring in the early stages of learning new material and indicating the pupil does not understand thoroughly. One approach is to provide hints or ask simple questions, or reteach the material, explaining the stages used to reach the correct answer.

The conclusion to be drawn from this is that students learn better with feedback given as rapidly as possible; and that errors should be corrected before they become habitual.

In terms of independent practice, the most common practice in pupils of 6–13 years is individual practice or seatwork, where more time is spent working alone than any other activity (50–75 per cent of time). Since pupils are observed to be less engaged, or less 'on-task', during independent seat work than during group or class instruction, it is important to learn how to increase pupil task involvement. Again Rosenshine (1983) showed that student engagement during seat work is increased by the following procedures:

more time being spent on lecture, discussion and guided practice, that is, more time being spent *preparing* for seat work;

the teacher structuring seat work and directing the class through the first seat work problems;

seat work following directly after guided practice;

seat work being directly relevant to the demonstration and guided practice;

the teacher actively circulating during seat work, providing feedback, asking questions, and giving short explanations.

Rosenshine concluded that seat work took place in all classrooms, but successful teachers spent more time demonstrating what was being taught and leading pupils in guided practice. Contacts should be short, 30 seconds or less, to allow for the maximum circulation, as Fisher *et al.* (1980) found: when teachers had to give a lot of explanations during seat work, student error rates were higher.

Another effective procedure for increasing engagement in seat work, particularly for difficult material and/or for slower learning children, is to break instruction into two or three segments of instruction and seat work during a single period. In terms of the effect on behaviour, as Brophy (1983) pointed out, circulation during seat work ensures students are held accountable, too.

(e) Variety and challenge in independent seat work

Kounin (1970) suggested that successful lessons maintained appropriate interest in work which, in turn, influenced task engagement. This he felt was achieved by planning variety and challenge in content and level of difficulty of subject matter, in materials used, location of activity, use of teaching aids and by the effective use of delegation of responsibility for work to pupils.

More recent work on effective learning and teaching has suggested that challenge in seat work or independent practice must be seen within the context of research indicating that learning is most effective when pupils have high levels of success in academic tasks, particularly low-achieving pupils or pupils with special educational needs. Even when teachers are present to monitor responses and provide feedback, success rates of at least 70–80 per cent should be expected (Brophy and Evertson, 1976). However, when pupils are working independently or working on homework, success rates of 95–100 per cent should be required (Fisher *et al.*, 1980). Such work demands application of hierarchically-organized knowledge mastered to the over-learning level. Observational research indicates that when pupils are given inappropriate tasks they are more likely to be too hard than too easy. *The implications of this are that several learning routes requiring tasks at different levels of difficulty are essential in many classrooms, particularly those which contain low-achieving pupils.*

Not only is inappropriate behaviour reduced by effective classroom management but during the last few years there have been numerous studies showing that teachers can be trained to increase academic achievement of students and/or higher academically engaged time in effective instruction.

Whilst it is most important that children master content of basic skills to the point of over-learning, over-learning is also necessary for higher cognitive processing. These procedures also work for older, skilled learners and it seems students do not automatically acquire a learning skill simply through experience in a subject matter. Rosenshine (1983) suggested a list of six instructional functions:

1. reviewing and checking the previous day's work (reteaching if necessary);

2. presenting new content or skills;

3. giving initial student practice (and checking for understanding);

4. giving feedback and correction (and reteaching if necessary);

5. giving independent practice;

6. having weekly and monthly reviews.

In presenting new material to be learned teachers frequently give demonstrations of new tasks or skills. Emmer *et al.* (1980) showed 10–to 14-year-olds learned mathematics, for instance, more effectively when more time was spent on lecture, demonstration and discussion. The most effective mathematics teachers spent 23 minutes per day in lecture, demonstration and discussion compared with 11 minutes for the least effective. Effective teachers spend time on presenting explanations, examples and sufficient instruction to obtain good results from pupils' independent seat work, with additional checks for understanding.

However, in other areas of the curriculum, demonstration is not necessarily as frequently used. Durkin (1981) noted there is seldom a demonstration phase in reading comprehension. In a study of twenty-four teachers of 10-year-olds instruction in this area was less than 1 per cent of the time. Equally, whilst teachers are exhorted to ask higher-order cognitive questions (calling for application, analysis and synthesis) they seldom demonstrate to students how to engage in such activities.

Communicating Authority

The Teacher Education Project referred to earlier (Wragg, 1981) compared experienced and student teachers and found experienced teachers were clear about rules, quicker to respond to infringements and used their eyes to scan the classroom effectively. Establishing dominance in the early days seems to be an effective response and what pupils expect in the 'testing of limits' time which takes place in early lessons. Wragg (1981) summarized pupils' views of the characteristics of a skilful teacher which frequently emerge from the literature:

1.   keeps order by being firm without being frightening,

2.   explains clearly to help pupils learn,

3.   is fair without having favourites or unfairly picking on pupils,

4.   is friendly, good humoured and approachable,

5.   is interesting through the provision of varied and stimulating work and willingness to incorporate pupils' views.

Robertson (1981) drew attention to both verbal and non-verbal behaviour which is particularly significant in a teacher establishing authority and control and sustaining attention through effective communication. He again stressed the importance of the first few meetings with a new class in establishing his definition of the situation and conveying his authority and status. On the verbal plane, talk is directed by the teacher towards the whole group and used both to maintain the social context and to develop the lesson content. The rules for this communication are that the listener must make himself or herself heard effectively and be sensitive to those wishing to contribute. Pupils on the other hand must give attention and feedback, and convey the wish to speak appropriately.

Status is conveyed largely through *relaxation of body posture*, in terms of sideways tilt of the head and body, assymmetrical and open limbs and *level of immediacy*, in terms of body orientation, proximity, eye contact and touch.

Because of the association of upright and tense body positions with respect and attention, teachers tend to associate an overly relaxed and casual approach from a pupil as indicating lack of respect and attention from the lower status person. However, if pupils *do* behave in an inappropriate way, a relaxed attitude and an easy, relaxed body posture from the higher status teacher may not be sufficient to maintain the status difference, suggesting status is conveyed as much by the *response* of the lower status person as the *action* of the higher status person.

In fact, a fixed and tense attitude, far from conveying aggression, may indicate insecurity on the teacher's part, whilst a closed, bowed position with feet and hands together may convey uncertainty, diffidence or submission, neither appropriate to the teacher.

Dominance can be increased through immediacy. The teacher moves freely and informally round the classroom, but the way of entering another's personal space is associated with emphasizing differences of status and may be perceived as challenging or threatening. So, while the teacher usually circulates freely in the classroom in a friendly, non-threatening and collaborative way and pupils' personal space is respected, at times, entering a pupil's personal space, picking up his or her belongings or touching the pupil's shoulder, for instance, can be an effective way of conveying a dominant attitude. The advantage of this is that this behaviour does not necessarily interfere with lesson flow or divert the attention of other pupils to a minor interruption.

Eye contact, too, is a powerful means of communicating intentions and feelings. When a higher status teacher is reprimanding a lower status pupil, s/he will expect to control eye gaze. On the one hand, lack of visual contact may convey lack of respect or attention and, on the other hand, a long, unflinching return gaze can be equally challenging and disrespectful. A pupil's averting from the teacher's gaze often conveys deliberate uncooperativeness, or at least gives little positive feedback, and hence little control to the teacher.

Facial expression also conveys meaning about the speaker's message — disbelief, anger, surprise, amusement — and little variation in facial expression conveys lack of interest or attention. Variation in timing, pitch and volume of voice, too, have a vital role in extending the meaning in communication. Slowing speech can convey emphasis, rapid or flat tone may convey less involvement, softness can convey calmness, attraction or threat.

Escalating a conflict may limit the options open to restrain; on the other hand a greater danger may lie in the fact that tension, arousal and threatening behaviour may actually have the paradoxical effect of *reducing* the teacher's status and authority.

Pik (1981) suggested that confrontations develop and progress in four, possibily overlapping, stages: a build-up, a trigger event, a rapid escalation and a finale, with the teacher having a feeling of no alternative, and both pupil and teacher preoccupied with winning/losing. He offered four rules for handling a confrontation:

1.   decide if the incident is worth a confrontation;

2.   leave yourself and the pupil a gracious way out to save face;

3.   remember threats — particularly of physical force — by the teacher will escalate the conflict very quickly;

4.   leave a reasonable time after the confrontation, but before the next lesson with the pupil, to talk privately.

Show of inappropriate feelings can have a devastating effect on classroom control. Inappropriate aggression and dominant behaviour may signal weakness, insecurity or reduced control. Lack of interest and involvement with material, conveyed to pupils by monotonous and unchanging speech and non-verbal behaviour, can lead to classroom boredom. Tenseness or anxiety may be conveyed in lack of smiling, rigid body posture, lack of eye contact, speech hesitations or fidgeting movement. At best this behaviour can elicit unease in the classroom, at worst it may lead to challenge which will further unnerve the teacher.

Status and authority will need to be demonstrated when the teacher requires rapid attention and silence in the classroom in order to talk to pupils. Not only is this essential for the communication to be delivered but, more importantly, it demonstrates the control and authority of the teacher. With a new class before a teacher-pupil relationship has been established, the novelty of the situation is likely to carry the pupils' interest. Later, effective strategies are essential. If it is necessary to raise the voice in order to command attention by a short, sharp instruction, it is essential that the delivery is not made before silence is obtained and that the voice recovers normal or even quieter tones to retain attention.

Reprimands where given should be brief, measured and considered, to avoid hesitations or pauses and to avoid lessening the impact of the communication or reducing the attention of pupils. Short, clear and unambiguous instructions avoid undue pupil attention to the teacher and the teacher's behaviour, which can give the whole incident too much emphasis and deflect from the main purpose of lesson content and pupil learning.

The onus for establishing and maintaining rules lies with the teacher and, as Hargreaves (1972) pointed out, the teacher must define the situation on his or her own terms through what Robertson (1981) would define as effective communication and appropriate use of status and authority. The work of Duke (1978) in US schools suggested that many students' behaviour problems arose from inconsistencies in school rules themselves and pupils claimed this was a major source of dissatisfaction.

Classroom organisation and management skills identified by Kounin (1970) and by Emmer *et al.* (1980) and effective communication skills described by Robertson (1981) confirm that effective management entails prevention of problems occurring rather than special techniques for dealing with arising problems. Throughout, classroom management is fully integrated with effective instruction which allows teachers to avoid most serious problems and to deal swiftly and briefly with infringements that do occur. For pupils with more extreme and intransigent problems additional strategies are available to supplement basic management and organizational techniques outlined above.

Teacher-pupil Relationships

The focus of the teacher as manager of group relations indicates how the behaviour of the class and the teacher is affected by the group context and the teacher's dual responsibility to the individual child and to the class group. Skills have been identified which enhance the teacher's group leadership role. One technique for achieving this is for the teacher to place some leadership responsibility on the pupils, as shown in the school effectiveness literature (Reynolds, 1976; Reynolds and Sullivan, 1979; Rutter *et al.*, 1979) whilst maintaining the thrust in instructional leadership.

Recent research has focused on breaking down social barriers associated with class, sex, race or achievement by involving students from different groups in cooperative activities, particularly activities which foster interdependence and participation of all group members to ensure successful completion of the task (Aronson *et al.*, 1978; Johnson and Johnson, 1975).

The teams-games-tournaments (TGT) approach divides students into teams varied in sex, race and achievement, which compete for prizes for academic excellence. Team members contribute to team points though performance on independent activities is awarded points according to a handicapping system. This approach (Slavin, 1980) improves the quality and quantity of interactions inside and outside the classroom.

Approaches which allow individuals to show special skills or abilities can be used to enhance status or peer acceptance. The jigsaw approach (Aronson *et al.*, 1978) organized to provide each group member with one key item of unique information, essential to group success, can spur more dominant, brighter and 'pushy' team members to encourage more withdrawn or slower students to greater participation. Alternatively social skills training can be used to help socially-isolated or rejected children in order to increase their initiating interactions by reinforcement.

There is sufficient evidence for its effectiveness to warrant the inclusion of social skills teaching. Sometimes concern is expressed about the active teaching of obedient and controlled behaviour in the class, yet evidence from research suggests that such behaviours as attending, remaining on task and volunteering answers about schoolwork have been shown to have an association with teacher and pupil success in learning (Cartledge and Milburn. 1978)

Studies of teachers' opinions of pupils indicate that they prefer children who attend, follow directions and work hard, and specific teaching of these behaviours has resulted not only in positive teaching behaviour but also in increased academic learning.

Effective techniques for teaching social skills — modelling and rewarding approximations to the desired behaviour — are best taught in the classroom itself, since behaviour in one setting may not transfer to another setting or be maintained over time without specific training.

Another function of the teacher is as group leader of informal groupings. Hargreaves (1972) suggested teachers should identify informal group leaders of classroom 'cliques' since they are central in determining norms of classroom behaviour and the criteria influencing group prestige. This implies that classroom management should take account of the informal status of each pupil, or as Wragg (1981) pointed out, teachers should always have the initiative in management in relation to whether or not to react to pupil confrontations, according to pupil expectations.

If a teacher gives praise or responsibility to a rejected pupil of low informal status, thus conferring formal status, this can lead to a deleterious effect on teacher-pupil relations. Long-term goals would be to enhance the status of the rejected pupil, but it is important that teachers should be aware of the 'ripple effect' (Kounin, 1970). When a teacher reprimands a child of high informal status this can be positive if the intervention is regarded as fair, or negative and counter-productive, if pupils feel the teacher has been unfair.

Furlong (1976) distinguished between a friendship group and what she called an 'interaction set', where a group of pupils share the same view of what is happening and common ways of behaving. She concluded that interaction patterns could vary with the situation, so a disruptive pupil could be supported in one situation but not in another where there was not a common definition of the situation.

Knowledge of existing friendship patterns can help the teacher promote cooperative enterprise and utilising existing group interactions and norms can be part of the work of the effective classroom manager. Which pupils wish to work with which others in a group can be determined by sociometric techniques of asking children to write down their own name and the names of pupils with whom they would like and not like to undertake a specific activity. Pupils can be asked to list in order of priority and then a sociogram can be constructed on a sheet of paper to indicate stars, isolates, mutual pairs, cliques and chains. Each child's name is shown in a circle with arrows indicating direction of choice and continuous or dotted lines indicating choice or rejection respectively.

Additional Classroom Management Strategies

Behaviour Modification

Techniques of behavioural analysis are often recommended to the teacher to *increase* a range of desirable social or academic behaviours. These include the use of praise and approval, modelling, establishing clear rules and shaping by rewarding progressive approximations to the target behaviour, token reinforcement, self specification and reinforcement (Becker *et al.*, 1975). They may be used equally to *reduce* inappropriate and undesirable behaviour of individuals, groups or the class as a whole, by extinction through ignoring, reinforcing imcompatible acceptable behaviours, 'time out' or withdrawal from social reinforcement, response cost (removal of privileges) relaxation for anxieties or fears, self-instruction and self-evaluation.

Central to the success of these techniques is a recognition of the social and mental development of the children involved. Brophy and Evertson (1978) identified four broad stages of development which have implications for classroom management strategies employed.

Whilst at Stage One — 6 to 8 or 9 years, and Stage Two — 8–9 years to 11–12 years, children, although needing instruction and socialization into classroom expectations, rules and routines, are more oriented towards pleasing the teacher; in Stage Three — 11–12 years to 15–16 years — the years of secondary schooling — pupils enter adolescence and are more peer-oriented. Classroom management becomes more of an issue as more pupils question or reject authority and disrupt to gain attention or seek amusement *not* through lack of knowledge of rules and routines, as in Stage One, but through unwillingness to comply. After 15–16 years, in Stage Four, as in Stage Two, students become more personally settled and oriented towards academic learning, and management issues become less prominent.

The implications for use of applied behavioural analysis techniques are that whilst social, rather than material or tangible reinforcers are more appropriate, praise and social reinforcers have less effect on student behaviour after 7–8 years. Equally, the praise and ignore formula often recommended for shaping appropriate classroom behaviour, may be less effective than producing a specific programme for a target pupil. Similarly, ignoring inappropriate behaviour will be effective only if the behaviour was being reinforced by teacher attention, which may be less likely with the boisterous teenager who may be more effected or impressed by peer approval. Even if the unacceptable behaviour were reinforced by teacher attention — probably so in the minority of cases — as Kounin's (1970) work has shown, ignoring disruption may lead to escalation and spread of the undesirable behaviour. Reinforcement techniques then are likely to be more effective if resulting from a mutually-constructed and agreed programme between the teacher and the pupil and delivered to the target pupil as the consequence of appearance of the mutually-agreed-upon unacceptable behaviour. Topping (1983), reviewing research evidence, concluded that reward systems result in better outcomes than punishment and children favour rewards involving parents, time off lessons and extra preferred lessons. Pupils favour prizes as rewards, but Topping suggested that this was more effective with academic achievement than reduction of unacceptable social behaviour.

The valued reinforcers which most secondary teachers control are numerous but often not powerful, which underlines the need to develop self-monitoring and self-control of behaviour, leading to the creation of a formal contract, specifying performance criteria, which must be achieved in order to earn agreed rewards.

Individual Counselling

Whilst early models and interventions tended to stress psychodynamic approaches, more problem-solving, objectives-oriented approaches are now accessible. Gordon (1974) described the need to analyse the extent to which students and teachers involved in a conflict 'owned' their contribution to the problem and the extent to which they acknowledged frustrating the needs of the other. Student-owned problems entail sympathy and active listening where the teacher attempts to understand not only what the student says but importantly what s/he is feeling and the reactions conveyed which are reflected back. When the teacher communicates his or her owning of the problem, this entails making explicit the effect of frustration and disappointment such behaviour has on the teacher.

This stage helps the teacher and student to create a mutual and rational understanding of the problem and encourages a more positive and constructive problem-solving approach to goal-setting for a mutually-agreed solution. The six stages are:

1. define the problem;
2. generate possible solutions;
3. evaluate these solutions;
4. choose which is best;
5. determine how to implement this decision;
6. assess the effectiveness of the implementation of this solution.

Glasser (1977) has considered a 'ten steps to good discipline' problem-solving approach which he has claimed to be associated with reduction in referrals to the office, fighting and suspension. These are as follows:

1. Select a student of concern and list typical reactions to his or her disruptive behaviour.

2. Analyse the list and see which techniques work and which do not and resolve not to repeat the ineffective ones.

3. Improve personal relationships with the student by providing encouragement and sympathy and by giving responsibility.

4. Require the student to describe the behaviour in detail and continue while accurate, then request him/her to stop it.

5. Call a short conference, repeat 4. Consider how it conflicts with expectations and rules and encourage the student to describe alternative, incompatible appropriate behaviour.

6. Repeat 5 with a negotiated plan and include the student's commitment to the strategies to eliminate the behaviour.

7. Isolate the student or use 'time out' procedures. Whilst isolated the student will be required to devise his/her own plan to be followed in future. This must be agreed by the teacher and have the student's full commitment to be maintained.

8. If this is unsuccessful the next step is internal suspension. At this point another school authority figure will be involved who will repeat the earlier stages and encourage the student either to devise a plan to return to the classroom, complying with reasonable rules or recognize he will continue in isolation,

9. If the behaviour persists or in-school suspension is ineffective, the parents are called to take the pupil home for the day and the process is repeated the following day.

10. If all else fails and return through the previous stages is unsuccessful, it is recommended that an outside agency is involved.

Research, particularly that of Kounin (1970), and of Emmer *et al.* (1980), provides sound and detailed information about classroom and pupil management at the beginning of the year and on a daily basis. This includes advanced organization, specificity about rules, routines and procedures which are clearly taught at the beginning of the year and consistently maintained and the systematical use of group management techniques together with effective instructional organization. This entails a corresponding recognition of the individual teacher of responsibility for exercising authority appropriately, providing instruction, clearly communicating expectations, and where necessary resolving conflicts and problem-solving solutions to individual disruptive pupils.

This chapter has offered an overview of the main variables to be found in successful classroom management. Many teachers have not received specific initial or in-service training in these techniques, found to be associated with effective instruction and classroom management. What it lacks is the specific detail provided by developed materials and training manuals. The following list of materials gives details of some practical books, manuals and training materials which are available.

In-Service Training Materials for Classroom Strategies	Topics covered	Comments
1. Tweddle, D. (1986) *Preventive Approaches to Disruption*, Basingstoke, Macmillan.	Topics include lesson instruction/organization and class management, effective teacher communication skills, pupil management, observation and analysis of problem behaviour.	There is a video for analysis of teacher and pupil behaviour; individual self-check, pair and group activities. Checklists for observation of video and classroom are included.
2. Wheldall, K., and Merrett, F. (1988) *BATSAC*, Birmingham, Positive Products.	It deals with applied behavioural analysis: observation and analysis of problem behaviour in the classroom and teacher responses. Ways are sought to obtain positive change in classroom climates. The use of approval/disapproval, rules and sanctions, and self-recording to obtain change in both social and academic behaviour is examined.	Video activities observation and analysis; individual, pair and group activities. 'Take home' worksheets for background reading and workbooks.
3. Dawson, R. *et al.* (1985) *TIPS, The Macmillan Teacher Information Pack*, Basingstoke, Macmillan.	TIPS is a pack of 125 booklets, each dealing with a particular difficulty. The Behaviour booklet covers a wide range of behaviours, e.g. bullying, destructiveness, dependency, attention-seeking, truancy and friendlessness.	The booklet is in three parts including: information, techniques and procedures, and practical strategies to remedy the problem.
4. Wragg, E. (1981) *Class Management and Control: a Teaching Skills Workbook*, Basingstoke, Macmillan.	It deals with issues of class management: beliefs, context, rules and relationships, rewards and punishments. Classroom teaching tasks for secondary school PGCE students, handling individual and group work and difficult classes are also included.	Ideas and materials for self-directed study, peer and tutor-led discussion, observation checklists and 'tips' lists are covered.

5. Amphlett, D., Davies, J.D. and Jones, D. (Eds) (1985) *In the Heat of the Moment*, Oxford Polytechnic Press.	Three separate video modules showing: teacher responses to a pupil avoiding a lesson; a child passing through an escalating tariff of sanctions following work refusal for a supply teacher; a case conference to examine a problem pupil.	Three booklets: teachers' handbook, video transcript and support documents for module 3. Information, background reading, transcript of sequences topics for discussion are given.
6. Trainer Guide by John Lambert and Susan Weil (1984) *Focus on Adolescence Programme 3: In School*, The Centre for Staff Development in Higher Education, University of London.	A series of short video sequences show aspects of teacher–pupil interactions, seen from both perspective of teacher and pupil.	Video sequence of trigger incidents to act as springboard to discussion in training teachers and others in education who work with young people. The guide contains a review of education and training methods relevant, discussion of issues, verbatim transcripts and references.
Practical Books and Manuals for Teachers	Topics covered	Comments
7. Cheeseman, P.L. and Watts, P.E. (1985) *Behaviour Management. A Manual for Teachers*, London, Croom Helm.	This book offers a background to problem behaviour. It covers such topics as describing in observable and measurable terms, assessment, observation, measuring, and planning an intervention.	This is a practical book giving charts, tables, checklists to aid readers.
8. Emmer, E., Evertson, C., Sanford, J., Clements, B. and Worsham, M. (1984) *Classroom Management for Secondary Teachers*, Englewood Cliffs, New Jersey, Prentice-Hall.	Major researchers in classroom organization and management re-evaluate and develop Kounin's original work.	This is a classroom management manual.
9. Laslett, R. and Smith, C. (1984) *Effective Classroom Management. A Teacher's Guide*, London, Croom Helm.	It is a readable and practical guide to the four rules of classroom management. It covers teacher expectations, organization, reward and punishments, stress and teacher strategies for confrontation.	It is spiced with teaching tips and based on classroom experience and research findings.
10. Marland, M. (1987) *The Craft of the Classroom. A Survival Guide*, London, Heinemann.	This little book offers general and sensible advice on lesson organization and classroom management for less-experienced teachers.	This is a 'must' for all probationer teachers.

11. Robertson, J. (1981) *Effective Classroom Control*, London, Hodder and Stoughton.	It covers topics for which the author carries out workshops with video material concerning communicating authority and enthusiasm. Analysing and dealing with unwanted behaviour.	This is a useful book which deals with areas of teaching behaviour, classroom management and lesson organization found to be effective with successful teachers.
12. Westmacott, S., and Cameron, J. (1987) *Behaviour Can Change*, London, Macmillan Educational.	Like Book 7 this book gives advice on describing behaviour in observable and measurable terms and simple advice on setting up behavioural programmes.	Another practical and well-illustrated book giving charts and tips for setting up programmes.
Strategies for More Individual Problems	Topics covered	Comments
13. Spence, S. (1981) *Social Skills Training with Children and Adolescents*, Slough, NFER.	The role of social skills training is discussed. Social assessment is considered and specified techniques and activities for assessment are given.	This is a manual for a structured programme of training in social skills. Social skills assessment: with record forms, assessment charts and photographs are given.
14. Sprick, R. (1983) *The Solution Book*, Henley on Thames, Science Research Associates.	This is a compendium of applications of the applied behavioural analysis model. Activities for classroom management and sheets for individual social problems of pupils are included.	There is a folder of classroom strategies, a comprehensive range of individual programmes for problem behaviour and coping strategies for teachers, e.g. relaxation for stress.
15. Thacker, J. (1982) *Steps to Success*, Slough, NFER.	There are two main phases to this programme: (i) 6 class lessons of one hour where the pupils are taught problem-solving strategies; (ii) 3 short, individual phases for the pupil to apply the strategies to his/her own problems.	The manual has role-playing exercises. It is a short course in problem-solving designed to help 11–13-year-olds overcome problems in social life. Cartoons of problem-solving strategies. Forms for weekly targets and charting progress, pupil folders are included.

References

ANDERSON, L., EVERTSON, C. and BROPHY, J. (1979) 'An experimental study of effective teaching in 1st grade reading groups', in *Elementary School Journal*, 79, pp. 193–223.

ANDERSON, L., EVERTSON, C. and EMMER, E. (1980) 'Dimensions in Classroom management derived from recent research', in *Journal of Curriculum Studies*, 12, pp. 343–346.

ARONSON, E., BLANEY, N., STEPHEN, C., SIKES, J. and SNAPP, M. (1978) *The Jigsaw classroom*, Beverley Hills; Sage.

BECKER, W. C., ENGLEMANN, S. and THOMAS, D.R. (1975) *Teaching 1: Classroom Management*, Chicago, Science Research Associates.

BERLINER, D. (1984) The half-full glass: A Review of research on teaching, in HOSFORD, P.L. (Ed.) *Using what we know about teaching*, Alexandria, V.A., Association for Supervision and Curriculum Development.

BOWMAN, I. (1981) 'Maladjustment: a history of the category', in SWANN, W. (Ed.) *The Practice of Special Education*, Oxford, Basil Blackwell in association with Open University Press.

BROPHY, J. (1979) 'Teacher behaviour and its effects', in *Journal of Educational Psychology*, 71, pp. 733–750.

BROPHY, J. (1983) 'Classroom organisation and management', in *Elementary School Journal*, 83, pp. 265–286.

BROPHY, J. and EVERTSON, C. (1976) *Learning from teaching: a developmental perspective*, Boston, Allyn and Bacon.

BROPHY, J. and EVERTSON, C. (1978) 'Context variables in teaching', in *Educational Psychology*, 12, pp. 310–316.

BROPHY, J. and PUTMAN, J. (1979) 'Classroom management in the elementary grades'. In DUKE, D. (Ed.) *Classroom Management. The 78th Yearbook of the National Society for the Study of Education, Part 2*, Chicago, University of Chicago Press.

CARTLEDGE, G., and MILBURN, J. (1978) 'The Case for Teaching Social Skills', in *Review of Educational Research*, 1, 1, pp. 133–156.

DEPARTMENT OF EDUCATION AND SCIENCE (1978) *Behavioural Units*, London, HMSO.

DEPARTMENT OF EDUCATION AND SCIENCE (1981) *Education Act*, London, HMSO.

DUKE, D. (1978) 'Adults can be discipline problems too!', in *Psychology in the Schools*, 15, 4, pp. 522–528.

DURKIN, D. (1981) 'Reading comprehension instruction in 5 basal reading series', in *Reading Research Quarterly*, 4, pp. 515–544.

EMMER, E., EVERTSON, C. and ANDERSON, L. (1980) 'Effective Management at the beginning of the school year', in *Elementary School Journal*, 80, pp 219–231.

EMMER, E.T., EVERTSON, C., SANFORD, J. and CLEMENTS, B. S. (1982) *Improving classroom management: an experimental study in junior high classrooms*, Austin, R. and D. Centre for Teacher Education, University of Texas.

EVANS, M. (1981) *Disruptive Pupils*, London, Schools Council.

EVERTSON, C. and EMMER, E. (1982) 'Effective management at the beginning of the school year in junior high classes', in *Journal of Educational Psychology*, 74, pp. 485–498.

EVERTSON, C., EMMER, E. and BROPHY, J. (1980) 'Prediction of effective teaching in junior high mathematics classrooms', in *Journal of Research in Mathematics Education*, 11, pp. 167–178.

FISHER, C. W., BERLINER, D. C., FILBY, N., MARLIAVE, R., CAHEN, L. and DISHAW, M. (1980) 'Teaching behaviours, academic learning time, and student achievement: an overview', in DENHAM, C. and LIEBERMAN, A. (Eds) *Time to Learn*, Washington, D.C., National Institute of Education.

FURLONG, V. J. (1976) 'Interaction sets in the classroom: towards a study of pupil knowledge', in STUBBS, M. and DELAMONT, S. (Eds.) *Explorations in Classroom Observation*, London, Wiley.

GLASSER, W. (1969) *Schools without failure*, New York, Harper and Row.

GLASSER, W. (1977) 'Ten steps to good discipline', in *Today's Education*, 6, pp. 61–63.

GOOD, T. and BROPHY, J. (1980) *Looking at classrooms*, 2nd ed., New York, Harper and Row.

GORDON, T. (1974) *T.E.T.: teacher effectiveness training*, New York, McKay.

HARGREAVES, D. H. (1967) *Social Relations in the Secondary School*, London, Routledge and Kegan Paul.

HARGREAVES, D. H. (1972) *Interpersonal Relations and Education*, London, Routledge and Kegan Paul.

JOHNSON, D. and JOHNSON, R. (1975) *Learning together and alone*, Englewood Cliffs, New Jersey, Prentice-Hall.

KOUNIN, J. (1970) *Discipline and group management in classrooms*, New York, Holt, Rinehart and Winston.

LASLETT, R. B. (1977) *Educating Maladjusted Children*, London, Crosby Lockwood Staples.

LUNZER, E. A. (1960) 'Aggressive and Withdrawing children in the normal school', in *British Journal of Education*, 30, pp. 1–10.

MINISTRY OF EDUCATION (1946) *Special Educational Treatment (Pamphlet No. 5)*, London, HMSO.

MINISTRY OF EDUCATION (1955) *Report of the Committee on Maladjusted Children (The Underwood Report)*, London, HMSO.

PIK, L. (1981) 'Confrontation Situations and Teacher-support Systems', in GILLHAM, B. (Ed) *Problem Behaviour in the Secondary School*, London, Croom Helm.

REYNOLDS, D. (1976) 'The Delinquent School', in HAMMERSLEY, M. and WOODS, P. (Eds) *The Process of Schooling: a sociological reader*, London and Henley, Routledge and Kegan Paul/Open University Press.

REYNOLDS, D. and SULLIVAN, M. (1979) 'Bringing schools back in', in BARTON, L. and MEIGHAN, R. (Eds) *Schools, Pupils and Deviance*, Nafferton, Driffield, Nafferton Books.

ROBERTSON, J. (1981) *Effective Classroom Control*, London, Hodder and Stoughton.

ROSENSHINE, B. (1983) 'Teaching Functions in Instructional Programs', in *The Elementary School Journal*, 83, 4, pp. 335–351.

RUTTER, M. (1965) *Helping Troubled Children*, Harmondsworth, Penguin.

RUTTER, M., MAUGHAN, B., MORTIMORE, P. and OUSTON, J. (1979) *Fifteen Thousand Hours*, London, Open Books.

SKINNER, B. F. (1953) *The Science of Human Behaviour*, New York, Macmillan.

SLAVIN, R. (1980) 'Co-operative learning', in *Review of Educational Research*, 50, pp. 315–342.

SQUIBB, P. (1981) 'A Theoretical Structural Approach to Special Education', in BARTON, L. and TOMLINSON, S. (Eds) *Special Education: Policy, Practices and Social Issues*, London, Harper and Row.

STOTT, D. H., MARSDEN, N. C., and NEILL, S. J. (1975) *Taxonomy of Behavioural Disturbance*, London, University of London Press.

TATTUM, D. P. (Ed) (1986) *Management of Disruptive Pupil Behaviour in Schools*, Chichester, Wiley.

TOPPING, K. (1983) *Educational Systems for Disruptive Adolescents*, London, Croom Helm.

WOOLFE, R. (1981) 'Maladjustment in the context of local authority decision-making', in BARTON, L. and TOMLINSON S. (Eds) *Special Education: Policy, Practices and Social Issues*, London, Harper and Row.

WRAGG, E. (1981) *Classroom management and control. A teaching skills workbook*, London and Basingstoke, Macmillan Educational.

Chapter 16

The Role of Language in the Creation of Special Educational Needs
John Harris

The School as a Social Setting for Language

Schools exist to provide children with sound educational experiences, and they do this principally through the medium of spoken and written language. Formal education involves organizing children into classes or smaller teaching groups within which effective instruction can take place. It is also understood that if learning experiences are to be properly structured and systematically presented teachers must exert a considerable degree of control over pupils' behaviour (see preceding chapter). From the point of view of the pupils, school organization, the techniques employed to achieve social control and the priorities of formal instruction create a social environment which is unlike anything they will have experienced before. Because language is above all a social activity and schools are complex social institutions, formal education is associated with special ways of using language which differ from the ones found in other settings outside the school. It is suggested in this chapter that it is the ways in which language is used in schools and the attitudes of teachers towards different forms of language which are very often instrumental in the creation and maintenance of special educational needs.

Consider some of the social characteristics of schools compared with the features of social experience the child will have been exposed to outside school. First, most children will have been cared for in the relatively stable environment of the home in which each child will share a relatively long-lasting and intimate relationship with a small number of adults. In turn the adults assume responsibility and develop a special relationship with a relatively small number of children. In contrast at school there is a much larger proportion of children to adults, and when pupils are organized into

232

classes, each adult will have responsibility for a large number of pupils but only for a small part of each day. Consequently, children and adults need to come to terms with the social and communicative demands which this form of organization imposes upon them. Secondly, whereas the social activities within the home are organized around care-giving and nurturance, the organization of schools reflects its concern with instruction, learning and social uniformity. Furthermore, while teachers are professionals who are trained and paid to act responsibly and reasonably with respect to their pupils, parents are, as it were, volunteers. As the eminent American psychologist Urie Bronfenbrenner has pointed out, one of the important characteristics of parents, which sets them apart from other adults in the child's life, is that they are prepared to go to *unreasonable* lengths in pursuing what they regard as their child's best interests. Thirdly, the organizational constraints of schools emphasize that pupils must go to particular places at pre-set times in order to carry out certain activities. The school timetable regulates the child's activity on the basis of time and location. Once again this stands in marked contrast to the situation at home where, apart from certain activities such as meal time and bed time, the child has more freedom to arrange activities on the basis of inclination and interest.

The organizational constraints of schools shape and regulate the social activities which can occur and these in turn will influence the kinds of language employed by pupils and teachers. Before describing in more detail the different ways in which language is used in schools, it is important to describe one further feature of schools which influences the language of teachers and pupils. One of the primary functions of schools is instruction, that is, the transmission of culturally valued knowledge from one person to another. Within schools, language is the pre-eminent medium for instruction and as such formal education practices which are created to assist learning have major implications for language use. Schools expose children to ways of using language which arise from the instructional process. Most children will have had only a limited experience of language being used in this way before and to some children the language of formal instruction may be completely new. However, it is clear that if children are to succeed in school they must extend their control of language to meet the new demands which are made by schools. Children who, for various reasons, cannot cope with the language of the classroom will inevitably face difficulties in school-based learning and on the basis of linguistic difficulties may come to be viewed as low attainers. Such pupils are not uncommon in secondary schools.

The Role of Language in Schools

This section describes in more detail some of the special ways in which language is used in schools. One essential requirement for good order in schools is that pupils generally do as they are told by the teachers. This will frequently involve one teacher giving verbal instructions to a large number of pupils all of whom are expected to hear, understand and follow the instruction. Groups of pupils may be addressed formally by their group name, e.g. 'Class 4', or more obliquely, as in 'I want you all to stop work' or 'If you have finished you may go'. The ability to follow such instructions is dependent upon the child recognizing that he or she can be a member of the group labelled 'Class 4' 'you all' and indeed 'those that have finished'. This in turn implies a sensitive appreciation of the way in which linguistic meanings are related to the context. Following instructions like these requires that the child is able to operate flexibly within the classificatory frameworks established by the teacher and to locate himself or herself within one of the designated classes (for example, finished assignment, assignment not finished). Furthermore, the child must read into the statement an unspoken presupposition — those not in Class 4, those who have not finished may not leave. While these problems are initially confronted by primary school pupils, those who do not extend their understanding of language to such uses will continue to face problems on into the secondary school.

As has already been suggested, schools set up special social contexts for teaching and learning, and the process of instruction creates its own special forms of language. The American psychologist Jerome Bruner has observed that when knowledge is communicated within the classroom an extra burden is placed upon the role of language. At home or in other non-formal contexts of education there is likely to be a greater emphasis on showing a child what to do and encouraging the child to gain mastery of a particular skill. For example, a child at home may help with the preparation of food for a meal, with gardening or with the repair of tools and machines. Each of these activities would involve a real problem within a particular physical and social context. In schools the problems are selected by the teachers because of their assumed value in promoting certain kinds of learning. Children need to accept these artifical problems and the importance of trying to achieve solutions if they are to succeed in school. At school the context of problem-solving is the classroom, since it is easier to bring the problems to the children rather than taking a class of thirty pupils to the problems to be solved. As a result the problems which teachers present to children in classrooms are different from the problems which they will have met outside school, and are presented differently, and they require a different type of solution. For example, Mercer and Edwards (1981) give the following examples of the kinds of classroom problems in which language is used to express abstract formal relations:

1. It takes three men six hours to dig a certain sized hole. How long would it take two men working at the same rate?

2.   John runs faster than George. Nigel runs slower than George. Who is the fastest?

3.   Who was the more successful King of England, George IV or George V?

School-based problems are different from the problems met outside the school because they are artificial problems. The value of the child solving the problem is not related to immediate practical needs which are apparent to the child (as might be the case, for example, in mending a puncture in a bicycle tyre). Instead, the importance of the problems is derived from a series of educational judgments regarding what children need to learn and how they should learn. In short, although the problems may be justifiable in terms of a curriculum, to the child they are isolated from the real world of experience and arbitrary. Getting the right answer will not be motivated by practical problems and the advantages associated with problem-solving in the real world but rather the social satisfaction of pleasing the teacher, and the intrinsic rewards which may follow from solving a puzzle or a brain teaser.

In setting the classroom problems teachers must overcome the organizational problem posed by larger groups. Very often this is done by describing the problem rather than introducing practical problems into the classroom. Sometimes the introduction of a real life problem would simply be impractical, in terms of size, space, time and equipment. But even where it might be practically possible to present children with real problems, this is either not done, or done in order to illustrate a principle. And here we come to another feature of the traditional formal school-based instruction. Children are expected to do more than acquire practical knowledge which might be necessary for solving the real problems they come across in their ordinary lives. They are expected to learn abstract principles associated with systems of knowledge which have very little bearing on the experiences of our daily lives.

Not only this, but in learning abstract principles pupils are also often required to learn a specialist vocabulary for stating these principles and explaining the underlying process. Because specialist vocabulary is often introduced at the same time as the phenomenon to which the words refer, it is often easy for children to draw inaccurate inferences as to what particular words mean. For example, Margaret Donaldson (1978) cites the example of the child who defined 'liquid' as something which is thick and green (Fairy Liquid). It is also very confusing when one technical term is explained in terms of another. For example a physics textbook defines liquid as 'the state of matter which has definite volume, but no definite shape'. But to understand this requires an existing understanding of 'volume', 'shape' and 'definite'.Examples of arbitrary problems which are introduced into the classroom to demonstrate abstract principles and which require the mastery of specialist terms may be found in almost all areas of the secondary school curriculum.

Not only will such problems be described, rather than presented physically, but instruction will also take the form of telling rather than showing. Verbal description and associated verbal explanations will therefore constitute both the problem and its solution. Thus in many classroom exercises, success in understanding what the problem is and learning how to arrive at an appropriate solution will rest entirely upon the child's command of language. As I will indicate below, there are good reasons to believe that the language of formal instruction is actually different in significant ways from the language of everyday experience, and that children or young people who do not have a strong grasp of the language of formal instruction will be at a serious disadvantage.

Not only is language central to the process by which teachers provide children with learning experiences, it is also an essential if pupils are to demonstrate competence in different curriculum areas. For example, having presented pupils with learning experiences, a teacher is likely to check on what has been learned by asking questions or by setting a piece of written work. A fundamental assumption underlying this use of language is that both teachers and pupils understand the special 'tutorial' nature of the questions posed. Teachers do not ask these kinds of questions because they do not know the answers, rather they ask them because they do know the answers, and they want to establish whether or not the pupils also know the answers. Similarly, when pupils provide written answers to questions, they invariably present information already familiar to the teacher so that the teacher can evaluate the pupils understanding. It has been suggested that classrooms and teachers operate on the basis of an implicit set of ground rules which among other things determine what kinds of language constitute legitimate contribution to a lesson (Mercer and Edwards, 1981). Once again, if children are to succeed in school they must learn these ground rules and the forms of language which are sanctioned by those rules.

Language Variations

The special ways in which language is used in schools would be of less concern if all pupils shared a common linguistic background and broadly similar abilities when they entered schools. However, this is not the case. One of the central features of language is its diversity, and throughout the school years and beyond there are considerable individual differences in terms of linguistic ability. Such differences raise fundamental issues within the educational system. However, in order to understand why this is so, it is necessary to explore in more detail both the nature of linguistic variations and the way in which schools categorize and evaluate pupils.

Language is often described as an abstract symbol system which can be manipulated to express meaning. Here the emphasis is placed upon the grammar of a language which enables a speaker to order sounds and words to create meaningful sentences. However, language can also be viewed as part of a process for managing social interactions. Just as people in different countries speak different languages and learn different grammatical systems, so cultural differences (and sub-cultural differences) give rise to different kinds of social interaction and different ways of using language. Language variation therefore embraces both differences in the ways in which sounds are organized within the grammar to produce meaning, and the different ways in which language may be used within different social contexts.

Accent

Accent refers to the variations within a language in terms of how individuals produce words. For example, 'cold', 'coal', and 'dole' share a common vowel which in some accents is pronounced as a single syllable while in others it is realised as two distinct vowel sounds. Similarly in many parts of London the 't' following a vowel is pronounced with a glottal stop thus producing typical 'cockney' realisations of 'water', 'butter' and 'later'. Accent varies geographically and also across social classes. Social class variation has given rise to a socially prestigious accent often referred to as received pronunciation or RP. This is not the accent associated with the upper middle classes, public schools and aristocratic families but the accent most commonly found among BBC announcers and professional people in the home countries.

Dialect

Dialect reflects variations in the grammatical rules by which meanings are expressed in sentences and by the words which may be used. While schools tend to be particularly concerned with prescriptive rules of grammar — that is, telling pupils how they ought to construct sentences — the study of dialect is concerned with the rules which are actually used by different social groups and the variations which exist in terms of words selected to express concepts or ideas. This *descriptive* approach to dialect emphasizes that there is no dialect which is intrinsically better or worse than any other. Prestigious dialects — for example Standard English — may be highly valued, but they are no more or less effective in terms of communication than any other dialect. Similarly, although Standard English has become the accepted dialect for both educational discourse and written langauge, this is simply a matter of history and tradition and in no way implies that Standard English is better suited for educational practices than any other dialect. Dialects tend to be associated with particular geographical regions and frequently coincide with variations in accent. However, at least in theory, it is possible to distinguish accent (pronunciation) from dialect (grammatical rules and vocabulary).

Style

Whereas it is usual to think of accent and dialect varying from person to person, style is concerned specifically with the ways in which individuals modify their speech according to the social setting. For example, if you wished to excuse yourself from a social gathering you might choose different words and sentences depending upon whether you were at lunch with professional colleagues or at a children's birthday party. Stylistic variation involves choosing appropriate language forms to match the social situation. It involves not only knowledge of how to say things in different ways but experience and accurate perception of a wide variety of social settings. Pupils perceived to be school failures at secondary level are frequently those who have difficulty in matching appropriate language forms to a situation. In many cases this is due to lack of experience.

Function

Functional variation is also concerned with the ways in which language may change in response to different settings. However, whereas style is particularly concerned with achieving similar outcomes by slightly different means, functional variation describes the ways in which language can be used to do different things. Because language is part of a social process, different kinds of social experience will lead to language being used in different ways. On the other hand, lack of experience of certain kinds of social activity will mean that the opportunity to learn about associated language patterns will not be available. Shirley Brice-Heath (1983) provides a vivid description of three communities in South Carolina, USA, where the patterns of child-rearing and social activity in and around the home provided the children in each of the communities with different experiences of using language. In each community the children were provided with rich social experiences and they all developed a sophisticated command of English. However, because the social experiences were very different, the children's linguistic abilities developed in different directions. When the children reached school age, those children who had not been introduced to the educational uses of language experienced considerable difficulty. This question of language use is explained in more detail below. But first it is necessary to consider how linguistic variation achieves prominence in schools.

Language and Educational Values

Language variation among pupils in schools is important for two reasons. First it provides a potential source of information for categorizing pupils in terms of implicit educational values. Secondly, it means that when children come to school there will be differences in the extent to which individual children will have experienced the kinds of language which are valued in schools. I will consider each of these issues separately.

Language and Social Categories

Schools are concerned with both educating children and classifying children. Indeed appropriate forms of classifications are often regarded as a *sine qua non* for effective teaching. Children may be grouped into classes, and into sub-groups within classes, on the basis of characteristics such as 'academic ability' 'intelligence' 'maturity' 'ability to get on with others' and so on. Furthermore, the way in which a teacher perceives an individual child in terms of those characteristics is likely to influence the teacher's behaviour towards the child. Some researchers go further than this (see Chapter 2) and argue that teachers' views of children's ability actually contribute towards school performance. This is the self-fulfilling prophecy which states that children who are *perceived* by teachers to be more able actually *do* better than children who are perceived as being less able, even when on the basis of objective testing the children are of similar levels of ability.

Different research studies have shown that teachers are strongly influenced by accent, dialect and voice quality when asked to make judgments about pupils (see Edwards, 1979, for a review). These judgments derive from social stereotypes in which certain types of behavioural and psychological traits are erroneously assumed always to occur together. Stereotyping is thought to happen because it enables people to categorize others on a wide range of personal characteristics with only minimal objective information. Once having categorized individuals on a range of characteristics it becomes easier to organize our own behaviour towards them. Stereotyping is thus inimical to an appreciation and concern for individual differences. If a teacher has built up a stereotype of a low-ability child as one who, among other things, speaks with a certain accent or dialect, then, in the absence of contradictory evidence, the linguistic evidence alone may be sufficient for the child to be categorized as being of low ability.

Attitudes towards language may be particularly entrenched when varieties of dialect and accent coincide with other important social markers, for example, pupils whose behaviour and dress marks them as coming from a low-prestige group or is suggestive of an anti-authority stance (for example punk or skinhead hairstyles). Similarly young people from ethnic minority groups, particularly those in which ethnicity is emphasized (Rastafarians) or where the cultural traditions are very different to those found among the ethnic majority, are particularly vulnerable to the influence of social stereotypes.

Social categories derived from linguistic variation may also influence educational objectives. If teachers believe that children are likely to be disadvantaged because of a regional accent or dialect, they may well seek to modify a child's language so that it approximates more prestigious forms. For example, it is often argued that since most written language is in Standard English dialect, a child will be better prepared for reading if he or she is already familiar with the spoken forms of Standard English (Romaine, 1984, pp. 207–209). It has also been suggested that children with regional dialects and accents experience disadvantages in the competition for employment after school, and that teachers ought therefore to help children to acquire more prestigious ways of talking.

The influence of negative attitudes towards dialect and accent does not however only extend as far as the teacher. All of us come to understand ourselves as social beings in terms of the way in which other people respond to us. If pupils become aware that because of their language they are regarded as less able or less important as people, they may come to regard their own language as inferior and cause for embarrassment. This in turn will discourage pupils from expressing themselves in written or spoken language and may lead to a gradual withdrawal from all educational activities which involve linguistic communication. Needless to say, children who appear to be tongue-tied and resistant to learning within formal settings such as the classroom, may be extremely voluble and competent communicators in other social situations (Labov, 1969; Brice-Heath, 1983).

Linguistic variation therefore can have an important impact on a child's learning experiences within school simply because of erroneous beliefs about the implications of different forms of language (stereotyping on the basis of accent and dialect) or because of the status which attaches to certain socially prestigious ways of speaking.

Language Inside and Outside the School

At home and in many non-educational environments language occurs within familiar social and physical settings and between people who know each other well. In such settings the meanings which are communicated are not always expressed in the words and sentences spoken; it is possible to communicate more than is actually expressed in the language structure. This is possible because over time people build up a shared knowledge which enables both participants in a conversation to predict what kinds of messages are likely to be communicated. Secondly, the physical context and the social activities in which conversational partners are engaged place constraints on the messages which are likely to be communicated. Together, shared knowledge and the immediate physical and social context make it possible to understand complex meanings, even when relatively little meaning is expressed in language. To illustrate this example, imagine two friends talking together while drinking in a pub. At one point one of the friends says 'same again?' with a questioning intonation. Here the pub and the activity of drinking (which includes social knowledge about how many drinks one is likely to consume and about turn-taking in the purchase of 'rounds') provides a physical context for the interpretation of this utterance. The shared social knowledge which exists between the two drinkers, means that the type of drink, and the size of measure does not need to be specified. Not only is this kind of contextually-based use of language natural and endemic to many social settings, it is also a major part of the experience of young children learning language. Thus from a developmental perspective, learning to communicate where only a part of the intended meaning is expressed in the words spoken comes before being able to formulate more explicit utterances. Expressing complex ideas in language so that the meanings can be understood from the language alone, is an important part of language-learning which depends upon children having appropriate experiences. These experiences include hearing language being used to make meanings explicit and being encouraged to express meanings in language, even in situations where the physical and social context might make such explicit meanings redundant.

At home children will have been exposed to different ways of using language and they will have had different experiences of decontextualized language — that is, language where meanings are made explicit and rely only minimally on the social and physical context. (See, for example, the work of Brice-Heath mentioned above.) However, when a child begins to attend school he or she will be immersed in the educational uses of language — that is, language for organization, language for instruction and language for demonstrating competence. In all three cases the child will be confronted by decontextualized language where the meanings conveyed must be clear from the words spoken (Donaldson, 1978; Mercer and Edwards, 1981, and above). Children who have already had some experience of language being used in this way will obviously be at some advantage in following instructions, in understanding teachers' descriptions and explanations and in providing 'correct' answers to questions (Romaine, 1984). Children who have not been exposed to this formal use of language may become confused and experience a feeling of alienation and failure (Bruner, 1966). It is also easy for adults to categorize such pupils as stupid — that is, innately less intelligent than linguistically more able pupils — or as suffering from a verbal deficit which will inevitably hamper their educational progress (Edwards, 1979). Neither of these interpretations provide a useful foundation for designing interesting and challenging educational experiences. However, it is important to recognize that schools make selective demands upon children and that experiences outside the school will influence how children are able to respond to these demands. Similarly a failure to respond to the different linguistic needs of pupils within schools will only reinforce and compound these problems.

Summary

This chapter began by suggesting that language needs to be considered both as an abstract system of communicating ideas and as part of a social process. Schools are complex social organizations within which certain kinds of activities are promoted, and these activities give rise to special ways of using language. Among the most important uses of language in schools are organization and control, instruction and the demonstration of competence.

The second part of the chapter considered the ways in which language varies across individuals. This included a consideration of accent, dialect, style and function. In the third section it was suggested that the special uses to which language is put in schools together with the existence of variation across individuals create the conditions for some pupils to experience difficulties. The first level of difficulty arises solely from the attitudes which some teachers may hold about the significance of accent and dialect. If children and young people who speak in a particular way are assumed to be less able than others, then they may experience educational disadvantages and perform less well in the classroom.

The second kind of difficulty arises from the status which the community outside the school attaches to certain dialects and accents. If teachers believe that a pupil with a regional accent or dialect is likely to suffer from discrimination in terms of post-school employment they are likely to encourage the acquisition of alternative more desirable accents and dialects.

This in turn may cause pupils to perceive their language as being of low status and inferior within the school setting. Such views may lead to antagonism towards more accepted ways of speaking and withdrawal from situations involving talking or writing.

The third area of difficulty concerns the way in which education depends upon a decontextualized use of language. Children who have not had experience of language being used in this way before entering school are likely to be at a disadvantage compared to other children who have had different linguistic experiences. Such differences and experiences will be compounded if children are judged as being innately less intelligent or linguistically deficient on the basis of these differences. It is also important to remember that a central theme of formal education is accomplishment of certain ways of using language. Language may be likened to a tool of thinking (Bruner, 1966) and children as apprentices who need to become proficient tool users. Proficiency in using language, however, will depend upon appropriate experience and good teaching.

References

BRICE-HEATH, S. (1983) *Ways with Words*, Cambridge, Cambridge University Press.

BRUNER, J.S. (1966) *Towards a Theory of Instruction*, Harvard, Harvard University Press.

BRUNER, J.S. (1966) 'Language and Cognition II', in BRUNER, J.S., OLIVER, R.R. and GREENFIELD, P.M. (Eds) *Studies in Cognitive Growth*, New York, Wiley.

BRUNER, J.S. (1976) 'Nature and Uses of Immaturity', in BRUNER, J.S., JOLLY, A. and SYLVA, K. (Eds), *Play: Its Role in Development and Evolution*, Harmondsworth, Penguin.

DONALDSON, M. (1978) *Childrens Minds*, London, Fontana.

EDWARDS, J.R. (1979) *Language and Disadvantage*, London, Arnold.

LABOV, W. (1969) 'On the Logic of Non-Standard English', reprinted in GIGLIOLI, P.P. (Ed.) (1972) *Language and Social Context*, Harmondsworth, Penguin.

MERCER, N. and EDWARDS, D. (1981) 'Ground Rules for Mutual Understanding: A Social Psychological Approach to Class-Room Knowledge', in MERCER, N. (Ed), *Language in School and Community*, London, Arnold.

ROMAINE, S. (1984) *The Language of Children and Adolescents*, London, Blackwell.

Chapter 17

Both Sexes Lose Out: Low Achievers and Gender
Sara Delamont

Sexism is a negative value, better swept out of schools... Let us hope that 1986 sees the following complaint, printed in the *TV Times* (3.7.1976) as a quaint reminder of an outmoded view of males and females:

> My brother and I are twins aged nearly sixteen. My mother wants me to leave school and wants my brother to stay on for a better education as she says girls don't need it — they get married. I'm very interested in French and am doing well in it at school. Do you think it is fair that I should have to leave and my brother stay on?

Let us hope no one believes it is fair in the 1980s (Delamont, 1980).

Introduction

The passage quoted above is the conclusion to a book I published in 1980 called *Sex Roles and the School* which raised a set of issues about the ways in which both boys and girls suffer from over-rigid sex-role stereotyping in schools. The book was intended for practising teachers and those training for teaching, and is still representative of my opinions on the subject. Since 1980 a great deal more research has been done on the topic including Powell and Littlewood (1982) on boys and foreign languages, Whyte (1986) on the Girls into Science and Technology project, a group of authors calling for *Girl Friendly Schooling* (Whyte *et al.*, 1986), and two useful collections on sex-differentiation and schooling (Marland, 1983; Whyld, 1983). Despite the research that has accumulated since 1980 the conclusion quoted above appears too optimistic. There are still plenty of parents, teachers, heads, advisors, governors, employers and adolescents who hold sexist views and act in ways that discriminate against one sex or the other, without even being aware of what they are doing. The research that has been produced often fails to reach pre-service teachers, or those on in-service courses, and there is very little about how sex-differentiation and/or discrimination occur among low-attaining pupils in secondary education. This chapter raises some of the issues which teachers need to consider, especially those where addressing sex inequality might lead to improved school performance and better attitudes to schooling.[1]

There are statistical studies of sex inequalities in education revealing the lack of girls in science and CDT after the age of 14, and maths after 16; balanced by lack of boys in foreign languages, home ecomonics and office skills courses after 14. There are job vacancies for young people with skills, but the early evidence from research into TVEI and CPVE is that boys and girls are being offered *different* training and vocational preparation which is based on outmoded ideas that the labour market is sex-segregated. The sceptical reader can easily find such statistics in the educational press and government publications. Here the emphasis is on the social relationships that continue every day in schools, where individual teachers can begin to change and challenge sex-role norms. Individual teachers can do little to alter the national statistical picture, but we can all change small things in the content and process of our lessons.

There are five main ways in which schools differentiate between boys and girls to the disadvantage of both sexes. These are: the organization of the school; the teacher's strategies for controlling and motivating pupils; the organization and content of lessons; the informal conversations between pupils and their teachers; and leaving unchallenged the pupils' own stereotyping and self-segregating of activities. Some of the material presented will display the sexes being segregated, and the differences between males and females highlighted and exaggerated; some will reveal either males or females being disadvantaged. The central arguments of the chapter are that schools should be actively concerned with sex equality, even if that means confronting stereotyped beliefs pupils hold; and that this is especially important for low-achieving pupils. I argue that the sex-stereotyping which is common in schools is more easily resisted by high-achieving adolescents, and such things as single-sex craft teaching have a particularly strong impact on low-achieving pupils.

In general, the higher the attainment level of secondary pupils the less sex-differentiation there is in their curriculum. There are examples of sex-stereotyping in sixth forms (e.g. Stanworth, 1981) and top bands, but the process is much more blatant and explicit in industrial training units for slow learners (Shone and Atkinson, 1981), in YTS schemes (Brelsford *et al.*, 1982;

Rees, 1983) and in the remedial classes of comprehensive schools (Burgess, 1983). It is easier for a clever pupil to opt for an unusual subject choice or career than for a low-ability pupil, one who is already in rebellion against the school, or one who is not achieving academic success. The other four types of sex-differentiation bear on pupils of all achievement levels with equal force, as the rest of the chapter shows and as I have argued elsewhere (Delamont, 1980, 1982, 1983a, 1983b, 1984 and 1986). The evidence that schools are places where a great deal of unthinking sex-discrimination goes on is examined later in this chapter, after an explanation of why it matters.

The Consequences of Sex-differentiation and Sex-discrimination

The consequences of sex-differentiation are slightly different for boys and girls. The boy who goes through school looking down on females, being allowed to adhere to the sexual double standard, unable to cook and sew, ignorant of childcare and equipped for a world where women wait on his emotional and domestic needs is handicapped for his future family and domestic life, and a lost cause for sexual responsibility and parenthood. He is primarily disadvantaged in his personal, emotional and home life. The girl who does not learn to assert herself, has not studied science, technology and 'heavy' craft is primarily handicapped in the labour market, because she lacks the skills (or confidence to acquire them) which lead to higher-paying jobs. However, both sexes are disadvantaged in both domestic and employment spheres if their schooling has left their ideas about sex-roles unchallenged and trapped in traditional stereotypes. Boys will be unwilling to enter occupations that are associated with women, even if such jobs (e.g. in the catering and retailing industries) are expanding. Women will face unhappy home lives if the men they marry are domestically incompetent and hold different expectations about marriage from their own.

This may seem to be an exaggerated, even hysterical, view. There is, however, too much evidence supporting it for the points raised about males and females to be dismissed (e.g. Guttentag and Bray, 1976; Best, 1983, Sadker and Sadker, 1982; Delamont, 1984; Whyte, 1986, Weis, 1988). For example Guttentag and Bray found that whereas girls were trying to plan their futures round more flexible sex-roles — that is, futures in which both parents had careers that mattered, and both partners shared housework, child-rearing and earning the household income — boys were not. Boys expected a future in which they did no housework, took no part in childcare, and supported a non-working wife. Lois Weis's (1988) recent study of adolescents in a city where the steel mills had closed found the same pattern of expectations. Young women saw themselves in an egalitarian marriage, boys envisaged a traditional one.

The schools that these adolescents attended were not dealing with such issues at all. The schools did not encourage the pupils to confront their divergent expectations, or fit the girls for the labour market by equipping them with vocational skills, or train the boys in childcare and housekeeping. Instead, the schools reinforced old-fashioned sex-stereotypes. They were encouraging pupils to become male and female adults fitted for a world that has vanished.

One particular issue – health education – will be used to explain what teachers could be doing, and why they should be challenging adolescents' sex-role beliefs. There is considerable British evidence that the sex education and health education that teenagers get fails to address boys' ideas about female sexuality, and consequently fails to change their behaviour. Sue Lees (1986), like Paul Willis (1977), Deidre Wilson (1978), Lesley Smith (1978) and Christine Farrell (1978) before her, found that teenage boys nearly all hold a polarized and a simplistic view of female sexuality. Boys believe there are 'good', 'nice' girls who are suitable as steady girlfriends, fiancées and wives and other women who are 'slags', 'tarts' and 'easy lays' who 'deserve all they get'. Old-fashioned as it may seem, teenage boys cling to such stereotypes, in which 'nice girls' are virgins until they are safely established in a steady, serious relationship; while 'bad' girls will have intercourse with many partners. Teenage girls do not necessarily believe that all females can be easily divided, but they accept that boys *do* have such views and realize that the male outlook has powerful consequences for their lives. One of Lesley Smith's (1978) respondents explained to her:

> Look I don't believe there should be one standard for a boy and another for a girl. But there just is round here and there's not much you can do about it. A chap's going to look for someone who hasn't had it off with every bloke. So as soon as you let them put a leg over you, you've got a bad name.

Similarly, Sue Lees was told:

> When there're boys talking and you've been out with more than two you're known as the crisp that they're passing around.... The boy's alright but the girl's a bit of scum (1986).

Girls have to avoid being 'slags' themselves, and they must not associate with other girls who have bad reputations. Lees was told:

> If someone for whatever reason has got a bad name,... you can't go with that girl. Because you get called the same name and if you're hanging around with a slag you must be one (1986).

Adolescent girls are careful to maintain their reputations as 'nice' girls and avoid being labelled 'slags' and 'sluts'. The latter can be spotted by a variety of signs, but one of them, in the boys' eyes, is a girl's knowledge and use of contraceptives. Teenage girls know that if they reveal any experience with contraception they will be labelled as 'tarts' and treated accordingly. In the girls' eyes, it is socially reasonable to risk pregnancy rather than be labelled a 'tart'. Studies on health and sex education (e.g., Rocheron, 1985; Measor and Woods, 1988) in comprehensive schools reveal that teachers do not challenge these adolescent beliefs. It is likely that if teenage pregnancy (Murcott, 1980), and even more importantly the spread of AIDS, are to be prevented, teachers will have to find some way of persuading boys to re-think their double standard, and of encouraging girls to risk social ostracism and preserve their health. The work of Aggleton and his colleagues (1988) discusses these issues specifically in relation to AIDS. Pupils of both sexes must be challenged to rethink their positions on the double standard, so that health education takes place in a less stereotyped atmosphere. Simultaneously girls need to be encouraged to challenge male perceptions and use contraception whatever the social consequences.

Lower-achieving pupils are in particular need of good health and sex education, and are least likely to receive it from any source other than the teacher, such as books. Girls who under-achieve in school tend to be sexually experienced at younger ages than those who are in high bands and taking exams (see Delamont, 1980).

There is also the controversial issue of adolescents' confusions about male sexuality. For most adolescents any boy who cannot, or does not, fight, run, jump and struggle to be *macho* is labelled as 'soft', and even as a 'pouf', 'boff' or 'fruit'. (See Delamont and Galton, 1986; Best, 1983; Measor and Woods, 1984). These insults, which have nothing to do with real adult homosexuality, are desperately hurtful for the adolescent boy. On 7 June 1987 the *TV Times* problem page carried the following cry for help:

> *Name-callers*
> I am a 13-year-old boy at high school, and my problem is name-calling. I do not know why, but other children have started shouting 'gaylord' and 'fruity boy' at me, and I find it very upsetting... KK, N. Ireland.

If teachers systematically challenged pupils' simplistic ideas about male and female behaviour, and presented a clear vision of a world in which *all* skills and personal qualities are associated with both sexes, then such insults would have no force. A boy who prefers reading to cross-country, or sewing to soccer, has a right to his preferences, and schools should cherish and encourage them.

At present there may be other potential Bruce Oldfields hiding their talents for fear of being labelled as 'poofters', just as there are potential Rosalind Franklins avoiding science in case people tease them. Britain cannot afford to lose such talents, nor should schools be abetting adolescent misery by letting simplistic peer-group pressures rule pupils' lives.

The above example concerned pupils' own stereotypes about male and female behaviour, and the failure of the school to challenge them, rather than ways in which teachers and schools create and reinforce sexual differentiation. In the next section of the chapter, the focus changes to the ways in which schools and teachers frequently differentiate between the sexes and discriminate against either males or females, *often without being aware of what they are doing.*

Sex-stereotyping in Ordinary Schools

It is very hard to recognize all the ways in which perfectly ordinary schools segregate, differentiate, and even discriminate against some pupils on the basis of their sex. Most of us grew up in schools that divided us by sex, and we are all liable to perpetuate sexual divisions because we simply do not notice them. When some of the ways in which schools are sexually divisive are mentioned they seem trivial; others are seen as 'natural', and both labels prevent change. This section uses data from several studies of comprehensive schools in Wales and England to illustrate ways in which sexual differentiation and discrimination take place, and then explains why they matter and how they can be changed. The four main arenas for sexual divisions in schools discussed are: school organization, teacher control, lesson content and structure, and informal teacher-pupil relations. In all these areas of school life many teachers are teaching sex-role behaviour by default, because they are stereotyping and segregating the sexes. The lessons about sex-roles which are reinforced by organizational and managerial arrangements may not be those which staff want pupils to learn at all.

Some concrete examples will make these issues clearer. The data which follow are from an observational study of comprehensive schools in Wales in 1985–86, the ORACLE project done in six schools in England (Delamont and Galton, 1986), and the work of Measor and Woods (1984) on a midlands comprehensive.[2] The Welsh data were gathered while researching how pupils with learning difficulties (formerly ESN(M)) were being integrated into mainstream school life. Nine schools were visited, all of which, just as the six ORACLE schools and that observed by Measor and Woods together with all teachers and pupils, have been given pseudonyms in this paper. A list of all the sixteen schools from which examples are taken is given at the end of the chapter.[3] Sex-stereotyping was not the main focus of any of the studies from which data are taken for this chapter. The ORACLE project and the Measor and Woods (1984) studies were focused on how pupils manage the transfer from primary to secondary school, and the Welsh study was on the integration of statemented pupils into the mainstream. The examples of sexual differentiation, sexual stereotyping and sex-discrimination given below were thrown up while we were observing something else.

School Organization

The Sex Discrimination Act of 1975 included several clauses which were designed to stop schools offering different subjects or organizational arrangements to males and females. Yet schools observed in 1978 and in 1985–86 were breaking the law and organizing boys and girls into separate subjects. In 1978 Waverly School in Coalthorpe (an industrial city in the North of England) only offered woodwork and metalwork to boys, and only girls did needlework and cookery. In South Wales in 1986 two of our schools, Sharway Downs and Fosse, taught all the craft in single-sex groups, and boys and girls did different subjects. At Sharway Downs all the pupils observed were in single-sex and single-ability groups for craft, so the boys from Mr Whaddon's second year 'remedial and statemented' group did woodwork and metalwork, while the girls did needlework and cookery. This sex-differentiation was also found at Fosse. At a third school, Rushford, only boys did metalwork and woodwork, although both sexes got some 'survival' cookery. At Burminster, girls did 'typing' in a single-sex group while boys did 'keyboard skills' in an all-male class. Thus at Sharway Downs and Fosse, boys never learnt to cook themselves a meal or sew on a button; while at Fosse, Sharway Downs and Rushford the girls got no chance to handle tools, use lathes or work with wood or metal. Measor and Woods (1984) showed that many boys did not enjoy either cookery or needlework, believing them to be 'girls' subjects'. Keith told them: 'I don't really like doing needlework as much as other things like cutting up rats'.

However, adults know that pupils need to learn many skills that they do not enjoy acquiring: the girls in Keith's class mostly disliked science but all schools regard it as part of a core curriculum. There is little evidence on how common such segregation still is, or on how to encourage pupils of both sexes to enjoy non-traditional subjects. The burgeoning literature on sex-roles and the school (e.g. Delamont, 1980; Whyld, 1983; Marland, 1983) contains very little on sex-differentiation among children with learning difficulties. It is possible that the amount of sex-segregation and sex-differentiation we observed was less than we would have found in special schools before the Warnock Report (1978), or in special schools today. It is clear, however, that the sex-stereotyped activities in South Wales in 1985–86 were similar to those found in comprehensive schools in three English LEAs as long ago as 1977–78 by the ORACLE project (Delamont, 1980; Galton and Willcocks, 1983; Delamont and Galton, 1986). Carol Buswell's (1981) observational study in a Newcastle comprehensive found that pupils were divided by sex about twenty times every day, and the organizational arrangements in these nine Welsh schools were essentially similar. Pupils were listed separately on the register, went into assembly in single-sex lines, waited outside classrooms in single-sex lines, had separate PE, in several schools had separate craft, used different cloakrooms, changing-rooms and lavatories, ate lunch in different sittings, and so on. During the teachers' action, sometimes only one sex was excluded from a class. Boys and girls also wore different clothing — in that several schools enforced ties and blazers for boys and not girls, or made girls wear only skirts rather than trousers and so on. In organizational terms, the sexes were frequently separated and differentiated for administrative convenience, not for educational reasons. Of all the above separations only that of changing-rooms and lavatories would receive widespread public support. Outside schools females wear trousers, eat at the same tables as males, and hang their coats on neighbouring hooks without any comment.

The educational experience of the moderately learning-impaired pupils we observed was characterized by integration achieved at the cost of sex-segregation. Sometimes the aim of locational integration was achieved at the cost of sex-segregation, sometimes pupils were isolated into single-sex *and* single-ability groups. Two brief examples will illustrate these points. At Rushford, the first and second year children ate lunch at a different sitting from older children, and were further divided by sex, so that all the girls had lunch together, and then all the boys. Pupils of low ability (all statemented children) from Mrs Lavater's special class which we were observing were therefore separated from one another, so that the three girls went to the first sitting, and the boys were sent in later. Each set of children was observed mixing in the dining queue and at tables with friends from other classes — but never with children of the opposite sex. This is an organizational arrangement which segregates the sexes, and discourages them from interacting socially.

Listing the two sexes separately on the register may seem a neutral act. However if the register is used to organize classrooms serious consequences can arise. At both Waverly and Melin Court (schools in Coalthorpe) the boys were listed first on the register and this had a consequence in technical drawing at Waverly and in woodwork at Melin Court. The ORACLE observers wrote:

After break go to Technical Drawing with Mr Quill. He lines them up at the back and the side of the room, and allocates seats in alphabetical order. Boys first — leaving spaces for absentees. There are twenty-eight children on the class list — and only twenty-three proper drawing tables — so five girls get left without proper desks and are given slots on the side benches. Then they are told that when anyone is absent, they can sit in the absentees' seats (Waverly).

In the woodwork room the new pupils are being allocated places at the benches in alphabetical order, with the boys first. When Mr Beech found that he had twenty-three in the group it was girls left without bench places — about three girls left to work in any space left where someone was absent (i.e. changing seats each lesson/starting each lesson by trying to find a bench space to work at). (Melin Court).

Here the use of a sex-segregated register had two consequences: sex-segregated seating in the technical drawing classroom and woodwork room and inducing a feeling of unease and 'non-belonging' in girls. I am sure the masters did not mean to make the female pupils feel insecure in their rooms, but using the register to organize seating had that effect.

School organization is not neutral, even when we take it for granted. Constantly separating pupils by sex emphasizes sex differences, and when male and female pupils are occasionally required to cooperate they find it very difficult. (Elliot, 1974; Barnes and Todd, 1977; Tann, 1981; Delamont and Galton, 1986; Best, 1983)

Motivation and Control

In all the six schools where the ORACLE fieldwork took place we found teachers using gender-differentiation as a way of motivating and controlling pupils. For example at Gryll Grange we saw Miss Tweed try to hurry her class through a maths exercise by staging competition between the boys and the girls to see which sex could finish all the sums first (see Delamont, 1980). Using ridicule to enforce discipline was also common. For example when Miss Wordsworth at Melin Court told the girls in her form to line up for Assembly and a boy, Wayne, stood up, she said 'Oh Wayne thinks he's a girl'. Wayne sat down again immediately. Attempting to motivate boys to work by comparing them to girls was frequently seen. For example:

At Waverly Miss Southey had a class in the school library and when she saw most of the girls had borrowed books but none of the boys she said "All the girls are taking out books but not one boy yet. Can't the boys read in this class?'

A few boys then borrowed books but most did not, despite the teacher's comment. Similar teacher strategies were equally common in nine Welsh schools in 1985–86 both to maintain order or organize activities where no educational reason existed. For example at Gorston Hall the fourth-year remedial and statemented group had a rural studies lesson in which the boys were sent out, unsupervised, to wheel some barrow-loads of earth to a new flower bed while the master interviewed the girls and filled in their assessment profiles with them. As only one girl could be seen at once, and the others were left to chat, they could have been moving the earth with the boys. The sex-segregation served no educational purpose, only an organizational one. A common teacher strategy was to allow one sex to leave the room before the other as a control strategy. Thus, in Mrs Leithen's class at Gorston Hall:

> It is 3.30. Mrs Leithen says 'Nobody is going from here till you are all quiet'. When they are quiet they are allowed to leave a small number at a time, girls first, then the boys in small groups.

This may work as a control strategy, but at the cost of emphasizing that boys and girls are different, and reinforcing their own prejudices. Schools should be challenging pupils' sex-stereotypes, not encouraging them. At Sharway Downs when the Senior Mistress of the Lower School was doing a history lesson on Pompeii with the remedial and statemented first years she found that Royden was doing nearly all the answering, so she suggested, 'Let's ask the girls for a change'. When the class moved on to RE, Royden again volunteered answers to most of the questions and this teacher too suggested that, 'Now the girls in front are sitting awful quiet'.

Here again the reasonable teacher strategy — getting other pupils to share in the progress of the lesson — is realized in a sex-segregating way. Other pupils are 'girls' — not individuals — and the other boys in the class were equally unresponsive to the teacher's questions and needed to be encouraged to answer. Singling out 'girls' serves only to reinforce their difference from Royden and other boys, and does nothing to encourage all the other pupils to participate in the discourse.

Teaching Strategies and Lesson Content

The content of much of the curriculum, and the ways in which teachers taught the material, is also full of sex-stereotyping. Carol Buswell's (1981) research in a Newcastle comprehensive included an analysis of the humanities materials used in the lower school. There were 326 pages of text, including 169 pictures of men and only 21 of women, and 102 individual men were described as against 14 women. Among the tasks for pupils were the following:

(1)   Look at the pictures of the clothes the Romans wore. Would they be easy for your mother to wash if you were a Roman?

(2)   Find the name of this make of car. Your father or brother will probably know, ask them.

(3)   Make up a poem about a very rich man or a very poor man.

The ORACLE project observers found equally stereotyped curriculum content in its six schools. In English, for example, a typical exercise involved pupils making up sentences around words given by the teacher to learn and practise sentence construction, punctuation and parts of speech. For example:

> In Mrs Hind's class, pupils are required to invent sentences, each including three words the teacher has put up on the board:
> boy, football, window:
> gorilla, cage, keeper;
> monkeys, coconuts, hunters;
> soldier, army, tank.
> Several pupils ask her about the words so Mrs Hind reads through them aloud. Says of 'soldier, army, tank' 'That's one for the boys really I suppose'.

This comes from Gryll Grange in the second week of term, but could be seen in any of the schools. We see an entirely gratuitous comment by a teacher re-confirming a stereotype the pupils already have instead of challenging it. It is also clear that the sets of words, and the sentences they will result in, are predictable and dull. Thirty-five children will probably produce 'The boy kicked the football through the window'. Much more interesting sentences, and more pupil attention being paid to the task, would be produced from '*girl*, football, window' and '*WRAC*, army, tank'.

At Guy Mannering one class were being taught about 'the book' by Mr LeGard who told them:

> on the title page there will be the author's name, and that tells you something about the book. You may recognize the author and therefore know he is a good one. 'If you get a chemistry book by a senior master at a big school he ought to know what he is talking about, but if it is by someone who is just a housewife, *well!*'

Winter (1983) has highlighted the restricted number of female characters in reading materials for slow learners in the secondary age-range, and the limited range of occupations and low ambitions the women characters have. Frances James, a remedial teacher, made the same point in a letter to the *Guardian* (17 February 1987).

Sexual stereotyping was also common in the textbooks, worksheets and teaching in the Welsh schools in 1985–86. So for example at Fosse when the second year were doing an exercise on healthy eating with Mrs Barralty, she discovered that none of the children knew what stock was.

> Mrs Barralty asked 'What's in a stock? Come on, girls, you do cookery...?'
> Vaughan replies 'OXO'

This interaction was doubly interesting. It confirmed for the observer that boys did not do cookery at Fosse, and stereotypes the girls. Interestingly a boy (Vaughan) was the only child in the room to have any idea how gravy was made, so the teacher's expectation — only girls who could be asked about cooking — was confounded.

Sometimes one teacher would try to avoid sexism and be frustrated by another. At Fosse we saw the girls from the remedial and statemented class join those from one of the 'B' band forms for PE. The teacher, Mrs Varrinder, sent those girls who had forgotten their kit down from the upstairs gym to the downstairs one, where the boys were having PE, to fetch back the benches that were normally kept there which had been 'borrowed' before half-term. They returned empty-handed, followed by boys carrying the benches, detailed by the PE master, who had been teaching male PE in the main hall. Mrs Varrinder's attempt to get some girls to carry benches was frustrated by the PE master, who chivalrously assigned boys to do it for them, stressing female dependence. Some of the boys assigned were smaller than the girls they were 'helping', which made the sexual division of labour appear silly.

One day at Sharway Downs the first year boys were scheduled for woodwork, but because they had been so badly behaved in the workshop in previous lessons the master took them to the graphics (TD) room, to design a poster instead. While discussing how a 'For Sale' poster should be designed the master said: 'If I was selling a car to a woman I'd put the colour first', (that is, before the make, price or mileage). Such stereotyped comments serve only to reinforce sexual prejudices that pupils already have.

One particular 'blind spot' that pupils have concerns the use of the words 'man' and 'men' to mean human beings rather than just males. This is a common flaw in teaching materials and in the oral parts of lessons. There is ample research evidence that pupils and students hear 'man' to mean 'males' unless they are explicitly told that it covers people of both sexes. There are forty-four articles on this point in Thorne *et al.* (1983): including Schneider and Hacker (1973) who found undergraduates studying social science interpreted 'men' in that way and Harrison (1975) who reports adolescents making the same mistake studying 'the evolution of man'. Teachers need to explain to pupils, especially those who are low achievers, that 'man's evolution' means human evolution, and 'great men of science' includes Marie Curie, Rosalind Franklin and Barbara McClintock, but few currently do so.

There are authors who claim that teachers allow boys to dominate the talk in classrooms, taking three-quarters of all the teacher's attention and making three-quarters of the pupil contributions (e.g Spender, 1982). As I have argued elsewhere in some detail (Delamont, 1984), such claims do not stand up to close scrutiny. However, studies do show differences in the ways teachers respond to male and female pupils. Shuy (1985) studied a teacher who regularly challenged things his male pupils said ('why did you say that?') but never the responses from his female pupils. The girls got positive or neutral feedback ('Okay', 'Alright' ' Very nice', 'terrific', etc.). A great deal more research is needed on this area, but all teachers can tape themselves and examine whether they are treating the boys and girls in their rooms differently and if so, in what ways.

Teacher-Pupil Banter

When teachers engage in informal interactions with pupils they may inadvertently be reinforcing stereotyped sex-roles. Carol Joffe (1974) found that teachers complimented girls on their personal appearance far more often than boys, and that girls received more compliments when they were wearing dresses than they did when in trousers. Classroom jokes may also be based on sexual stereotypes:

> The top French set are in the language lab, and the pupils were answering questions in French about their families. A boy who says he has four sisters gets the cheery comment from the master 'Poor Lad' (Waverly)

Similarly when Miss Tweed's class came back from having their school photographs taken she said to the girls:

> You've done enough fussing. I know you're all filmstars. Did he faint with delight at such loveliness?

Jokes such as these would not be such a source of sex-stereotyping if all other aspects of schooling were more thoroughly egalitarian and free of sex-segregation, sex-differentiation and sex-discrimination.

The picture outlined so far is a negative one and may have left the reader feeling depressed about schools and schooling. In the final section of the chapter some solutions and proposals for change are outlined.

Strategies for Change

Whyld (1983) has an excellent section (p. 295–313) in her book packed with realistic ideas for ordinary teachers to draw on to change sexist schooling. Winter (1983) has written a useful paper on how teachers of remedial pupils can combat sexism in their classrooms, and there are practical handbooks by Sadker and Sadker (1982) and Whyte (1985). Raphaela Best (1983) has produced a lively account of how she changed the sex-stereotyped attitudes of a class, so that they went on through secondary school struggling against the sex-differentiation they met there. One of her pupils — Jonathan — even managed to be elected class president (form captain) with the slogan 'vote for Jonathan: He campaigns for women's rights'.

Various proposals have been made to reduce sexism in schools. One interesting set of such reforms was proposed by Susanne Shafer (1976):

(1)   Co-education
(2)   Co-educational sex education
(3)   Additional maths and science for girls
(4)   Non-sexist textbooks in all subjects
(5)   Promotion of women teachers to senior posts
(6)   Basic domestic survival skills for all boys
(7)   Counselling for girls to encourage achievement

Shafer is an East German, who claims that there is greater sex equality in schools in the GDR: a belief that is not supported by the evidence in Lane (1983) and Sutherland (1985). One major American project which tried to change teachers' classroom behaviour and pupils' stereotypes is discussed in Guttentag and Bray (1976). This project included pupils in kindergarten, and 10 and 14 year olds, and studied attitude change and classroom behaviour before and after curriculum materials on sex-roles were introduced. They found that teachers who were both skilful and convinced of the desirability of the materials could change pupils' views. However, a poorly-planned curriculum package, or one that was badly taught, was likely to reinforce the boys' negative views about girls rather than change them. The classroom observation data showed that after the non-sexist materials had been introduced, girls became more active participants in classroom interaction. Guttentag and Bray (1976) offer the following nine generalizations based on the action research:

(1)   Sex-role attitudes are hard to change in children of any age
(2)   Children are generally non-sexist about themselves
(3)   Children are somewhat sexist about same-sexed peers
(4)   Children are very sexist about opposite sex peers
(5)   Children at kindergarten can learn to be occupationally non-sexist
(6)   Girls are trying to create lifestyles that integrate home and career
(7)   Boys generally disregard or squelch non-sexist values
(8)   As perceived by children, the male's role is tight, while the female's role is more flexible
(9)   A little intervention is/may be dangerous; a strong intervention has/can have powerful positive effects.

There is a lesson here for British schools. Only teachers committed to changing sex-role relationships in schools are likely to be able to shift pupils' attitudes, and then only if they are skilful in their use of materials. No point would be served in sending non-sexist materials into the schools where teachers were not interested in using them. Similar conclusions can be drawn from the Girls into Science and Technology project in Britain (Whyte, 1985) and the Schools Council's Reducing Sex Differentiation in Schools project (Myers, 1987).

At classroom level there are things individual teachers can do, such as the German master at Waverly:

> Mr Baden goes over the difference between 'Frau' and 'Fraulein', and adds that he does not know if the Germans have a word for 'Ms' now. He sees blank looks from the pupils, and asks what 'Ms' means. Pupils volunteer 'Miss' and 'Mrs', no one knows. Mr Baden explains to them that Ms is deliberately designed to avoid the distinction and compares it to Mr.

A junior-school teacher, Sally Shave (1978) wrote an article on how she struggled to be non-sexist in her classroom, and some of her suggestions are equally applicable to secondary pupils, especially those who are low achievers. Shave's list includes:

(1)   a varied reading scheme of non-sexist books
(2)   discussing the sexism in traditional stories like *Cinderella*
(3)   reversing the sex-roles in traditional stories
(4)   *never* dividing the children into males and females for any activity (use 'blue jumpers', or 'black shoes', 'birthdays in March, May and September' or some other non-sexual division)
(5)   train girls to do their own lifting and carrying
(6)   assign the strongest pupils to heavy duties
(7)   encourage girls to get dirty if necessary

All these are practices that can be used by any teacher in any school.

Conclusion

Pupils who are not achieving in their secondary schools will be disadvantaged in many areas of their adult lives: employment, health, marriage, housing, and so on. Their problems will be greater if they leave school expecting to find a sex-role system of the kind common in the 1950s. Teachers have a duty to prepare them for the world which actually exists beyond school where AIDS, unemployment and divorce are major social problems thay must face. In all those areas a more egalitarian set of beliefs about sex-roles, and competences in a range of skills that includes both traditionally 'masculine' and 'feminine' ones, will enable low achievers to survive better in the wider world.

Notes and Acknowledgements

1. Elizabeth Renton prepared this paper from my scruffy and incoherent manuscript for which I am grateful.
2. The observation conducted in Wales was funded by the Welsh Office, and conducted by Frances Beasley and myself. The ORACLE project was funded by the SSRC and conducted by Maurice Galton, Janice Lea, Margaret Greig, Sarah Tann, John Willcocks and myself.
3. The nine schools visited in Wales were:
   Artinswell, Burminster, Clipperstone, Sharway Downs, Earlsfield, Fosse, Gorston Hall, Hanham and Rushford.
   The six ORACLE schools were:
   Gryll Grange, Guy Mannering, Kenilworth, Maid Marion, Waverly and Melin Court.
   The school studied by Measor and Woods (1984) was Old Town.

References

AGGLETON, P. (1988) 'Health education, sexuality and AIDS', in BARTON, L. and WALKER, S. (Eds) *Politics and the Process of Schooling*, Milton Keynes, The Open University Press.

BARNES, D. and TODD, F. (1977) *Communication and Learning in Small Groups*, London, Routledge and Kegan Paul.

BEST, R. (1983) *We've all got scars*, Bloomington, Indiana University Press.

BRELSFORD, P. *et al.* (1982) *Equal Opportunities in the Youth Training Scheme*, Sheffield, MSC.

BURGESS, R.G. (1983) *Experiencing Comprehensive Education*, London, Methuen.

BUSWELL, C. (1981) 'Sexism in school routine and classroom practices', in *Durham and Newcastle Research Review* 9, 4, pp. 195–200.

DELAMONT, S. (1980) *Sex Roles and the School*, London, Methuen.

DELAMONT, S. (1982) 'Sex differences in classroom interaction', in *EOC Bulletin*, 6, pp. 30–37.

DELAMONT, S. (1983a) 'The conservative school', in WALKER, S. and BARTON, L. (Eds) *Gender, Class and Education*, London, Falmer Press.

DELAMONT, S. (1983b) 'A woman's place in education: myths, monsters and misapprehensions', in *Research Intelligence*, 13, pp. 2–4.

DELAMONT, S. (1984) 'Sex roles and schooling: or See Janet Suffer, See John Suffer Too', in *Journal of Adolescence*, 7, pp. 329–335.

DELAMONT, S. (1986) 'From lettuce to lasers: changing the curriculum for women' in *Journal of Curriculum Studies*, 18, 4, pp. 457–461.

DELAMONT, S. and GALTON, M. (1986) *Inside the Secondary Classroom*, London, Routledge and Kegan Paul.

DES (1978) *Special Educational Needs (The Warnock Report)*, London, HMSO.

ELLIOT, J. (1974) 'Sex roles and silence in the classroom', in *Spare Rib*, 27, pp. 12–15.

FARRELL, C. (1978) *My mother said*, London, Routledge and Kegan Paul.

GALTON, M. and WILLCOCKS, J. (1983) *Moving from the Primary Classroom*, London, Routledge and Kegan Paul.

GUTTENTAG, M. and BRAY, H. (Eds) (1976) *Undoing Sex Stereotypes*, New York, McGraw Hill.

HARRISON, L. (1975) 'Cro-Magnon Woman — In eclipse', in *Science Teacher*, 42, 4, pp. 9–11.

JOFFE, C. (1971) 'Sex-role socialization and the nursery school', in *Journal of Marriage and the Family*, 33, 3, pp. 276–291.

LANE, C. (1983) 'Women in socialist society with special reference to the GDR', in *Sociology*, 17, 4, pp. 489–505.

LEES, S. (1986) *Losing Out*, London, Hutchinson.

MARLAND, M. (Ed) (1983) *Sexual Differentiation and Schooling*, London, Heinemann.

MEASOR, L. and WOODS, P. (1984) *Changing Schools*, Milton Keynes, The Open University Press.

MEASOR, L. and WOODS, P. (1988) 'Sex education and adolescent sexuality', in HOLLY, L. (Ed) *The Sexual Agenda of Schooling*, Milton Keynes, Open University Press.

MURCOTT, A. (1980) 'The Social construction of teenage pregnancy', in *Sociology of Health and Illness*, 2, 1, pp. 1–23.

MYERS, K. (1987) *Genderwatch*, London, SCDC Publications.

POWELL, R. and LITTLEWOOD, P. (1982) 'Foreign languages: the avoidable options', in *British Journal of Language Teaching*, 20, 3, pp. 153–159.

REES, T.L. (1983) 'Boys off the street and girls in home', in FIDDY, R. (Ed) *In Place of Work*, London, Falmer Press.

ROCHERON, Y. (1985) Unpublished Ph.D. thesis, Warwick University.

SADKER, M. and SADKER, D. (1982) *Sex Equity Handbook for Schools*, London, Longman.

SCHNEIDER, J. and HACKER, S. (1973) 'Sex-role imagery in the use of the generic "man" in introductory texts', in *American Sociologist*, 8 pp. 12–18.

SHAFER, S. (1976) 'The socialisation of girls in the secondary schools of England and the two Germanies' in *International Review of Education*, 22, 1, pp. 5–24.

SHAVE, S. (1978) 'Ten ways to counter sexism in a junior school', in *Spare Rib*, 75 p. 42.

SHONE, D. and ATKINSON, P. (1981) 'Industrial training for slow learners', in *Education for Development*, 6, 3, pp. 25–30.

SHUY, R.W. (1985) 'Secretary Bennett's Teaching', in *Teaching and Teacher Education*, 2, 4, pp. 315–324.

SMITH, L. S. (1978) 'Sexist assumptions and female delinquency', in SMART, C. and SMART, B. (Eds) *Women, Sexuality and Social Control*, London, Routledge and Kegan Paul.

SPENDER, D. (1982) *Invisible Women*, London, Writers and Readers Publishing Cooperative.

STANWORTH, M. (1981) *Gender and Schooling*, London, WRRC (reprinted by Hutchinson in 1983).

SUTHERLAND, M. (1985) *Women who teach in Universities*, Stoke-on-Trent, Trentham.

TANN, S. (1981) 'Grouping and group work', in SIMON, B. and WILLCOCKS, J. (Eds) *Research and Practice in the Primary Classroom*, London, Routledge and Kegan Paul.

THORNE, B., KRAMARE, C. and HENLEY, N. (Eds) (1983) *Language, Gender and Society*, Rowley, MA., Newberry House.

WEIS, L. (1988) 'Youth in a de-industrialising economy', in BARTON, L. and WALKER, S. (Eds) *Politics and the Process of Schooling*, Milton Keynes, The Open University Press.

WHYLD, J. (Ed) (1983) *Sexism in the Secondary Curriculum*, London, Harper and Row.

WHYTE, J. (1985) *Gender, Science and Technology: Inservice Handbook*, York, Longman.

WHYTE, J. (1986) *Girls into Science and Technology*, London, Routledge and Kegan Paul.

WHYTE, J. et al. (Eds) (1986) *Girl-Friendly Schooling* London, Methuen.

WILLIS, P. (1977) *Learning to Labour*, Farnborough, Saxon House.

WILSON, D. (1978) 'Sexual codes and conduct', in SMART, C. and SMART, B. (Eds) *Women, Sexuality and Social Control* London, Routledge and Kegan Paul.

WINTER, M. (1983) 'Remedial education', in WHYLD, J. (Ed) — see above.

Chapter 18

New Initiatives
Tina Frost and David Frost

The use of 'jargon' in this section is not intended to confuse or make this piece accessible to only those in the know. It is used only to make the chapter shorter than it would otherwise be. We have provided a short glossary of terms at the end.

The purpose of this chapter is to look at some of the changes in curriculum and teaching styles that are now working their way into schools and colleges, and to consider their implications for teachers and lecturers. Although for the purpose of this book we concentrate on the low achiever, we see these implications as relating eventually to the whole spectrum of student ability.

The background to these changes is partly in response to pressure from employers and government, aware that the schools product was not meeting the needs of industry, and partly from the EEC. Many people are unaware of the amount of resources that have come from Brussels to try to bring the British standard of training into line with that of the rest of Europe — only Spain and Greece at present receive more aid than Britain.

In a climate of poor industrial performance, education seems to have become the scapegoat. There has been a widespread view that schools have been producing exam-ridden, perhaps factually aware pupils, with few skills relevant to the world of work. In short, their 'training' was seen to be largely irrelevant — even basic maths and English classes were criticised for not providing the tools: employees who could not work out percentages and spell

The absence of jobs has affected the morale and motivation of the average fifth year student. Increasingly, in the early 1980s, it seemed that a student who worked hard to achieve Grade 3 CSE would have nothing more to offer than someone who had never bothered with school work at all — both would end up on a 'Scheme'. The government, with 'supply side' ideas on the working of the economy and aware of this country's low level of youth training compared with our European competitors, pressed for a post-16 approach which would prepare young people for a rapidly changing job market — not, of course, for unemployment. This market would be characterized by flexibility: frequent changes of employment accompanied by varied but perhaps lengthy unemployment periods. Training at the ages of 16–18, it was felt, would cut down on future training time. Job analyses done throughout the country led to pronouncements on what skills were common to all jobs — these were the Core Skills at the basis of the YTS — Number; Communication skills; Planning and Problem solving; Practical and Computer skills.

At the same time as the MSC was setting up YTS courses, BTEC; CGLI and the RSA were active in developing courses which reflected many of the elements in YTS. Put simply, the approach was to be student centred and based on negotiation. Each course had in common some form of profiling system as a method of assessing individual progress.

It is fascinating to see, at a time of such high unemployment, that the requirements of industry appear to have taken so much precedence over the curriculum theorists' views of what ought to be taught. We might have expected it to be the other way round. It is argued of course that the so called transferable skills (based on job analysis), either vocational or pre-vocational, are really the same things as skills for life. In addition it is clear that traditional courses in schools have lost their role in terms of sifting people for jobs at 16. Many pupils at this age consider themselves as school failures and end their final year hating school, unable to see the relevance of much that goes on there. This really is not surprising because much of it is neither entertaining (except of course for disruption which can be highly entertaining), nor relevant in the sense of getting or holding down a job. Teachers who have tried the new approaches outlined in this chapter have noticed often almost miraculous improvement — the previously bored, disinterested student has become involved and motivated. Courses such as CGLI 365, BTEC General Diploma and some RSA courses as well as TVEI within schools seemed to do this and students achieved unexpected results. Good YTS courses also showed what different teacher expectations could achieve. There is undoubtedly a Hawthorne effect here: teachers who have worked at and evolved a course may subsequently put in more effort to see that it works.

It is fairly clear that the new approach referred to here is effective in terms of motivating students and in allowing them to take real responsibility for their learning, as well as the general direction it is taking. It requires considerable commitment from the teacher, not only in terms of time to meet pupils one to one but also to make sure tasks match the skills required in the course. It does beg the question: if teachers were able to spend this much time monitoring and directing the progress of other pupils, on 'ordinary' courses, how much improvement would be seen then? What we are talking about is the beneficial effect of individual attention which due to large class sizes in most schools has been almost impossible to implement.

One other factor should be mentioned here — the Council for the Review of Vocational Qualifications intends to standardize the present variety of examinations and their requirements. CPVE, YTS, Open Learning — all will fit into a modular programme. There are implications here for the timetable; for the school year; for teacher conditions of service and for syllabuses. The transition period will be hard and the teacher's job will change. No longer will the requirement be to prepare materials but rather to help the students through them. This could provide a great freeing of teacher time to enable them to facilitate learning but if done well it could involve more time.

The intention is presumably to centralize the control of education as is common in Europe. There will be a system of modules which can be picked up at any age. Course content will be established nationally. CPVE and YTS will link into this process — at the moment being concerned with initial diagnosis and assessment, they will hopefully, in the future, encourage motivation and teach self study methods so that the individual can follow further programmes. The money recently channelled into Open Tech. and the emphasis on Distance and Open Learning shows how interested the present government is in developing materials that stand alone, that once produced apparently reduce the need for teachers. There is also the added 'bonus' of easier standardization. Work-based projects implemented in the workplace during YTS have the same intention, but it is increasingly evident that the need for teachers' support has been underestimated. The main role that we see for teachers in the future is as motivators. Materials cannot, however good, stand alone. Open Learning in North Yorkshire, given a recent investment of £100,000 for materials, is according to the Director dependent for its success on the skills of its tutors. One of us was involved in writing Work-Based Projects for a large nationalized corporation. After two years of helping trainees with the projects, they were then left to work unsupported. The resulting apathy and lack of progress of the trainees resulted in the company again recruiting professional support on an 'outreach' basis.

We expect to see this approach initiated in CPVE and YTS moving down the school system to link with the accepted primary school models.

Although the MSC is still moving things ahead because they have the money, most schools and colleges are struggling to keep up with some of the ideas because the resources have not been directed towards them. The Government seems to be moving towards getting industry to take over‘

responsibility for training — so staff development time and resources have been allocated this way rather than to schools and FE which are left to find things out for themselves. The present situation is that schools and FE are frantically trying to prepare new courses to retain students in a contracting market — we are in the numbers game.

It may help at the moment to focus on some of the major elements in these courses and look at their implications. The idea of a negotiated curriculum for example seems quite straightforward at first sight — students negotiate the course content with their tutor — they do not of course dictate their requirements — and a type of implied contract is agreed. Periodic 'reviews' also mean that course content can be modified if the 'clients' are not satisfied. This may seem a big change for a traditional teacher who likes to work to a set syllabus. One established rule of control in classrooms has been to make clear requirements in terms of conduct, acceptable standards of work and subject areas to be covered. Negotiation would seem to remove the last of these props.

There may also be some degree of hypocrisy — good negotiators will know the constraints acting upon them and try to direct the students whilst leading them to believe it was their decision. Is this manipulation valid? Tutor credibility could easily be lost. Anyone who has been on negotiated courses themselves knows that the process of one's opinion being continuously sought can be very wearing — it has to be skilfully done unless one is to feel manipulated. Course after course of negotiation could easily become a tedious diet.

The second aspect which is crucial to the new courses is the degree of flexibility required. It is difficult for a TVE, CPVE, or YTS tutor to give a really detailed syllabus breakdown. Each course will vary because it depends on the needs of the students, their starting point, the local labour market situation and other factors. What will be common to the courses will be the aim of extending core skills. The work done will have validity as long as it appears to involve these skill areas. To some extent these two approaches are coming together as YTS is designed to offer transfer onto other schemes and perhaps into other OTFs (Occupational Training Families). How this will work out in practice, in two-year YTS courses with increasing pressure from managing agents to keep 'bums on seats' and to maintain a rolling programme, due to the costs involved — remains to be seen. Trainees may actually be deterred from transferring from schemes because of the detrimental effect this could have on the rest of the group and the extra effort required to coping with an 'infill' who will not be at the same stage of development as the others and will need more attention. Heaven help us, trainees may even be deterred from applying for a job!

The implications of this student-centred, flexible approach are likely to be viewed with alarm by an administrator or timetabler who likes to see things set out well in advance — and perhaps even more so by the secondary school teacher who has invariably had a set syllabus to work to. Many indeed have used the time constraint involved as an excuse for not following student-centred 'red herrings'. Student teachers who have always been told to prepare each lesson carefully, may find it extremely uncomfortable to walk into a room full of adolescents without a well-rehearsed 'lesson' up their sleeves. It is the awareness of core skills which changes the situation. The teacher must now broaden the students' rather limited skills: memory, accuracy, neatness, etc. The range of skills required on the new courses generally include other areas, such as the ability to explain to groups and to take responsibility for planning an activity. The more one reflects on the skills required from the teacher the more difficult it becomes to be optimistic. In the present climate most teachers are very concerned about control, some are mainly judged on it. A didactic style; a clear enunciation of the rules at the outset; a consistent approach to reward and punishment — these are all techniques of control, for what can you teach that anyone will listen to without control?

Now, teachers are not necessarily going to set themselves up as founts of wisdom. If the course is flexible they must admit ignorance in some matters and yet must have credibility with their students. For YTS this may mean getting up at 5 a.m. to deliver the early mail with a trainee or crawling with them through a muddy pothole on a CPVE residential. They are now in the business of building relationships which has become something of a prerequisite to developing the skills of their trainees. In many cases the 'control' model above has been found wanting for low achievers. Teachers now need to be using or at least thinking in terms of the jargon words 'managers of the learning situation' and 'facilitators' helping and working alongside their pupils. Our point of course is that many teachers have been criticised in the past for not actually teaching a subject very well with the more limited range of skills involved in that communication process. How much more difficult will it be to do all that when needed, but also develop the other things — student autonomy and self-confidence in particular. One thing is certain, without reasonably small groups, and by that we would say perhaps ten, it cannot be done.

So far we have written about only two essential aspects of the new courses, negotiation and flexibility. However there are others. One of these is the movement towards criterion-referencing and away from norm-referencing. Although there is an emphasis upon the process rather than the product, the outcomes are still important — increasingly as with the two year YTS stress on competency achievement. The intended 'modularization' throughout the educational structure is planned to make this more attainable and more obvious. Both YTS and CPVE are concerned with personal improvement measured agaist a yardstick; YTS is moving towards competency-based criteria in work-related skills in the second year whereas CPVE and TVE are pre-vocational and largely concerned with progression in transferable skills.

It must be added here — at the moment there seems to be a great rush amongst managing agents in YTS to gain the support of the national examining bodies for the competency objectives of their courses. City and Guilds, etc., have been working overtime to provide examinations in the workplace that will meet the criteria of the MSC — a recently-written examination, for example, ranges from multiple-choice factual questions on geography (e.g. which is the capital of Fance (a) Berlin (b) Paris (c) Madrid (d) Rome) to a practical test for tying a mailbag (this is a competency test for postpeople). So the aim now is not only to expect more of industry in providing training, but also to expect them to work out their own examination system, taking that too away from FE — the worry is whether they can cope with this. Present examples seem to show a rather worrying trend towards factual testing and emphasis on recall — and so the wheel turns full circle — industry could become exam-ridden and the methods of 'teaching' and 'instruction' that teachers have been criticised for, may again be in vogue.

The differences between YTS and CPVE appear to be less important at the moment than the similarities. Both involve experiential learning; both emphasize activity-based learning; and both seek to provide experiences whose outcomes are indeterminate, trusting in the 'Review' procedures to link them to the structure of the course and to emphasize the learning.

There are difficulties with these concepts. The attempt, for example, to provide a competency-based criterion of a task such as building a brick wall may be easier than 'talking effectively to a group'. Which group? About what? At what level? etc. There is the further difficulty that students themselves may tend to compare their performance with the rest of the group. You do not have to be moderately competitive to do this. If we as adults learn to ski and everyone else appears to do it better than us, do we measure ourselves simply against an objective criterion?

However, there are other reasons why courses such as TVE should help to motivate the low achiever. Firstly, the courses concentrate on 'doing' rather than 'listening' and 'recording'. You can of course lecture a group of young people on safety standards in the workshop, and the physical and chemical processes associated with welding, but what they really want to do is get on with making 'something'. This is the meaning of the terms 'participative' or 'experiential' learning: making use of real situations and experience to encourage motivation, and to form an effective partnership between teacher and learner. In the process of 'doing' they will pick up many other core skills such as listening and recording but they will also have experience of planning and communicating. It is an expensive process because it will mean making mistakes, and materials cost money. Of course TVE has been centrally resourced and there are implications for resourcing in this whole approach. The second fundamental reason for increased motivation is that instead of the rather limited range of skills that conventional schooling validates and reinforces, many others can be validated. A 'low achiever' may be a low achiever on memory, recording, neatness, etc., but nevertheless a reasonably high achiever in terms of, say, leadership/ organizing ability. The approach outlined does stand a better chance of finding areas of competency in pupils and boosting these in order to increase self-confidence and personal effectiveness.

We do have a very clear hierarchy of knowledge. It took the sciences a long time to become respectable, and ancient languages fought a long rearguard action. To some extent, perhaps especially in Oxbridge, the battle is still being fought. Hierarchies of knowledge will be with us for a long while and pupils will be aware of them.

The problem in the past and perhaps the future is that 80 per cent of the population may have different views on whether it is more important to weld *well* or to analyse Shakespeare.

Another relatively new concept in schools and colleges, although not exclusive to the courses so far mentioned, is assessment by profile. The 'formative' profile is a checklist of statements about competency in core skills, which is measured against the student's performance. Essential to this process is the one to one dialogue with the student. Some sort of agreement is found about the level of a student's performance and a further 'contract' entered into to improve it in future. Thus the assessment becomes part of the process of improvement. The 'summative' profile takes the form of a set of achievements reached by the end of the course.

YTS has a similar process. Trainees are encouraged to record their own progress and experience. Records of the four outcomes — work skills, examples of transfer of these skills, experience of the world outside work and personal effectiveness — are now kept and used as a discussion point during reviewing sessions. Then at the end of the course these are recorded on the final certificate. This indicates the development in various skill areas as well as stating achievements during the course according to the four outcomes. The CPVE certificate looks very similar.

A summative profile is a lot more specific than, for example, an 'O' level pass in sociology. At least it is specific in terms of skills and does not aim to be specific in terms of knowledge. Certainly the possession of an 'O' level in sociology tells an employer something about a student's knowledge of sociological data and techniques and will imply the possession of various unspecified skills, as, for example, the ability to write a reasonably lucid analytical essay. For many business people it appears to say something about 'general intelligence' (if we could agree what that is). This still may be the case when only those judged unable to get a good GCSE grade may be allowed the luxury of taking other courses. Whilst this competition exists between GCSE and other courses, the former may continue to be a more useful passport than a summative profile after a YTS, CPVE or TVE course.

The two-year YTS course will aim to record 'competencies'. GCSE claims to be offering a course much more to do with skills in handling knowledge than retention of knowledge, and many teachers will certainly welcome this. Very many old CSE courses, perhaps in the interests of tightening up on the reliability of the examination process, had become little more than memory exercises. Perhaps it is an exaggeration but one gets the impression that whilst schools are moving into the relatively uncharted waters of trying to encourage and assess the development of skills — and perhaps in the process throwing the baby out with the bath water — two-year YTS is moving towards specific knowledge of specific areas. What is of concern is that, only a few years ago, just this ethos prevailed — the emphasis was on the process, not the result. The present emphasis, led by government and industry, is on competency, reaching a 'standard' which one either reaches or fails — and will this soon be applied to CPVE?

The degree to which all the courses mentioned so far, and including TVE, are actually taken up by the 'low achiever', varies from one part of the country to another. Courses are not designed specifically for the low achiever. They are designed for a spread of ability which may range from the student unable to read to those capable of 'A' levels. It has been argued that a CPVE year prior to 'A' level for a 'high achiever' might fill a gap in terms of pupil confidence, research skills, etc. In actual fact, of course, an average CPVE group will contain quite a high proportion of students who have been low achievers, just as TVE often does, and who would not perhaps have been in mainstream education at all after the age of sixteen. In some parts of the country where unemployment is very high the choice is only one of YTS or staying on vocational or pre-vocational courses. As many college vocational courses become over-subscribed and take the relatively high achievers, a 'low achiever' eschewing YTS will take the pre-vocational option.

In conclusion, most successful courses that have already taken place have had certain common characteristics: a flexible timetable; a student-centred curriculum; an ability to meet student needs; and, most important, they have only involved small groups. The simplest analogy of trying to motivate, and help individually a group of young people, is to see them as the 'plates on sticks' trick seen on stage — the teacher/tutor is the manipulator and has to keep the plates from dropping by dashing from one to another, keeping them going — the more plates the more energy expended. We would hate the 'new ideas' on education to be misunderstood by those who might not appreciate the skills involved in this process. We feel that good teachers have been underestimated, and teaching skills have been undervalued. Some would argue that the 'magic' that is promised by these new systems could equally well have occurred with more flexibility; more thinking time and particularly smaller class sizes in schools in traditional courses. However we believe that the best chance of achieving self-confident and well-motivated young people able to adapt to a changing work pattern and able to enjoy living in society peaceably, is most likely to be achieved by the types of courses outlined here.

Glossary

ESF	European Social Fund
YTS	Youth Training Scheme
CPVE	Certificate of Pre-Vocational Education
CGLI	City and Guilds of London Institute
(365)	'Pre-Vocational GCLI Course
BTEC	Business and Technical Educational Council
OTF	Occupational Training Families
Negotiation	The process of establishing a dialogue with students to reach agreed objectives
Formative)	Ongoing Analysis of Achievements
Profiles)	
Summative)	Final Record of Achievement
UVP	Unified Vocational Preparation (forerunner to YTS)
RVQ	Review of Vocational Qualifications
Outreach	Working with students in Industry
TVE	Technical and Vocational Education (previously TVEI)

Bibliography

Cox, M. (1983) 'Influence on in-service training of secondary school teachers. Breaking with tradition', in *Youth Society*, No. 76.

F.E.U. (1978) *Experience, Reflection and Learning*, Curriculum Review and Development Unit.

Jones, A. (1982) 'Where have all our comprehensive principles gone', in *Education*, Vol. 160, No. 25, December.

Lancaster, M. (1982) 'The new training initiative', in *Coombe Lodge Report*, Vol. 15, No. 2.

MILLER, J.C. (1982) *Tutoring*, F.E.U.

TOLLEY, G. (1985) 'The new curriculum: Towards the primacy of the vocational', in *Economics*, Autumn.

YOUNG, D. (1982) 'Helping the young help themselves', in *Times Educational Supplement*, No. 3465, November.

YOUNG, M. (1871) *Knowledge and Control*, London, Collier-Macmillan.

Training Manuals

YTS L51 (1984) Core Skills in YTS, Part I (Manual)
YTS L52 (1985) Core Skills in YTS, Part II (Manual)
YTS Practitioners Guides (1985) Numbers 1–5
MSC Core Skills: Learning, Guidance and Personal Effectiveness

A wide range of published materials on aspects of YTS is available from MSC, Moorfoot, Sheffield.

Contributors

Arlene Ramasut — Lecturer in Special Educational Needs, University College, Cardiff. Previously worked with school leavers with special needs in the F.E. sector and with SEN pupils in secondary schools.

Derek Phillips, Ph.D. — Lecturer in Special Educational Needs, University College, Cardiff. Educational Psychologist who has worked with behaviourally disturbed adolescents.

David Galloway, Ph.D. — Lecturer in Special Educational Needs, University of Lancaster. Previously Educational Psychologist in Sheffield and Australia.

Tony Kloska — Special Needs Coordinator, Lockleaze High School, Suffolk. Previously Head of Special Unit for Behaviourally Disturbed Adolescents in Bristol.

Mike Farrell — Head of Special Needs Department, Cynfartha High School, Mid Glam.

David Reynolds — Lecturer in Education, University College, Cardiff.

Colin Johnson and Mike Newman — Lecturers in Science Education, University College, Cardiff.

Glyn Johns, Ph.D. — Lecturer in Mathematics Education, University College, Cardiff.

Barry Johnson — Senior Lecturer in Special Educational Needs, Gwent College of Higher Education.

Mark Fowler — Senior Research Officer, National Language Unit of Wales, Pontypridd.

William Salaman, Ph.D.	HMI. Previously Senior Lecturer in Music Education, University College, Cardiff.
Dilys Price	Senior Lecturer in Movement Education, South Glamorgan Institute of Higher Education.
David Fontana, Ph.D.	Reader in Educational Psychology, University College, Cardiff.
Graham Upton, Ph.D.	Professor of Special Education, University of Birmingham. Previously Senior Lecturer in Special Educational Needs, University College, Cardiff.
Carol Aubrey	Lecturer in Special Educational Needs, University of Durham. Previously Educational Psychologist, Shropshire LEA.
John Harris, Ph.D.	Lecturer in Psychology and Child Development, University College, Cardiff.
Sara Delamont, Ph.D.	Senior Lecturer in Sociology, University College, Cardiff.
Tina Frost	Lecturer in Communication Studies, Thomas Danby College, Leeds.
David Frost	Head of Sixth Form, Lawnswood School, Leeds.

Index

Caerleon
Library